DATE DUE

FEB 2 3 2003   MAR 2 2 2004
NOV 2 7 2004

Demco No. 62-0549

METROPOLITAN COLLEGE
OF NEW YORK LIBRARY
75 Varick Street 12th Fl.
New York, NY 10013

A COGNITIVE-BEHAVIORAL APPROACH TO COUNSELING PSYCHOLOGY

A COGNITIVE-BEHAVIORAL APPROACH TO COUNSELING PSYCHOLOGY

Implications for Practice, Research, and Training

Gerald L. Stone

PRAEGER

PRAEGER SPECIAL STUDIES • PRAEGER SCIENTIFIC

Library of Congress Cataloging in Publication Data

Stone, Gerald L   1941-
   A cognitive-behavioral approach to counseling psychology.

   Bibliography: p.
   Includes indexes.
   1. Counseling. 2. Cognitive therapy. 3. Behavior therapy. I. Title. [DNLM: 1. Counseling. 2. Psychology. WM55 S877c]
   BF637.C6S776   158'.3   80-21344
   ISBN 0-03-055926-X

Published in 1980 by Praeger Publishers
CBS Educational and Professional Publishing
A Division of CBS, Inc.
521 Fifth Avenue, New York, New York 10017 U.S.A.

© 1980 by Praeger Publishers

All rights reserved

0123456789 038 987654321

Printed in the United States of America

FOREWORD

The principal reason for writing this book emerged as an attempt to reassert the legitimacy of cognition within the helping profession. Such an attempt appears necessary within the fields of counseling and psychotherapy. On the one hand, popular theories of therapy have emphasized unconscious processes, feelings, and behaviors, while many practitioners and researchers have separated practice and research in a misguided response to the call for relevance. These factors have combined, resulting in a de-emphasis or in some cases the denigration of the cognitive domain.

Recently a cognitive emphasis has developed within psychology and sociology as a major influence. It would seem to be an appropriate time for the therapeutic profession to reconsider the importance of symbolic processes and to examine the implications of new cognitive models.

This book was an attempt to overcome the avoidance of cognitive phenomena by psychologists and others involved in therapeutic endeavors through a systematic elaboration of the implications of cognitive science for the specific functions traditionally associated with counseling and psychotherapy. These functions include establishing rapport, identifying concerns, setting goals, implementing change strategies, conducting research, and facilitating professional development. *Cognitive-Behavioral Counseling* was written primarily for counseling psychologists and other psychology- and counseling-related professionals (for example, clinical psychologists, psychotherapists, counselor educators, social workers, mental health workers).

The organization of the book reflects an effort to interrelate the implications of a cognitive-behavioral perspective with the generic functions of the therapeutic enterprise. Chapter 1 provides an introduction to a cognitive-behavioral perspective and to the generic functions of the helping process. Chapters 2 through 6 describe each helping procedure in the context of a cognitive-behavioral perspective. Theory, research, and practical examples are included within each of these chapters. A postscript concludes the book with a brief outline of research projects that serve to review major points of the book and to give direction for future exploration of the topic.

ACKNOWLEDGMENTS

The completion of a first book, such as this, gives me an opportunity to reflect and comment on the contributions made in the production of this book. At a very broad level, I would like to thank at least four groups of people who have been particularly helpful and stimulating. The first group helped me learn how to think about counseling: Bill Hinds, Norm Stewart, Bob Winborn, Bill Farquhar, Andy Porter, Dozier Thorton, John Schneider, Herb Burks, Dick Johnson, and Jim Engelkes at Michigan State University. A second group consists of a dedicated group of peers and former graduates of Michigan State who have sustained me in my endeavors and continue "to think" about counseling: Ken Lafleur at the University of Virginia, John Horan at Pennsylvania State University, Wayne Rowe and Avi Scherman at the University of Oklahoma, Geoff Yaeger at the University of Cincinnati, Mark Hector at the University of Western Ontario. A third group helped me move from speculation through research to publication. Within this group, my former colleagues and students in the Department of Psychology under the able leadership of Bill McClelland at the University of Western Ontario have provided support and stimulation to this project. In addition, Sam Osipow, Charlie Gelso, and their legion of anonymous reviewers at the *Journal of Counseling Psychology* have helped me translate my past thinking and research into efficient written communication. A fourth group represents individuals who have had an impact on the content of my thinking through their writings: Michael Mahoney at Pennsylvania State University, Don Meichenbaum at the University of Waterloo, Albert Bandura at Stanford University, Albert Ellis at the Institute for Advanced Study in Rational Psychotherapy, and Jerome Frank at the Johns Hopkins University. With respect to the preparation of the book, I am particularly indebted to Gail Koff at the University of Western Ontario and Ginny Volk and Reta Litton at the University of Iowa for the typing of the manuscript. Finally, I would like to thank my wife, Cheryl, and my children, Corby and Carrie, who provide a loving and "crazy" atmosphere in which I can avoid the hazard of taking myself too seriously.

CONTENTS

FOREWORD v
ACKNOWLEDGMENTS vi
LIST OF FIGURES AND TABLE ix

1 COGNITIVE-BEHAVIORAL COUNSELING 1
   The Cognitive Movement 1
   Cognition and Counseling 5
   Plan of the Book 12

2 ESTABLISHMENT 18
   Generic Goals 18
   Establishment Goals 19
   Sources of Establishment 20
   Influence Processes 25

3 CONCEPTUALIZATION 32
   Background 32
   Traditional Assessment Models 33
   Contemporary Assessment Models 34
   Summary of Models 37
   A Cognitive-Behavioral Model 38

4 INTERVENTIONS 49
   General Considerations 49
   Cognitive Restructuring 50
   Self Instruction 58
   Self Management 61
   Additional Interventions 74
   Summary 83
   Implications for Vocational Psychology and Prevention 84

5   **RESEARCH**   87
    Point of View   87
    Internal Validity   91
    Construct Validity   95
    Statistical Conclusion Validity   100
    External Validity   105
    Priorities   107
    Illustration   108
    Design Strategies   123
    Priorities   131

6   **PROFESSIONAL DEVELOPMENT**   133
    Science Education   135
    Practical Education   139
    Integration   146
    Research   148

POSTSCRIPT   150
BIBLIOGRAPHY   152
AUTHOR INDEX   178
SUBJECT INDEX   184

LIST OF FIGURES AND TABLE

Figure 1.1	A conceptual framework for counseling.	16
Figure 5.1	Counselee perception of counselor helpfulness as a function of interview structure and counselee conceptual level (CL).	116
Figure 5.2	Satisfaction as a function of counselor interview structure and counselee conceptual level (CL).	117
Figure 5.3	Expressions of self awareness as a function of counselee conceptual level (CL) and degree of counselor-offered structure.	118
Figure 5.4	Counselee talk time as a function of interview structure and counselee conceptual level (CL).	119
Figure 5.5	Simulated data.	126
Table 5.1	Summary table for F ratios.	115

A COGNITIVE-BEHAVIORAL APPROACH TO COUNSELING PSYCHOLOGY

1
COGNITIVE-BEHAVIORAL COUNSELING

THE COGNITIVE MOVEMENT

A popular development in the psychology of the 1970s and 1980s has been the rediscovery of cognition. Whether the development is revolutionary is debatable, but the trend shows all the indications of becoming a significant conceptual and methodological approach. In Kuhnian terms (Kuhn, 1962), a cognitive-behavioral perspective, at least in applied psychology, has many of the symptoms of a paradigm entering into the normal science phase. Specialized journals and newsletters have been published (for example, *Cognitive Therapy and Research, Cognitive-Behavior Modification Newsletter,* and others). Books have appeared (Mahoney, 1974; Meichenbaum, 1977). Courses have been introduced into the curricula of many graduate departments of psychology and related disciplines. National conventions and workshops have been held. All these signs of the times have concerned the role of cognition in behavior change.

Convergences

Increased attention on cognitive systems is not restricted to a few areas of psychology. Rather it appears that psychology in general has become cognitive, with many fields of psychology showing a convergence of interest. The same can be said for sociology (see Schutz, 1970). Developmental psychologists have become interested in Piaget's research and theory (Piaget, 1970). Interest in cognitive development has extended to the area of social cognition (see Shantz, 1975). Social psychologists talk about attributions and the influence of such causal perceptions on human affairs (Heider, 1958; Kelly, 1967). Implications from attribution theory are being used to understand academic achievement (Weiner, 1974) and depression (Seligman, 1975). One of the few substantive contributions to learning and personality in recent years has been the writings of Bandura (1969) and Mischel (1973) on a social learning orientation, emphasizing the role of central mediational processes in human experience. Human motivation investigators have shown renewed interest in the psychological significance of events (Dember, 1974). Lazarus (1974) has focused on the appraisal process that mediates between environmental events and stress reactions. Atkinson and his collaborators (Birch, Atkinson, & Bongart, 1974) have formulated a theory that integrates cognitive and motivational factors. In psychotherapy, researchers and therapists have been influenced by cognitive variables (Aaron Beck, Albert Ellis, Jerome Frank, George Kelly, Julian Rotter). The extent of the influence can be seen in the recent attempt to examine client-centered therapy and theory from an information-processing point of view (Wexler, 1974). In psychoanalysis, writings (Erickson, 1950; Hartmann, 1958; Kris, 1951; Rapaport, 1958) have emphasized the ego functions. Moreover, numerous behavior modification strategies have been developed that rely on cognitive processes. Such procedures include self control (Goldfried & Merbaum, 1973), attribution theory (Kopel & Arkowitz, 1975), self instructions (Meichenbaum, 1977), rational-emotive psychotherapy (Ellis, 1962), cognitive restructuring (Goldfried, Decentecea & Weinberg, 1975), biofeedback (Shapiro & Schwartz, 1972), imagery (Singer, 1974), covert therapies (Cautela, 1967), and problem solving (D'Zurilla & Goldfried, 1971). This latter converging of behavioral and cognitive psychologies is of main interest here.

Historical Background

Cognitive psychology has been experiencing a renaissance. Some even describe the history of psychology as an evolution from mechanism to cognition (see Weiner, 1972). While such an accretion theory of scientific development does not fit the popular Kuhnian interpretation nor appear consistent with the facts (Bolles, 1974), it does highlight the importance of cognition in contemporary psychology. It can be argued that psychology has not become cognitive, but has been more or less cognitive throughout its history. One can certainly view cognition as a salient area of study in the early years of psychology. It is true that interest in internalism subsequently subsided due to conceptual and methodological deficiencies and the advent of behaviorism. Yet work in cognitive psychology continued. Important cognitive studies were conducted in Europe by Bartlett in England, Piaget and Jung in Switzerland, Gestalt psychologists (Koffka, Köhler, and Wertheimer) and Lewin in Germany, Luria in Russia, and Binet in France. Another major influence on European psychology and its investigation of private experience was psychoanalysis. In North America, Tolman (1932) attempted to reintroduce cognitive mechanisms into mainstream psychology. His work on expectancy has been continued and extended by Rotter (1954). Moreover, the development of a psychometric approach to personality, psychological testing, and industrial psychology, given impetus by the forces of war and economic depression, focused attention on cognitive abilities.

In many ways, the growth of cognitive psychology can be credited to the technological innovations after World War II. The creation of the digital computer and early work on information theory (Shannon, 1948) led to signal detection theory (Peterson & Birdsall, 1953), information processing (Neisser, 1967), and computer modeling (Miller, Galanter, & Pribram, 1960; Newell, 1961).

A few pioneering works that relied on the growth of such cybernetic literature furthered the cognitive renaissance. Hebb (1949) published a book concerning a neural model of behavior. Even though computer models were not developed during this time and many of his constructs are inadequate, Hebb's book can be credited with introducing psychologists to an alternative to the positivistic input-output models often associated with behaviorism. His work stressed internal systems and led to extensive studies in sensory deprivation that indicated the influence of mediational processes. Broadbent (1958) clearly indicated the importance of cybernetics through his research on such cognitive processes as selective attention and memory. In the area of language, Chomsky (1957, 1959, 1964) has suggested that the central focus of inquiry should be on constructions and rules. Such a structural model has had wide impact on linguistics and cognitive systems (see Miller & Chomsky, 1963). Proposals for a more constructivist psychology were given classic expression by Neisser (1967) and introduced into contemporary clinical psychology by Kelly (1955) and Frank (1961/1973).

Albert Ellis was another influential voice in therapeutic psychology. Relying more on psychoanalysis and stoic philosophy than on information processing, Ellis forcefully underscored the impact of irrational ideology on human behavior. Meichenbaum (1977) has extended such a content-based, cognitive therapy by focusing on internal dialogues and self instructions, while Beck (1967) has found irrational thinking a major component in clinical depression.

Such recent contributions highlight the convergence of cognitive and behavioral perspectives in applied psychology, a convergence that represents seemingly divergent trends. On one hand, psychological explanations are relying more heavily on cognitive processes. On the other, use of performance treatments and self-control strategies is proving to be a powerful behavior-change methodology. While these two positions have been pitted against each other in competitive encounters, a third position has emerged that endorses a convergence of trends. That is, the convergence recognizes the impact of mediational processes on personal adjustment while emphasizing the role of environmental variables on perception and performance. Such an interactionalism is apparent in the relationship between expectancy and performance accomplishments discussed by Bandura (1977). At the practical level it is revealed by cognitive therapists' (Ellis, Meichenbaum, and Beck) use of performance-oriented homework assignments in conjunction with their cognitive exploration methods.

The preceding discussion suggests a cognitive perspective has emerged that has a significant history, wide popularity across many areas of contemporary psychology, and, converging with behavioral psychology, application to therapeutic concerns. It should not be inferred, however, that this represents a definitive and comprehensive history of cognitive psychology. Nor is it appropriate to assume that there is a single cognitive approach. There are many conceptualizations of the cognitive process and, furthermore, these constructs are generally not sufficiently conceptually understood, empirically verified, or critically appraised. Some of the conceptual hypotheses and practical applications have more support than others. What is being suggested is that an exposition of a specific cognitive approach, a cognitive-behavioral perspective, broadly and pragmatically defined, be integrated systematically with a particular model of the helping process. It is hoped that such an endeavor will specify the implications of a cognitive-behavioral perspective for the helping professions and will stimulate the critical assessment of such a contribution.

Themes

As has been pointed out, cognitively oriented psychologists have not escaped the semantic problems and myopic tendencies of other scientists. There are no unequivocal definitions nor one legitimate orientation in psychology. The following thematic description, then, is a particular attempt to list the major themes representative of a cognitive-behavioral perspective. Much of the description will be adapted from other such attempts (Mahoney, 1977) and from work in information processing (Neisser, 1967) and social learning (Bandura, 1969). For purposes of theoretical exposition, the themes concern mediation, phenomenology, construction, reciprocity, and information. That is:

> The world of experience is mediated by the person who experiences it. The person primarily responds to mediated information about his or her world rather than to the physical world.
> Such information is more or less actively constructed by the person.
> Yet such information is generated within a reciprocal person-environment context in which the thoughts, feelings, and activities of the person are related to the stimulus environment.
> Information is the basic factor in most human learning.
> The response systems of the person, including cognition, emotion, and motor behavior, are interdependent.

These broad generalities are interrelated, if not overlapping. Briefly, the themes revolve around the central position of mediation. That is, the mediational model, similar to a Kantian orientation, suggests that there is quite a lot of action going on between input and output. The person does not have direct access to a real world of tables, chairs, and people. The only knowledge available about reality is mediated information. Thus the perspective is phenomenological with behavior being related to perceptual processes. That is, individuals respond to the world in terms of their symbolization of it. Thus the stimulus world is more or less transformed in its contact with sense organs and the more complex systems of information processing. Such transformations occur through the person actively contributing to the production of his or her experiential world by "actively" seeing, hearing, imaging, thinking, and remembering. And it is information, the basic unit of learning in a cognitive-behavioral perspective, that is attended to, transformed, stored, and retrieved.

One may wonder if such a heavy mediational position tends toward neomentalism with consequent reduction in the influence of the real world of objects and people. However, the next theme, emerging from the confluence of cognitive psychology and behavior modification, stresses the reciprocal impact of the environment and the person. Even though the person—as a complex, interactive organism—acts upon the environment, the environment (including behavioral consequences) is a major source of influence on mediational functions. Such reciprocity between person and environment is not easily reduced to isolate causative components. The interdependent nature of the human organism adds to the complexity. Human learning is influenced by the current stimulus situation, the physiological state of the organism, and the interactive cognitive processes (for example, selective attention and expectancy).

Many of these globally described themes have implications for the therapeutic process and will be described more specifically later. Moreover, these assertions have parallels in the historical and theoretical development of counseling psychology.

COGNITION AND COUNSELING

Counseling psychology has a history of cognitive influence, as does general psychology, but the role of cognition in counseling has not been prominent. Leon Levy's (1968) seminal contribution that describes the process of counseling and counselor education has been neglected. In addition, while some of the cognitive themes seem parallel to many of the counseling theories, it appears on closer inspection that the relevant themes are defined differently. In other instances, cognition has either been neglected or established as a counterproductive process. Let us take a closer look at the major counseling theories in relation to the cognitive-behavioral themes (mediation, phenomenology, construction, reciprocity, information, and interdependence). These theories include trait and factor theory, client-centered theory, and behavioral theory. All have changed throughout their development. Consequently, any broad description of these theories will inevitably miss many important points and lack the analytical insight afforded by more in-depth study. No attempt is made to provide such in-depth treatment. Rather the focus is on the relationship and meanings of certain cognitive-behavioral themes within each of the broadly outlined counseling theories.

Trait and Factor Theory

The precursors of the trait and factor point of view included Parsons' early formulation of vocational guidance (1909), differential psychology, and the work of such individuals as Patterson, Darley, and Williamson at the University of Minnesota. Trait and factor theory has been discussed in many books and journals, but the most influential treatment has been given by Williamson (1939, 1950, 1965; Williamson & Biggs, 1979).

Basically, the trait and factor approach as outlined by Williamson emphasizes the relationship between an individual's personal characteristics and the developmental choices associated with education and work. Individuals differ in terms of abilities, interests, attitudes, and temperament. Educational and work environments can be interpreted as requiring different levels, kinds, and patterns of such characteristics. In order to enhance personal satisfaction and maximize efficiency in human resource allocation, individuals should make wise educational and vocational decisions based on scientific procedures. In facilitating such decision making, Williamson suggests the client must be encouraged to use appropriate problem-solving skills and be provided valid information about the client's personality and about the world as defined by social consensus. Williamson suggests a six-step method (Williamson, 1939) by which to accomplish these goals. The steps (analysis, synthesis, diagnosis, prognosis, counseling, and follow-up) appear to be an adaption of Dewey's problem-solving approach to education. That is, many of the problem-solving steps recommended by Dewey parallel Williamson's six-step method. In Dewey's summary (1916), these steps included information gathering ("sense of a problem" and "observation of conditions"), hypothesis generation ("formation of a suggested conclusion"), and experimentation ("active experimental testing"). The collection of valid information from a wide range of sources seems to be congruent with the first steps of analysis and synthesis. Diagnosis and the formulation of a hypothesis appear parallel. From a Williamson orientation, the counseling step can be seen as the testing of a new approach or alternative in solving a problem with evaluation and follow-up procedures assessing the process.

In the counseling process, Williamson did not hesitate to advocate the more directive practices of giving advice, instructions, and persuasion. Advocacy of directive counseling was based on Williamson's dissatisfaction with the Rousseauian philosophy of permissiveness and his recognition of the importance of social criteria. The importance of external criteria can be seen in the use of external reference groups in the trait and factor methodology (for example, Minnesota Multiphasic Personality Inventory and Strong Vocational Interest Blank).

Although social adjustment goals may seem dominant, Williamson does speak about the importance of affect within the counseling process. At the same time, it can be argued that such discussion was ill-conceived and that to a large extent Williamson considered most emotional issues far more germane to the more affectively oriented psychotherapies than to the problem-solving process of counseling.

In reviewing the trait and factor theory, it is apparent that Williamson adopted a problem-solving orientation. This orientation suggests the importance of scientifically based information, of an active problem-solver, and of person-environment interactions as a context for decision making and self development. These characteristics can be seen as more or less parallel to some of the cognitive-behavioral themes previously discussed. The person as an active problem-solver is characteristic of a mediational and constructivist model of human behavior. The stress on information and person-environment interaction is similar to its importance in a cognitive-behavioral framework. Yet there are critical differences. Compared with contemporary cognitive psychology and the development of information processing, Williamson's approach can be seen as less than mediational. Williamson tends to define many of the seemingly parallel mediational themes into stimulus and social categories. Information is discussed more in terms of stimulus properties, such as test results, observations, and the like, than in terms of mediational qualities such as personal meaning. Even though he talks about person-environment interactions, the focus suggests that problem-solving encounters in counseling situations are directed more toward adjustment to social reality than to the transactional quality of reciprocal determinism. Such emphasis is understandable when one considers the implications of an approach developed in a university setting and based to a large extent on Dewey's philosophy. This does not mean that adjustment is necessarily good or bad, but that the seemingly parallel cognitive-behavioral themes in trait and factor theory are defined more different than parallel.

Client-centered Theory

Client-centered theory, in contrast to trait and factor theory, is based more on an internal frame of reference. This reflects its association with the personal adjustment tradition of counseling and represents an extension of phenomenology, existentialism, and Gestalt and dynamic psychologies. Carl Rogers is the major spokesman and originator of client-centered therapy (Rogers, 1942, 1951, 1959). As are most theoretical systems, the Rogerian approach is difficult to describe; it is especially difficult and can easily become a caricature because the Rogerian approach has been popularized with consequent distortion. It is an eclectic approach with elements from most psychological systems. Moreover, the approach has been discussed in numerous publications over time by Rogers and adherents, both faithful and not so faithful, with resulting changes and errors.

Basically, the client-centered method is derived from Rogers' clinical experience that led him to observe the orderliness and positive value of human nature. Since human nature is assumed to be basically good, Rogers inferred that releasing the natural developmental process (actualizing tendency) of human nature was all that was necessary. Thus directive methods of coercion, traditional diagnosis, interpretation, and others must be avoided because they prejudge and devalue. Rather nondirective counseling practices and the counselor's personality were seen as major factors in facilitating growth through the client's self-awareness and understanding. Such factors were elaborated into a theory of therapy with emphasis on the process of counseling, including therapist attitudes and subjective experience.

Rogers' theory of personality was developed later, reflecting his belief that theory proceeds from practice. It is not possible to discuss all of his explanatory concepts. Four concepts that appear to be of major influence are concerned with knowledge, feelings, the self, and incongruence. In terms of knowledge, Rogers put a premium on internalism, believing that an internal frame of reference was the most appropriate vantage point in understanding human behavior. He was not opposed to more objective endeavors. In fact, Rogers has always encouraged the scientific study of counseling. He has directly and indirectly contributed to such investigations through the introduction of audiotape recordings of interview sessions, the development of content analysis procedures, and the construction of measures (such as content scales, self-ideal card sort, and others) for the evaluation of counseling process and outcome. But, according to Rogers, knowledge and personal effectiveness are not limited by external criteria. There are other ways of gaining knowledge, with subjective experience being the predominant mode.

To a large extent Rogers' view of experiencing is dominated by the experiencing of feelings. The awareness of feelings is seen as a crucial step in the development of a fully functioning life. There is a strong tendency in client-centered thinking to use effective experience and nonexperience as a comprehensive explanatory concept in discussing healthy and unhealthy living. That is, at the lower stages of human development feelings are not fully recognized (incongruence), whereas at higher stages the richness of feelings is fully owned and experienced in awareness (congruence). Such a conceptualization puts a premium on effective experience.

Another facet of subjective experience in client-centered theory is Rogers' concept of self. Stated in a more informal way, the self construct includes internalized social values (conditions of worth), self perceptions, and self evaluations. The self develops out of the individual's earliest experiences. It becomes differentiated through the natural developmental process and becomes elaborated through interactions with significant others. Such transactions lead to a self concept and a need for positive evaluation.

With the development of the self concept, the stage is set for understanding how human nature so often fails to manifest its positive destiny. Rogers' response is that incongruence develops between the self concept and the natural way of regulating behavior (organismic valuing process) because positive valuing from significant others is made contingent upon the individual introjecting certain values from the interpersonal environment. The values that have been adopted can be more or less contradictory to an individual's natural processes. Such incongruence leads to conflict between the basic natural processes (actualizing tendency) and the actualization of a self concept based more or less on external and alien conditions. Because of early developments and early social learning, the self can become progressively divorced from experience, which leads to rigidity, anxiety, and other neurotic behaviors. To change the process of threat and defense, a corrective relationship is needed to desensitize the client to denied experiences, enabling the client to slowly assimilate distorted experience. As a result, the self concept becomes more congruent with experience.

In summary, Rogers emphasizes the subject as opposed to the object of knowledge. His view of congruent with the mediational themes (mediation, phenomenology, and construction) associated with the cognitive-behavioral perspective. Reality for the individual is perceptual reality. The individual appears to be an active processor, symbolizing, organizing, and evaluating experience. Although mediation plays a central role in the Rogerian approach, there are significant distinctions between a more contemporary cognitive-behavioral perspective and client-centered theory. It seems that the Rogerian active processing qualities are usually a function of defense. That is, experience is mainly symbolized and evaluated in terms of its threat to a self concept based on internalized values acquired through socialization. On the other hand, Rogers speaks of an openness to all experience as characteristic of a fully functioning person. This would suggest that active processes such as selective attention are not operative under nondefensive conditions.

Futher distinctions between Rogers' model and a cognitve-behavioral perspective can be seen in his use of the notion of feelings. His use of feelings as abstract entities seems to mask information and cognitive organization underlying these abstractions (see Wexler, 1974). An uncritical extension of a premium on feelings has tended to denigrate cognitive operations and enhance an irrational approach to applied psychology (see Strupp, 1976). Moreover, feelings are described by Rogers as independent of other experiences and as existing outside of awareness. Such descriptions are at variance with the theme of interdependence of response systems. Thus the Rogerian theory shares many common characteristics of a mediational model, but emphasis on an individual's emotional experience and lack of conceptual clarity tends to erode the theoretical and practical influence of cognitive processes.

Behavioral Theory

Antecedents to behavioral thinking include the learning theory tradition (Pavlov, Bekhterev, Watson, Thorndike, Guthrie, Hull, Skinner, and others) and the development of an object-oriented philosophy (Descartes, Locke, Hume,

Comte, and so on). In the area of counseling, Krumboltz, Thoresen, and Hosford have been influential in describing the applications of learning theory to the counseling process (see Hosford, 1969; Krumboltz, 1964, 1966a, 1966b, 1967; Krumboltz & Thoresen, 1969, 1976; Thoresen, 1966). In discussing a behavioral approach, there is considerable potential for ambiguity and confusion. As a result of the stridency of recent debates between so called behaviorists and humanists, there is a tendency to distort the behavioral position by both adherents and critics. A behavioral approach, as described in most counseling texts, is often associated with a multitude of counseling procedures, more or less with a relationship to appropriate learning theory rationale. Moreover, there are wide theoretical and procedural divergencies among behavioral viewpoints, calling in question any consensual agreement that may be implied from such statements as "a behavioral approach" or "based on learning theory." Thus it will be necessary to limit our discussion of behavioral theory to operant conditioning while realizing the risks of dated caricature and distortion.

The discussion would be more contemporary and comprehensive if it described other viewpoints and interventions including the influence of cognitive variables, but cognitive-behavioral modification and its implications for the counseling process are the topics for the entire book. The selection of operant conditioning does not indicate that the behavioral theory is solely defined by this specific viewpoint, but it does suggest that such an approach (for instance, reinforcement) is often used by behavioral counselors and, is in all probability, the behavioral procedure most often cited in counseling-oriented publications.

Behavioral counselors are primarily characterized by the following assumptions.

> Human behavior is a function of the interaction of heredity and environment.
> Most human behavior is learned and is therefore subject to change.
> Observable behavior constitutes the data base for behavioral counselors.
> Environmental manipulation is the basic behavior-change strategy used to develop relevant changes in client behavior.

Reinforcement, defined as creating appropriate consequences that facilitate specific behaviors, is the environmental-manipulation procedure most often employed by behavioral counselors with an operant orientation. Such assumptions and procedures have resulted in a significant challenge to traditional counseling practices and other traditional mental health approaches. In general, there has been a shift in understanding psychological problems from infectious disease analogies and internalism to learning models and externalism. Such an assumptive world has had many implications for the counseling process. Psychological assessment is seen more in terms of a functional analysis than in terms of the traditional categories of psychiatric classification (see Kanfer &

Saslow, 1969). Goals are described in more specific language (Krumboltz, 1966a). Interventions are not limited to traditional interview therapy, but include a wide range of performance strategies (see Krumboltz & Thoresen, 1976). Finally, accountability is stressed. Empirical research is the method of arbitrating differences of opinion and is the criterion used to make therapeutic decisions. Unfortunately, many of these assumptions and implications become involved in the sterile debates of the 1950s and 1960s between self-described behaviorists and adherents of a more medical and psychotherapeutic perspective, resulting in unproductive labeling and uncritical thinking.

Behavioral counseling is conceptualized in learning terms with the counselor as a facilitator in the learning process. Most problems concern inappropriately learned behaviors, and such behaviors can be unlearned through the use of many behavioral procedures. Reinforcement is one. The first step is the accurate assessment of the client-presented problem in terms of the problem itself (frequency, intensity, duration, behaviors, and response patterns), the situation (physical, interpersonal, social, institutional, and cultural characteristics), and the client (motivation, learning history, and biological condition). Generally, the reinforcement counselor will rely on response-reinforcement contingencies to explain the maintenance of behavioral problems. In step 2, client goals are specified through collaboration between client and counselor. Goal statements are stated in performance terms and use step-by-step criteria for purposes of accountability. Step 3 involves counselor use of environmental events in promoting the desired behaviors. Data is systematically gathered throughout the process for client and counselor use, especially in the final step of evaluating the outcome of counseling.

Thus behavioral counseling could be described as using an external frame of reference that is characterized by quantity and measurability. It shows certain similarities (such as external orientation) with a trait and factor approach, but the level of inferences (central or peripheral), units of analysis (traits or observable behaviors), and methodologies (group comparisons or within-subject comparisons) make for significant differences. In terms of the mediational perspective and related themes, it is obvious that behavioral theory, with methodological and at times philosophical preoccupation with an input-output model of human behavior, does not emphasize mediational processes. Thus many cognitive themes (mediation, phenomenology, and construction) are not relevant to the more radical behavioral position. Earlier works in behaviorism used stimulus-response relationships rather than information as the basic unit of learning. The themes of reciprocity and interrelatedness have emerged from a behavioral perspective but, historically, emphasis has been on the external control of behavior and consequently not on the impact and interrelationship of internal response systems.

Therefore, it is the examination of the nonmediational model of behavioral theory that provides the clearest contrast to the cognitive-behavioral themes. Such themes are not stressed more as a result of methodology (measurement) than of philosophical assumption. It should be reiterated that many psychologists and counselors identified as behaviorists are considering intervening constructs that mediate learning. It must be remembered that many authorities in the field (such as Mischel, Bandura, Mahoney, Krumboltz, Thoresen, and others) are attempting to expand the philosophical and procedural dimensions of behavior modification to include cognitive phenomena, while remaining faithful to its empirical stance. A similar trend of expansion is apparent in client-centered thinking (see Wexler, 1974) and in vocational psychology (see Vroom, 1964).

PLAN OF THE BOOK

The remaining chapters of this book will examine the implications of cognitive-behavioral theory in terms of the specific functions of counseling. Before discussing these implications, it is necessary to develop a framework of the counseling process in order to appropriately translate cognitive-behavioral theory into implications for counseling practice. In addition, such a framework will provide the structure for the book.

The Need for a Model

Although counseling has been influenced by many information-rich historical conditions and theories, counselors have lacked an adequate framework for conceptualizing the counseling process. Such a state of affairs probably reflects the more pragmatic interests of many counselors who question the value of theory. It is as though counselors have believed that counseling is something one does, not something one studies. That is, counseling has often been described as a spontaneous and creative experience that is guided by intuition and bodily wisdom. This description is often labeled (mislabeled) art and usually implies the neglect, if not the denigration, of rational inquiry. Such a formulation fails to demonstrate an adequate understanding of the meaning of art. Most art is not characterized by an absence of reflection. Quite the contrary, art generally displays structure, discipline, and effort. Art is associated with the structure of Bach's music. Art emerges through the discipline and effort required by Wyeth to paint the same picture more than 100 times or of Hemingway to spend several weeks on a single paragraph. Without reflective study, structure, discipline, and effort, chaos rather than art reigns. To a large degree, counseling has become more chaotic than artistic due to its neglect of a conceptual model.

As many have noted, there is nothing as practical as a good theory. Many of the arguments are familiar. No individual is without implicit theories about human nature. Theories make sense out of a confusing and complex world. Theories enable choices to be made. Theories guide practice and research.

To summarize, the question is not whether to use theories, but what theories to use and how to use them. This latter assertion raises a paradox. Although theory can improve vision, it can also blind. Mahoney (1976) has summarized much of the evidence concerning the distortions resulting from rigidly holding specific theoretical positions. Theoretical predilections of a counselor can make the counselor insensitive to data that are not compatible with, or not articulated within, the counselor's system. Under these paradoxical conditions, the counselor may reject systematic conceptualizing activity and become muddleheaded or may adopt a specific and meaningful conceptual framework that often leads to erroneous and incomplete conclusions.

The dilemma is real. The first task for counseling psychologists is not so much the development of other theories of human behavior but the development of a generic framework that specifies the characteristics of the counseling process.

A Way of Thinking

Theory and *conceptual framework* have been used rather loosely up to this point. Some distinctions need to be made. The preceding discussion concerned the need for a basic framework for conceptualizing the counseling process and the dilemma of whether to adopt specific theories of counseling. In a recent book, *Systematic Counseling* (Stewart, Winborn, Johnson, Burks, & Engelkes, 1978) the distinction is noted between models for examining theoretical implications and theory itself. It is the former discription of "models for utilizing theories" that is of major concern. Such a model suggests how a specific theory can be used within the counseling process. It does not replace theory, but provides a framework for translating theory, in this case cognitive-behavioral theory, into implications for counseling practice, research, and training. Much of the following discussion will be based on such a "models way of thinking," used in education (for example, Gagné & Briggs, 1974; Glaser, 1962; Joyce & Weil, 1972) and counseling (Stewart et al., 1978).

Joyce and Weil (1972) discuss a number of recent overlapping trends that have contributed to such a distinctive way of thinking. These trends have had a significant impact on education, government, and business. They include training psychology, cybernetic psychology, and systems analysis. While overlapping in many respects (for example, post-World War II phenomena), each trend has a somewhat different history and has emphasized different processes. Briefly, training psychology developed in response to military needs for training programs concerned with complex learning (such as submarine crew training). Training psychologists emphasized the breaking down and sequencing of performance and task analysis. Cybernetic psychologists emerged as translators of the rapidly developing computer technology and transformed such technology into human engineering terms. Such psychologists were also involved in training military personnel (for instance, flight simulation). They emphasized dynamic feedback and self regulation. Systems analysis can be traced to many sources (such as Bertalanffy, 1968), but the most influential has been the operations research conducted by the military and extended by business. Systems analysis has been primarily concerned with conceptualizing system components and their management.

Contributions have converged and have provided a methodology for conceptualizing a generic framework for the counseling process. First, these converging trends share a problem-solving orientation in which a system is developed, implemented, controlled, and evaluated. Secondly, such an orientation emphasizes the relationship of parts of a system to one another and to the system itself. Thirdly, the orientation relies on systematic knowledge of the learning process derived from scientific psychology. Finally, behavior change is its goal.

As mentioned, this methodology has been applied to education and counseling. In education, Robert Glaser (1962) has developed a basic model of teaching in which he describes four interrelating parts: instructional objectives, entering behavior, instructional procedures, and performance assessment. Instructional objectives concern what the student should be able to demonstrate at the end of an instructional event. Entering behavior describes the student's level of functioning before instruction begins. The teaching strategies used to bring about the desired changes are the focus of the instructional procedures component. Finally, performance assessment consists of procedures used to determine the student's progress in relationship to the instructional objectives. Each of these components is related through feedback mechanisms that provide smooth coordination and regulation. With slight modifications, such a model has great similarity to the counseling process. Operationally, the functions of counseling have been described in similar terms: counseling goals (instructional objectives), assessment (entering behavior), interventions (instructional procedures), and evaluation (performance assessment).

In counseling, Stewart and associates (1978) have used a systems approach in developing a detailed model of the counseling process. They have provided a flowchart model that indicates a basic optimal sequence of counseling functions.

In relating the systems orientation (way of thinking) to the counseling process, certain characteristics appear relevant. As discussed earlier, many of the recent trends in educational technology share a problem-solving perspective with emphases on learning and behavior change. Such a perspective has historical roots in counseling psychology. Many counselors describe counseling as a learning process and focus on problem solving and goal setting.

Another relevant aspect revealed in these applications is the breaking down and sequencing of procedures. In this book, the counseling process is the whole to be analyzed into components and such components are to be interrelated through optimal sequencing. These factors, problem solving and component analysis, are relevant to the development of a framework for counseling.

A Framework for Counseling

In formulating the following schema, no claim of originality is made. In fact, much of the content is based on other attempts to identify the generic features of helping (for example, Frank, 1961, 1973). The schema reflects an attempt to identify and organize the generic functions of counseling. The organization and component structure will be based on problem-solving operations. Thus the major emphasis is on the translation of general problem-solving procedures into a counseling model rather than on the elaboration of a detailed model of counseling.

The problem-solving process, according to D'Zurilla and Goldfried (1969) consists of stages: a general orientation, problem definition and formulation, generation of alternatives, decision making, and verification. The first stage provides an orientation or set by which the individual can recognize and cope with a problem situation without being overwhelmed by stress and confusion. Then the individual faces the task of defining the problem situation. Such a task requires information gathering and conceptual learning in order to establish an adequate formulation.

The major task of the alternatives stage is to generate a number of operational alternatives. In light of the alternative solutions, the problem-solver now must make predictions about these possible action plans and carry out the optimal plan. In the last stage, active experimental testing of the plan is conducted to verify the efficacy of the individual's solutions.

Each of these stages has been translated into specific counseling functions. In the model proposed here, a general problem-solving orientation corresponds to establishment processes; problem formulation is labeled conceptualization; interventions represents the alternative-generation and decision-making stages; and, finally, verification procedures are included under research.

Before discussing the translation of such a stage approach to counseling, it should be remembered that D'Zurilla and Goldfried (1971) did not imply that problem solving occurred precisely according to such sequential steps. Rather they argued that typically the stages would overlap and interact. Thus this stage approach to counseling should not be viewed as a description of the actual counseling process, but as a way of organizing the counseling functions.

Figure 1.1 is a diagram of the counseling model. Each element will briefly be described here, and later chapters will give specific consideration to each component. Establishment (box A) is a process that many counselors describe in terms of a specific type of relationship between the client (client system)* and the counselor. Such relationship conditions are usually described

---

*Use of the term client does not necessarily imply a remedial and individualistic perspective. Implications can also be made for consulting and preventive perspectives that include groups and institutions. Use of such a term is for convenience. Further elaboration of a preventive perspective is in Chapter 6.

FIGURE 1.1 A Conceptual Framework for Counseling.

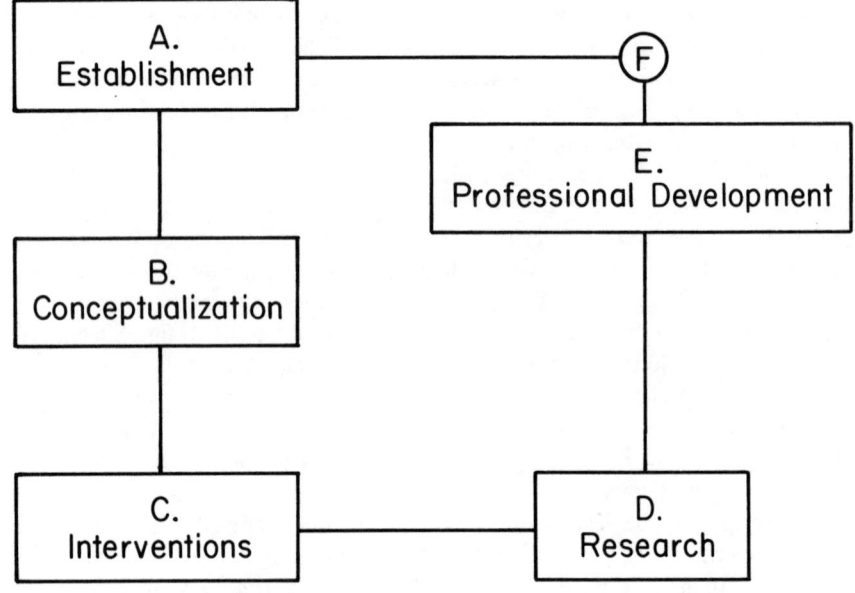

Source: Constructed by the author.

in client-centered terminology with the focus on counselor attributes (for example, competence, caring, and acceptance) and client experience of confidence in such attributes. These conditions can often reduce anxiety associated with problem situations and lead to positive expectations.

In addition to relationship conditions, the establishment phase involves a rationale or explanation concerning adaptive and maladaptive behavior. Such rationales are usually optimistic and highly plausible explanations of human behavior that tend to mobilize clients involved in crises and contribute along with relationship conditions to the establishment of a general problem-solving orientation. Conceptualization (box B) involves the systematic collection and critical survey of available information concerning the problem situation with consequent formation of a tentative hypothesis and plan of action. Such functions are often discussed in the counseling literature as assessment and goal setting. The conceptualization phase extends the establishment processes through elaboration of relationship conditions, which facilitates increased client participation and information gathering. Such a collection of information and its subsequent analysis aids problem interpretation, a further specification of the rationale process involved earlier. Such problem specification can offer understanding and explanation to reassure perplexed clients. Such problem definitions lead to the formulation of particular goals and strategies for change.

Interventions (box C) describe the specific implementation of a plan of action. These procedures require effort and active participation of both client and counselor. Such procedures afford an opportunity for clients to perform new skills, to receive feedback, and to observe their behavior and its effects. Research (box D) consists of the methodologies and measures used to determine the effectiveness of a particular plan of action. Professional development (box E) is the process that prepares the counselor for various counseling functions. Finally, lines which connect the boxes in Figure 1.1 are called feedback loops and indicate the interdependence of the various counseling functions. These feedback loops represent a mechanism for obtaining information that can be used in regulating and adjusting the counseling system.

The five parts of the model correspond to the remaining chapters of this book. Each chapter will examine the implications of cognitive-behavioral theory in terms of the specific counseling function. In addition to descriptive material, each chapter will contain implications for theory, practice, and research specific to each counseling function. A postscript will raise theoretical and professional issues with questions for future research.

2
ESTABLISHMENT

GENERIC GOALS

To a large extent, the process of counseling is determined by its objectives and by the needs of the client. If the various counseling functions, such as the establishment process, are largely dependent on goals and client needs, it is necessary to specify a generic goal of counseling. Once such a goal is described the various counseling stages can be defined in terms of their specific goal-related functions as they relate to the developmental needs of clients.

A generic goal is not readily revealed in the counseling literature. Counseling goals have been a subject of controversy (Krumboltz, 1964; Patterson, 1964). The type of goals recommended in the literature are diverse: self actualization (Boy & Pine, 1963), personal effectiveness (Blocher, 1966/1974), decision making (Williamson, 1950), and problem resolution (Krumboltz, 1965). Arguments about criteria have been endless. Client-centered goals are judged to be too subjective and incapable of accurate evaluation by behavioral counselors, while behavioral goals appear too specific and too concerned with environmental control for Rogerian counselors. Both may be right. Such diversity and controversy over goals leads to semantic arguments that may blind us to useful commonalities. One such commonality appears to be an emphasis on self management as a desirable therapeutic outcome. Most goal statements stress that counseling brings about changes and that clients use these changes to enhance their everyday lives. The emphasis in such satements is on equipping the client for self management (see Strong, 1978). While insight-oriented therapy goals have remained vague with consequent confusion concerning the counseling process and its effectiveness, such goals have emphasized the client as the agent of change. Client-centered counseling has focused on the client's responsibility for growth and maturity. Through the corrective experience of relationship counseling, the client's gain of insight and perceptual clarity are implemented by the client in everyday life. The client is the responsible agent with the counseling experience serving as a facilitator of self management.

Recent trends in behavioral psychology (Goldfried & Merbaum, 1973; Kanfer, 1975; Mahoney, 1974; Thoresen & Mahoney, 1974) are also beginning to emphasize a self management perspective. Even though earlier behavioral goal discussions may have stressed specific, one-dimensional objectives and environmental control, there appears to be wide support for a "personal science paradigm for the client" (Mahoney, 1974). Such a paradigm encourages the client to aquire a broad range of coping skills that the client can use independently. This focus on general strategies for independent use is congruent with the problem-solving conceptual framework adopted in this book. These convergences suggest that a promising approach to counseling goals would be to cast them in terms of self management. Specifically, counseling is viewed as an apprenticeship in problem solving through which the client is equipped for effective self management. Thus each stage of counseling is described in terms of its contribution to mobilizing the client's resources for effective self control.

ESTABLISHMENT GOALS

The first temporal stage of problem solving has been described as a state of doubt, confusion, and frustration (Dewey, 1916), not unlike the initial stage in counseling. The client who comes for professional help with personal problems is often described as anxious and/or depressed, the two most common complaints of people seeking therapy. Often in the literature the client is described as feeling helpless, lacking self control, immobilized, and unable to perceive accurately. For instance, the following exerpt from Fitts (1965) concerns the description of the experiences of a potential therapy client.

> I just had to do *something*! I've been scared to death; I don't know what's happening to me! I think I'm completely coming apart— sometimes I'm afraid I already have. I can't go on this way. I can't remember anything, I don't even know *what* I'm doing, half the time, and the other half I don't care! Nothing really matters anymore. (1965, p. 16)

Of course, this does not reflect the feelings of all clients. In fact, such descriptions rely more on clinical folklore than empirical investigations. Moreover, such descriptions appear to be a function of the type of problem; the previous characteristics are more often associated with personal adjustment problems than with vocational problems. Data on personality characteristics of counselees with different problems tend to support such a view (Minge & Bowman, 1967).

With such caution in mind, three characteristics of clients in the preparatory stage of counseling appear to inhibit their self control and thus become likely targets for change within the establishment phase. They are anxiety, information processing, and motivation.

As research suggests, high anxiety can inhibit performance, reduce information processing capacity, and lead to impulsive and/or rigid behaviors. For instance, the previous client description shows that the desperation of the client may be interfering with the client's memory (see Kaye, Kirschner, & Mandler, 1953).

The perception of events and processing of observations can easily be distorted in the initial stage of counseling. As mentioned, high anxiety can reduce information processing through selective attention, resulting in distortion of the problem and of alternative solutions ("I don't know what's happening to me!"). Causal attributions can also be affected. Feelings of hopelessness arise due to a sense of powerlessness ("I think I'm completely coming apart . . . "). That is, causes of events are perceived to be beyond the client's personal control.

Frank (1961/1973) talks about demoralization as a state common to many seeking therapy. Such individuals may be described as lacking the will power to carry out actions necessary for effective self management ("I don't even know *what* I'm doing, half the time, and the other half I don't care. Nothing really matters anymore"). These descriptions are akin to the condition of "learned helplessness" (Seligman, 1974, 1975). That is, prior perceptual experience of the client has led to the learning of the independence of behavior and its impact, resulting in motivational deficits and interference with the learning of new skills. The perception of noncontrol essentially inhibits the active problem-solving process.

It is apparent that these conditions—anxiety, information processing, and motivation—interact and overlap. There seems to be evidence that they often appear in the initial stage of therapy and inhibit the client's self-management capacity and the opportunity to learn and practice new skills. Of course, these conditions have different values and impacts depending on the client's situation and nature of the problem. Moreover, some of the characteristics mentioned, such as learned helplessness, may not be entirely adequate as a paradigm for human behavior (see Blaney, 1971). Yet, lacking conclusive evidence, these three conditions appear to be among the key targets for the establishment phase. That is, establishment processes should attempt to reduce anxiety, increase the effectiveness of the client's processing of information, and increase the client's expectancy of counseling effectiveness and personal power.

SOURCES OF ESTABLISHMENT

Relationship Conditions

Since the early 1950s, relationship conditions have been the predominant factor in discussing the counseling process. In fact, the terms relationship and counseling have increasingly become interchangeable through the influence of Carl Rogers. The stress on relationship conditions within the client-centered approach emerged through the confluence of philosophy (Dewey), progressive education (such as Dewey, Kilpatrick, and G. Watson), and social work (for instance, Rankians). This convergence led to a relationship therapy that stressed a positive evaluation of expressed feelings, the encounter of counselor and client, an emphasis on the present, a focus on the natural developmental process, and lack of emphasis on an authoritarian therapeutic attitude. The Rogerian view of relationship counseling was given specificity in 1957 when Rogers presented his description of the necessary and sufficient conditions for personality change (for example, genuineness, unconditional positive regard, and empathy). These conditions have been revised and increased in number through the work of Truax and Carkhuff (Carkhuff, 1969; Truax & Carkhuff, 1967). Even though there is controversy surrounding these relationship factors and the specific ways in which they interact with other counseling procedures is yet to be determined, these conditions appear to be recognized and accepted by a wide variety of therapists (for example, Goldfried & Davidson, 1976).

Relationship counseling has been primarily associated with an insight or release paradigm of behavior change. That is, the task of the Rogerian therapist is to provide the relationship-enhancing attitudes that release and facilitate the basic developmental process (actualization) that exists in all human beings. In the older and more psychoanalytic view, the relationship serves as a context for the elaboration of transference reactions of the patient toward the therapist onto whom the patient projects childish wishes and attitudes. Through such a process, the patient is enabled to consciously examine earlier attitudes leading to emotional insight. Both views put a premium on the client's/patient's experiencing of this relationship that permits growth and change.

In terms of the target goals of the establishment phase (anxiety reduction, processing effectiveness, and motivation), relationship counseling emphasized that the provision of an understanding atmosphere accomplished each of these goals. Anxiety reduction was thought to occur through catharsis or insight. That is, the discussion of the causes of one's anxiety was thought to reduce anxiety. As anxiety was being reduced, defenses (distortions) were being removed, enabling the perceptual field of the client to be enlarged (open to experience). Thus more accurate information was hypothetically accessible. In addition, the provisions of the relationship conditions stressing the positive value of the client and faith in the client's capabilities was thought to facilitate a commitment to change.

Although much of what has been discussed concerning the relationship conditions may have some general truth, such a view does not offer much insight into the specific processes that underlie the effects of relationship counseling. It is hoped that a more cognitively oriented model (information processing) may provide additional insight into the relationship processes and how they function during the establishment stage.

An Information Model

From a cognitive-behavioral perspective, relationship conditions are viewed as necessary but not sufficient. Such conditions are thought of as being present throughout the counseling process. Moreover, these conditions can be conceptualized in terms of their information-processing functions (see Wexler, 1974). If we limit our discussion to empathic responding (since the other traditional conditions of unconditional positive regard and genuineness may be redundant and/or involve little overt activity), Wexler (1974) suggests such activity involves three information processing functions: an attentional function, an organizing function, and an evocative function.

In order to understand these functions more clearly, it is necessary to specify empathic understanding and information processing. Traditionally, empathy has been concerned with subjective understanding. This is clear in Rogers' definition:

> an accurate, empathic understanding of the client's world as seen from the inside. To sense the client's private world as if it were your own, but without losing the "as if" quality—this is empathy . . . (1961, p. 84)

Empathy is a complex process and, as suggested before, a controversial construct. Empirical data concerning its measurement and influence is far from conclusive (see Chinsky & Rappaport, 1970; Gladstein, 1977). With such caution in mind, empathy has been usually construed to involve cognitive and affective dimensions. The process of empathic responding occurs in the following sequence: 1) perception of client communication, 2) processing of client communication (discrimination and integration—understanding), and 3) the communication of the counselor's understanding. Such a sequence leads to a communication that is usually described in terms of a levels-system of empathic communication (see Carkhuff, 1969; Truax, 1961). Three levels of empathic communication seem basic to most systems: subtractive, interchangeable, and additive. The subtractive level implies that the counselor's communication does not focus on the client's communication; the counselor diverts attention to another area instead (for example, advice giving). Interchangeable expressions between counselor and client refer to the similarity of affect and meaning contained in the counselor's response to client statements (for instance, reflective communication). Additive expressions of the counselor are viewed as reflecting a deeper level of experience than expressed by the client (similar to interpretative communication).

The levels-system of empathic responding has much in common with a recent conceptual development in memory research called a levels of processing approach (Craik & Lockhart, 1972). In terms of memory, Craik and Lockhart propose that rates of forgetting are a function of the depth of encoding (for example, semantic analysis). That is, memory is facilitated by enriched and elaborated processing. For example, after a word or phrase is recognized it may trigger images, stories, and associations that lead to deeper levels of processing. Words or phrases that are so elaborated are usually retained longer than others that have had impoverished processing. Thus there exists a continuum of processing, including the nonattended and partially analyzed, the rehearsal of material at a fixed level of processing (Type I), and the deeper analysis of material (Type II processing). Meaningfulness and information retention depend essentially on the level of analysis.

In relating the two levels-systems, the subtractive level in empathic communication is related to the phenomenon of nonattention or partial processing. If a client's expression is not attended to, the information is lost for the client due to inadequate processing. The interchangeable and additive levels are similar to Type I and Type II processing proposed by Craik and Lockhart (1972). Attention to the client's communication can be accomplished through counselor reflective responses. Such interchangeable communication appears to be similar to rehearsal operations at a fixed level of processing that serves to retain information, which has been called Type I processing. It is the additive level or Type II processing that should lead to improved memory and perhaps more effective therapeutic communication. Here the counselor's statements lead to deeper levels of analysis (termed Type II processing) by the client in which the client's learned cognitive structures interact with the counselor's communication. Such a communication may offer a more effective organization of information that enables the client to elaborate different facets of his or her experience in more meaningful ways. In terms of linguistics the counselor is more concerned with the client's deep structure (full linguistic representation of experience) than the client's surface structures (communications). At this deeper level, the counselor may be serving important organizational functions (providing new cognitive structures, new processing rules, and so on).

In terms of information processing, especially a level of processing approach, it can be seen how empathic responding has attentional and organizational functions. That is, nonempathic responding by the counselor to the client's problematic experience leads the client away from the problem. Counselor reflective communication on such client experience has the merit of focusing and maintaining the client's attention on the problematic situation. Finally, a counselor's additive communication can provide a more meaningful organization of information that the client can use for further elaboration.

The evocative function of empathic communication is related to the other functions. It too serves a role in facilitating the client's processing of information. The evocative function can best be described from a linguistic perspective (see Bandler & Grinder, 1975). Basically, the language of the counselor can influence the amount of analysis clients perform in processing their experiences. Inexpressive language may not stimulate the client to self explore in a meaningful way. For instance, many client expressions suffer from nominalization, the transformation of a process into an event. Compare the following statements.

Carol understands that she decides her own life.

Carol understands her decision about her own life.

In the second, the process version (the verb, decide) has been transformed into an event (decision). The possible effect of such linguistic distortion is to portray an ongoing and active process as a closed and finished situation. The counselor needs to be aware of distortions, such as deletions, permutations, nominalizations, and so on, and use evocative language to reconnect the event with the ongoing process. That is, the use of active verbs, vivid adjectives, metaphors, and imagery by the counselor enhances processing effectiveness by correcting distortions and stimulating client semantic analysis.

In returning to our establishment goals, how do the relationship conditions as potential information-processing variables reduce anxiety, increase processing effectiveness, and facilitate expectancies? From an informational perspective, anxiety may be viewed as a result of an inability to organize information. Clients may simply lack the ability or structures necessary to process the available information. As a result, they may appear bewildered and confused. They may be unable to concentrate and may eventually become depressed and passive. Another possibility is that they become rigid and rely on a few processing mechanisms. Such a condition may lead to vigilance in which the client actively attempts to fit information into impoverished cognitive structures. Whatever the cause or effects, anxiety results largely from the impact of inadequately organized information. If this is the case, relationship factors (such as emphatic responding), by providing attention and cognitive organization to the client's experience, can be effective in coping with inhibition and inadequate cognitive activity. It should be mentioned that increased empathic responding may not eliminate affect but may create affect through its stimulation of increased client cognitive functioning. Such increased functioning could lead to restructuring of the client assumptive world. This change, as in any change process, is likely to be associated with arousal. But the affective state associated with change appears to be qualitatively different from that associated with disintegration—that is, a hopeless condition based on confusion and disorganization compared with the hopeful condition related to elaboration, restructuring, and change. Similar to Schacter's research (e.g., Schacter & Singer, 1962), the specific affective state is not solely a function of the bodily condition condition but includes the influence of the person's construction of the present situation (that is, information and attribution). Thus the anxiety reduction goal needs to be clarified. Such reduction is not the elimination of arousal per se, but the reduction of arousal associated with information inadequacy and hopeless interpretations. At the same time, the counselor strives through evocative language to stimulate client cognitive activity resulting in arousal and increased motivation.

In summary, the information-processing view of relationship counseling specifies processes that may be involved in accomplishing establishment goals. These information processes help clients attend to and organize their experiences and stimulate them to explore and redefine their experiences in deeper and more meaningful terms. Such a view has been largely neglected by counseling psychologists. Unfortunately, little research is available to evaluate this view. There may be some promise in using various paradigms for exploring these proposals. For instance, paradigms from memory research could be used to investigate client retention of predetermined in-therapy material that had been systematically associated with various levels of counselor empathic responding. Content analysis of interviews using a transformational grammar perspective and/or nonlinguistic analysis using voice quality (for example, Rice & Wagstaff, 1967) could be conducted as procedures for assessing processing effectiveness. In conclusion, a more cognitive view of traditional relationship counseling appears informationally rich and offers useful research paradigms. Such a view merits further investigation.

INFLUENCE PROCESSES

A second source for the establishment process concerns certain influence processes that have been identified in social psychology. These processes, including credibility, rationale, and expectancy, have been associated with interpersonal influence and attitude change. Such processes have emerged from a social influence paradigm. Historically, the development of a social influence perspective owes much to Kurt Lewin and his students (Festinger, Cartwright, Kelley, Thibaut, Deutsch, Schachter, Back, and others). The Lewinian emphasis on the interrelatedness of person and environment was a major contribution to psychology and stimulated the generation of related social influence concepts, such as cognitive dissonance (Festinger), social power (Cartwright), causal attribution (Kelley), and group dynamics (Lewin, Lippitt, & White, 1939). Besides Lewin and his followers, Carl Hovland and his group at Yale University need to be mentioned for their contribution in reestablishing attitude research and persuasion as major focuses in experimental social psychology (Hovland, Janis, & Kelley, 1953). These trends have emphasized a paradigm that concerns itself with how the actions of one person become the conditions for the actions of another person (see Secord & Backman, 1974).

Five major components need attention in discussing the influence process: the source, the influence communication, the social setting, the receiver, and the target.

> The source. The source variables mean the attributes of the influencer, for example, the expertness, trustworthiness, or attractiveness of the influencer.
> The influence communication. Communication factors include the content and structure of the communication and the type of appeal used.
> The social setting. Setting characteristics have to do with contextual variables through which the influence communication is presented. Examples include sanctions and expectations associated with specific

settings (public, private, and so on), concerning the legitimacy of the specific influence process.

The receiver. The receiver (influencee) category describes the characteristics of the person receiving the influence communication. Such factors include personality, ability, and emotional condition.

The target. The behavioral acts and attitudes that are to result from the influence attempt are in this category.

A great deal of research has been done on these elements within experimental social psychology (see McGuire, 1969), but, until recently, little work has been done in applying such knowledge of the influence process to counseling and psychotherapy. It wasn't until 1961 when Jerome Frank, a student of Lewin, published his important book, *Persuasion and Healing,* that the social influence process was clearly applied to psychotherapy. A little later one of the first dissertations using persuasion methodology concerned with therapy-like phenomena within an analogue setting was published (Bergin, 1962). The extrapolation of concepts and results from social psychology to psychotherapy has expanded through the publication of a book by Goldstein, Heller, and Sechrest (1966). In the area of counseling, Stanley Strong has elucidated and investigated the potential of an influence process view (Strong, 1968, 1978). Such translations stress the similarities between the therapeutic situation and social persuasion. In terms of our major influence components, there does appear to be a good fit. That is, as described earlier, the potential client (receiver) for counseling is likely to be anxious and involved in an ambiguous and problematic situation. Under these conditions, the client would be expected to be susceptable to persuasive influence. Such a client seeking out a professional would find a socially sanctioned context for helping (setting), which would typically arouse expectations of relief. As therapeutic transactions commence, the client's perception of the counselor's competence and other attributes (source variables) would facilitate the effectiveness of the influence process. The transactions (communication) themselves can be construed as persuasion attempts. Through the communications, a type of relationship is established in which the confidence of the client in the counselor's competence and concern for the client is strengthened. Moreover, such therapeutic communications attempt to provide a rationale of treatment. Such explanations often attempt to influence the client's attitudes and behavior. For instance, such rationales are often optimistic and plausible theories of human behavior. Most rationales concern a two-step model of behavior change in which the client changes through therapeutic work with a counselor and such changes are implemented by the client in the client's broader life (Strong, 1978). Such rationales attempt to influence the client to actively participate in therapeutic work and attempt to induce positive expectancies (targets). Thus therapy can be construed as an interpersonal influence process.

From such an influence perspective, three variables appear to be relevant to a problem-solving model of counseling: credibility, rationale, and expectations. Such cognitively-oriented variables seem to be derived from a conceptualization of the client as a problem-solving individual attempting to resolve real life problems. Individuals attempting to solve problems are concerned about competence, strategies, and outcome probabilities. Of course, cases can be made for the inclusion of other influence sources, such as attraction, social power, trustworthiness, and others. In fact, the three variables selected are probably not exclusive categories and in the following discussion of each variable there will be a great deal of overlap. For purposes of clarity, each variable will be discussed separately.

Credibility

The most studied among source variables in attitude research is credibility. The credibility paradigm has typically involved a communication presented at a fixed level to several equivalent groups of subjects with different purported sources for each group. Significant group differences are interpreted to be due to these different sources.

Historically, credibility or the expertness facet of credibility had an early start in attitude research and has had somewhat of a repetitious research record. There may be several reasons for its early start. Undoubtedly, the ease of constructing expert sources (behavioral definitions) lends it scientific respectability. Moreover, the spirit of the recent past has been concerned with power (McClelland, 1975) and the suggestibility of people (Milgram, 1963). Whatever the historical background, one of the most straightforward and reliable findings is that the amount of attitude change is associated with different levels of socially desirable dimensions of the influencer such as knowledge, education, social status, age, and so on (Hovland et al., 1953; McGuire, 1969). That is, the higher the evaluation of the source, the more attitude change is produced. Two major sources of credibility have been identified: expertness and trustworthiness. Expertness usually means competence, status, education, and so on, and trustworthiness has to do with objectivity and disinterest. Both facets overlap, with expertness having more persuasive impact (see McGuire, 1969). Most of the following discussion concerns expertness.

In terms of counseling research, expertness manipulations have consistently produced the appropriate set (Dell & Dell, 1976; Schmidt, 1973; Scheid, 1976; Strong & Dixon, 1971; Strong & Schmidt, 1970). A number of analogue studies have also noted the persuasive impact of perceived expertness on opinions (for example, Bergin, 1962; Strong & Schmidt, 1970). Most of these analogue studies follow a paradigm very similar to attitude research. That is, external cues (diplomas, certificates, setting, and introduction) and/or behavioral cues (a relaxed, dynamic, and responsive counselor) are used to influence clients' attitudes and behaviors. Most of these attempts do have persuasive impact, behavioral cues being associated with the greater impact (Scheid, 1976; Strong & Schmidt, 1970). Such studies, however, have been mostly analogue studies that generally involved videotape ratings or one interview-like session, extreme dichotomies between expert and inexpert conditions, and questionable ego-invested attitude targets. These studies are subject to demand characteristics and have not yielded definite answers (see Dell & Schmidt, 1976).

Within these restrictions, it appears that expertness has a persuasive impact, at least a stonger impact than other possible source variables. It also appears reasonable that credibility would provide an important source for the establishment phase. Anxious clients wanting to solve their problems would be sensitive to counselor competence. Perception of counselor expertness might relieve initial stress and could increase and maintain the counselor's influence in attempting to deal with the establishment concerns of correcting distortions and inducing motivation. Moreover, such influence is not restricted to this phase, but is important to the whole counseling process. In summary, to the degree that counseling is an influence process in which the client lacks self-support resources, credibility would be a salient source of establishing counselor influence and initiating client behavior change.

Rationale

Social psychologists have investigated many aspects of the message (similar to the concept of rationale used here) in persuasion studies (see McGuire, 1969). Among these are fear appeals (Janis & Feshbach, 1953), verbal reinforcement (Ekman, 1958), arguments and counterarguments (Hovland, Lumsdain & Sheffield, 1949), and others. Frank (1961/1973) was one of the first to discuss the relevance of rationales in psychotherapy. He suggested that most psychotherapies had a rationale that included a general explanation of human behavior and an optimistic outlook. Other writers on counseling and psychotherapy usually discuss similar themes under structuring or preparing the clients for therapy. For instance, Wolpe (1973) carefully discusses the origins of neurotic fear and the practice of behavior therapy with his clients. Recently, Meichenbaum (1977) has spoken of the benefits of the conceptualization process in which clients are helped to redefine their problematic situations. He stresses that new self understanding and feelings of hopefulness are goals of such a process.

Two functions of therapy rationales appear salient: structuring and persuasion induction. The structuring function of rationales is similar to the use of advance organizers (Ausubel, Novak, & Hanesian, 1978). Organizers are introductory materials that establish a meaningful learning set in which the learner recognizes what the learner already knows, what the learner needs to know, and how such knowledge components can be interrelated for meaningful learning to take place. In terms of therapy rationale, the client is provided with a conceptual framework that usually stresses an optimistic viewpoint in which facets of the client's problematic situation are viewed as changeable through self mastery. At the same time that such rationales are providing conceptual structure for the treatment interventions to follow, an influence induction is occurring in which the client's active participation and expectation of help are targets. The rationale is not a hard sell directed to short-term motivational enhancement. It should involve active collaboration between counselor and client in order to avoid resistance and dependency attributions. Moreover, such rationales need to be tied to specific treatment procedures in order to facilitate client coping effectiveness.

The research supporting such a view of rationales is sparse. Most of the therapy studies involve the rationale as an aspect of a multimethod treatment. Educational research on advance organizers has been mixed (see Barnes & Clawson, 1975), with such studies having several conceptual and methodological problems (lack of consruct validity of the advance organizer design, criteria for an organizer, item difficulty, criterion tests, and so on). Related medical research on placebo affects indicates that explicit or inexplicit helping rationales are associated with symtom relief (Shapiro, 1959).

If rationales are effective in the establishment phase, such effectiveness may be a function of providing a meaningful interpretation of the disorganized and distorted field of an anxious client. Motivationally, as a result of an effective rationale, the client may increase self understanding and experience feelings of control and hope leading to the necessary acts of change.

Expectations

Historically, expectation of help emerged from the medical tradition. Expectancies also have been investigated within social psychology, particularly in cognitive dissonance studies and in the social role literature. But the placebo effect in medical research appears to be the tradition from which psychotherapists have borrowed most extensively in examining the expectancy effect in psychotherapy. Frank (1961/1973) and Goldstein (1962) have been instrumental in examining the effects of expectancy in psychotherapy research. Recent interest in the influence of expectancy has been reasserted through the work on self efficacy (Bandura, 1977), the role nonspecific treatment effects in systematic desensitization (Kazdin & Wilcoxon, 1976), probability learning (Estes, 1972), cognitive appraisal (Lazarus, 1966), and prediction (Kahneman & Tversky, 1973).

While this interest in, and empirical research on, expectancy is recognized, the expectancy construct in psychotherapy is troublesome (Wilkins, 1973). The evidence is not as strong as expectancy advocates indicate. Numerous methodological problems have been discussed (Wilkins, 1973). Advocates viewing expectancy as a trait have made inappropriate cause and effect statements between expected gain (pretherapy) and improvement (posttherapy) on the basis of self report and correlational data. Self reports can be transparent and subject to demand characteristics, and correlational data do not easily serve as valid bases for cause and effect statements. Experimental studies that manipulate expectancy through expectancy instructions may also be problematic. A question of parsimony has been raised. That is, is it efficient or necessary to discuss some hypothetical, internal cognitive process that is rarely evaluated independent of outcome? Instructions, the amount of information, and individual prediction seem to be more straightforward.

Whatever the status of expectancy as an explanatory concept, it is useful to continue to investigate its potential contribution to the counseling process. In this book, expectancy as well as the other establishment sources are viewed as being involved in all stages of the counseling process. In terms of expectancy, its potency is realized when it is closely allied with the performances involved in the interventions. As Bandura (1977) points out, performance provides the most influential source of expectations. As a source of establishment, expectancy of help can relieve anxiety and mobilize a client to perform the necessary therapeutic activities. Moreover, the therapist can present an expectancy schema that may alter the client's inappropriate patterns of information processing through selectively emphasizing certain facets of experience and altering the client's anticipated consequences.

An Informational Model

As with the relationship conditions, it seems important to explore the influence sources from an informational perspective. It should be pointed out that the influence sources—capability, rationale, and expectancy—as distinct from relationship sources, are primarily cognitive variables based on information. That is, these sources usually rely on information contained in environmental events, such as credentials, didactic rationales, or expectancy instructions. From a constructivist orientation, the impact of such external information in terms of the establishment functions will depend on how it is cognitively appraised. Much of the work on the influence processes neglects the information that is tranformed and available to the individual. In terms of theses processes it may be important to understand how various information sources (such as eye contact, credentials, setting, factors, self disclosure, and rationales) are perceived by the client. It seems the counselor should be sensitive to the intrinsic beliefs of the client before arbitrarily asserting influence on the basis of position, jargon, and highly discrepant communications.

Researchers involved with these and related influence processes support the importance of the client's perceptive world. Ausubel and colleagues (Ausubel et al., 1978) recommend that meaningful learning occurs when material to be learned is related to the student's existing cognitive structure. Thus an understanding of the student's existing cognitive structure is imperative before appropriate teaching materials can be developed and implemented. The same applies to the use of advance organizer-type rationales used in psychotherapy. Social psychology research (Secord &

Backman, 1974) indicates that a successful communicator must know if the position advocated is within the respondent's range of acceptance. Moreover, these intervals appear to vary according to a number of factors such as credibility. Again it appears that a counselor needs to become aware of the client's self statements and attributions, the amount of ego investment, and situational press before providing a potential highly discrepant communication. For instance, it may be that too much of an internal induction—self responsibility for a wide range of problems—might create unnecessary anxiety that could exacerbate the presenting problem. This would especially be true for persons involved in situations, such as racism, that may require external attributions for effective coping.

Expertness and expectancy sources could also benefit from an information processing view. Instead of solely relying on external events to define these factors, some recognition must be given to how these sources and related attributes are perceived by the client and how they influence continued participation and involvement in therapeutic activities. Both of these sources may be primarily determined by their association with client-perceived performance mastery during treatment. That is, initial expertness and expectancy effects may be a function of the obvious external and behavioral cues described previously. But the maintenance and strengthening of these effects may be a function of the evidence for personal efficacy perceived by the client. The initial effects may enhance attentiveness to treatment procedures (homework) and, through persuasion-induced selective perception, alter inappropriate processing activity. Whatever the processes, it appears that therapy as an influence process cannot neglect the potential importance of phenomenological analysis of the client. In terms of research, such analysis does not replace empirical studies, but provides additional data from which decisions about its usefulness (predictive utility) can be made.

3
CONCEPTUALIZATION

BACKGROUND

By establishing a general orientation in approaching the counseling situation, the problem-solving counselor moves toward the stage in which the client is helped to specify the problem(s). Such a process can be viewed as a conceptualization process in which clients are helped to interpret (redefine) their problems into a new language system that leads to understanding, a sense of self management, and eventual corrective action (see Meichenbaum, 1977).

Historically, problem specification activities in the helping field have been subsumed under such categories as diagnosis, assessment, psychological testing, and others. Assessment or psychological testing are broad concepts associated with measurement and differential psychology. Diagnosis is concerned with appropriate identification of a disease process based on specific data bases, such as laboratory workups, x-rays, and medical history. After the difficulty has been identified, an appropriate treatment is implemented and monitored. This has also been standard procedure in psychiatry. That is, problem specification is an act of classifying disorders by using psychiatric nosological labels. There has been some question about the therapeutic usefulness of diagnosis in counseling (see Tyler, 1969), at least in the narrow sense of characterizing individuals according to formal nosological systems. Indeed there have been attempts to develop classification schemes in counseling (Bordin, 1946; Callis, 1965; Pepinsky, 1948; Williamson & Darley, 1937), but Tyler suggests that diagnosis in counseling should refer to a broader enterprise of developing a comprehensive picture of the client. Although there may be some agreement about the value of developing a working image of the client through various assessment activities, unfortunately, little agreement has emerged concerning the appropriate approach or mode of assessment on which such activities rely.

TRADITIONAL ASSESSMENT MODELS

Traditional concepts of assessment have been associated with the dynamic and psychometric orientations. These two orientations continue to coexist in clinical assessment and provide conflicting perspectives. The psychometric approach is concerned with traits and standardized testing, assuming that a person's behavior is influenced significantly by relatively stable, enduring dispositions. These dispositions, believed to be quantifiable and scalable, are also assumed to have a large degree of consistency and generality. In identifying such dispositions, dispositional psychologists rely heavily on empirical methods. Emphasis is on reliability and validity, confirmed through sophisticated methodology and statistical procedures (factor analysis). Standardization and objective tests are highly valued. Clinical judgment and inference are minimized.

Typically, inferences about clients' dispositions are based on their reactions to sets of items with a limited number of presribed choices, such as "strongly agree," "frequently," "yes," "no." Such self-report questionnaires can then be mechanically scored, and interpretation of test results depends on the sum of various elicited reactions (additive model) in comparison with well-developed norms. The Minnesota Multiphasic Personality Inventory (MMPI) is a good example of the traditional psychometric approach. It consists of 566 items to which one may answer "true," "false," or "cannot say." These items have been sorted into ten clinical scales and four validity scales. Scales (except Scales 5 and 0) were devised on the basis of establishing empirically the items that significantly differentiated particular diagnostic groups from "normals." Results of an individual's MMPI are usually recorded in terms of converted scores (T scores) in profile form. This format, in which a T score of 50 represents the average score of a specific reference group, readily provides a quantitative comparison. Many handbooks (for example, Marks & Seeman, 1963) are available for more in-depth comparison of a single individual's profile and additional normative information.

Whereas intelligence tests, specific abilities tests, and personality inventories have been derived from a psychometric approach, interview and projective techniques are associated with a dynamic orientation. The findings educed from such techniques depend less on psychometric properties than on the interpretative skills of the clinician. All projective methods are based on the projective hypothesis, namely, individuals reveal themselves in the way they deal with ambiguous stimuli. Such a projective strategy involves making clinical inferences about unconscious processes based on observations of behavior that are assumed to be nonadditive. That is, various overt behaviors that are indicators of a specific attribute are not necessarily summed, as is the case in the psychometric approach, to indicate the strength of that attribute. Suppose Tina frequently helped others, volunteered for many public help projects, and was an ardent adherent of helping others, while Lee rarely offered aid to others and seldom volunteered for altruistic projects. According to the psychometric model, Tina would be considered more altruistic than Lee. If a nonadditive model is used, the same conclusion would not necessarily be reached. In fact, it could be inferred by a dynamically oriented assessor that Tina's behavior is indicative of a consuming power motive ("telling others what to do") and that her altruistic behavior masks a perceived character weakness. This example shows how central the clinician is in the dynamic model through the impact of inferences and interpretations.

In projective testing, the clinician presents an individual with ambiguous stimuli, such as inkblots (Rorschach), pictures (TAT), incomplete sentences (sentence completion), words (word association), ambiguous instructions ("Create the most imaginative story [show a picture] . . . ," "Draw a person . . ."), and/or ambiguous questions ("What could this be?"). Almost any test stimuli with different instructions can be used projectively. In fact, the projective orientation has been carried over into the interpretation of more objective tests. Thus, intelligence tests are not only used in the assessment of intelligence, but can be interpreted to reflect an individual's personality dynamics. Interview dynamics behavior, dreams, slips of the tongue, and most other incidental behavior can serve as behavioral signs for interpretation since such material is assumed to reveal more accurately the unconscious life than does intentional behavior, because intentional behavior is presumably based on control and defensive motivation. Attempts to relate these behavioral signs to unconscious dynamics are based on special scoring procedures, such as Rorschach (Beck and Molish, 1967), TAT (McClelland, Atkinson, Clark & Lowell, 1953), and/or the clinician interpreting the themes in accord with a paticular personality theory.

Psychometric and dynamic traditions have converged in clinical practice. Such practice depends heavily on clinical judgment and uses a battery of tests, including intelligence tests, self-report personality inventories, and projective techniques. The convergence of these traditions in contemporary practice is represented in the work of Murray (1959) and Rapaport (Rapaport, Gill, & Shafer, 1945) and is succinctly outlined by Korchin (1976).

CONTEMPORARY ASSESSMENT MODELS

In contemporary professional psychology, two traditional and conflicting models have emerged to challenge traditional assessment procedures, namely, the behavioral and phenomenological. Though clearly different from each other, both orientations have questioned the adequacy of clinical judgment and the meaningfulness of global personality contructs. To a large degree these questions arise because of differing underlying assumptions. The clearest assumptive contrast is between the behavioral and traditional strategies. As noted, traditional assessment procedures have been directed as measuring intraindividual variables, such as "instincts," "needs," "drives," or "traits," that would predict behavior. This general approach represents a centralistic perspective (Murray, 1938). In contrast, the more radical behavior assessors have rejected the predictive function of internal determinants and have focused on behavioral and environmental events. Thus observable variables, rather than personality constructs, are the major concern. As opposed to emphasizing the characteristics an individual "has," the behavioral view places greater stress on what a person "does" (Mischel, 1968). Since the centralist perspective is rejected, there is no reason to assume that overt actions are indicators of underlying dynamics; rather such actions are seen in relationship to various environmental events. Assessment is therefore limited to the study of an individual's responses to specific facets of the environment.

Behavioral assessment can be characterized as direct, analytic, and present-oriented. That is, behavioral assessors have been concerned with sampling present behavior, primarily particular dimensions rather than the total personality, and observing the relationship between behavioral acts with specific situational conditions. Moreover, such behavioral assessment is also additive in that the likelihood of a specific reaction to a situation is primarily a function of the frequency of that reaction to the same situation. To learn how a person acts in stressful situations, behavioral assessors observe how persons act in such situations and/or ask these persons directly how they behaved in these situations in the past or expect to act in future similar situations. For example, a phobic individual can be exposed to a performance measure of avoidance. Such a measure may include a number of tasks that represent more threatening interactions with the feared situation or object. Scoring would involve the number of tasks completed successfully (see Bandura, Adams, & Beyer, 1977). The individual may be given a self-report measure of fear (Fear Survey Schedule; Wolpe & Lang, 1964) that directly requests an indication of the degree of fear of various objects and situations. In addition, individuals may be asked to designate their expectations of performing successfully under various stressful conditions (see Bandura et al., 1977). Such expectations may be associated with a number of graduated tasks in which the individual indicates the degree of confidence in accomplishing each task.

Another behavior assessment strategy is to teach the client assessment skills. Such a procedure is associated with the self-control literature (for instance, Thoresen & Mahoney, 1974) in which the client is taught to carry out functional analyses—analyses of the covariations between changes in environmental conditions and changes in selected behavioral patterns. One skill involved in such analyses is the strategy of self observation, which requires individuals to carefully attend to and record their interactions for purposes of evaluation. Self-observation data can be collected via a diary, counter, or chart. Such recording procedures tend to enhance treatment effectiveness and lead to treatment evaluation. In addition, such self-control strategies provide a client with more data about the problem and a sense of self management, both germane to the conceptualization stage.

At the other extreme of contemporary assessment models is the phenomenological approach. This approach has no great affinity for behavior or intrapsychic constructs, but is concerned with the meanings people ascribe to their lives and world. Such assessment of meaning has some correspondence to traditional assessment in that phenomenological assessors are concerned about the internal life of the individual and primarily use self-report measures. In contrast to the traditional models, phenomenological assessment is relatively straightforward and contemporaneous, in that reports of subjective experience are usually related to the here and now and are taken more or less at face value. These reports are not considered signs of some inferred intrapsychic state or underlying disposition. Nor do they focus on the past as in the psychoanalytic strategy; information about the past is considered only in clarifying present perceptions. There is no need to infer underlying unconscious processes, since the phenomenological strategy assumes that subjective awareness of events largely determines behavior. The emphasis of such a strategy is to gain phenomenological knowledge of a person, that is, an attempt to understand subjective experience from the internal frame of reference of the individual relating such experiences. Adopting another's perspective is thought to be different from making inferences about a person based on the external frame of reference seemingly adopted by other formal assessment procedures.

In contrast to the more radical behavioral model, phenomenological assessment has stressed the complexity of behavior and the importance of perception of the internal and external environments. Instead of relying on observations of one-dimensional stimuli and discrete responses as in typical functional analyses, the phenomenologist has suggested the importance of how individuals interpret their experience in understanding human behavior.

The essence of phenomemological assessment involves understanding the person's experiences in terms of what they mean to that person. This means, among other things, suspending one's own meanings for words and phrases that the other person uses. Devices such as the semantic differential (Osgood, Suci, & Tannenbaum, 1957) and the Role Construct Repertory Test (Rep test) developed by Kelly (see Bannister & Mair, 1968) were developed in order to assess the meaning an individual assigns to particular concepts. In the semantic differential, the individual is presented a stimulus word ("me," "school," "my job") and asked to rate each stimulus on a graphic, 7-point, bipolar scale ("rough-smooth," "hard-soft") by marking the point that clearly indicates the personal meaning of the stimulus concept. On the Rep test, the individual is asked and/or assisted in listing many people or things that are personally important (self, father, spouse) and then asked to compare and contrast (sorting) these items in groups of three. That is, in each trial the person indicates how two items are similar to each other and different from the third. In this manner, a systematic and flexible assessment of the way a person construes the world is accomplished through evoking subjective dimensions of similarity and opposites among events.

The development of client-centered therapy by Rogers can be seen in the context of the assessment of phenomenological knowledge. Though rejecting concepts of formal assessment, Rogers' discussion of the interview conditions and use of the Q-sort methodology (Stephenson, 1953) are primarily aimed at understanding the client from the client's frame of reference. In terms of the interview, Rogers has discussed the importance of certain relationship conditions, such as empathy (Rogers, 1975), in which the counselor is urged to suspend judgment and formal assessment procedures and to learn from the client how the client feels, thinks, and behaves. In addition, a Q-sort (for example, Bloch, 1961) could be implemented to continue the empathic process. Such a procedure consists of a large number of cards, each containing a printed statement, such as "I am likable," "gets anxious easily." The Q-sort can be used for many different purposes: self descriptions (self sort), ideal self description (ideal sort), and others. Different instructions are presented depending on the nature of the sort. After appropriate instructions, the client usually sorts cards into a forced distribution along a continuum from items that are least characteristic to most characteristic of the target of the sort.

SUMMARY OF MODELS

Perhaps the most fundamental point to emerge from the brief review of assessment models is that they are incomplete. First, most models ignore environmental assessment. Behaviorists appear to consider the environment, but the unit of analysis is usually small and one-dimensional. Such an analytic standpoint may be useful from a methodological perspective, but certainly denies the multidimensionality of situations and the impact of larger systems on an individual's behavior. Such an individualistic focus has been the bane of most clinical assessment methods, often leading to a "blame the victim" orientation. Second, many of the widely used psychometric tests have failed to demonstrate either convergent or discriminant validity, sufficient control of response set bias, or theoretical relevance. Third, the more centralistic assessment methods have shown a disregard for behaviors except as they serve as signs of unconscious meanings and generalized dispositions. Finally, behavior assessors have neglected intraindividual variables though such neglect is not intrinsic to a behavioral conceptualization. To be sure, the models have been improved and broadened by such developments as the emphasis on an ecological perspective (Bronfenbrenner, 1977) and environmental assessment (Moos, 1976), the improved methodology in psychometric test construction (for example, Campbell & Fiske, 1959; Cronbach & Meehl, 1955; Jackson, 1970; Loevinger, 1957), the increased appreciation of situational impact in dynamic formulations (for instance, Wachtel, 1977), and the increased attention devoted to cognitive variables in the behavioral tradition (such as Mischel,

1973). These developments point toward an improved methodology that focuses on cognitive-behavioral-environmental data in which information about an individual's relevant cognitions and behaviors in relation to the conditions of the psychological situation is of particular concern.

A COGNITIVE-BEHAVIORAL MODEL

General Considerations

The cognitive-behavioral approach to assessment proposed will not be the comprehensive "working image" suggested by Tyler (1969) nor will it be able to satisfy the need for environmental assessment. The focus will be on information about client psychological processes provided by experimental procedures designed to bridge the gap between observable performance and client processes. Thus the importance of subjective experience is not assumed, but must be demonstrated empirically. Other valid assessment practices are not discussed because they are adequately covered elsewhere. Unfortunately, the theory and technology of environmental assessment are rudimentary, but an attempt to highlight some promising environmental evaluation procedures is included.

The neglect of cognitive analyses has many reasons. If one assumes the importance of unconscious distortions and defenses, it follows that self-report data will be highly suspect. If one assumes that cognitions do not enhance behavioral prediction and then primarily studies those situations in which cognition may be relatively unimportant from a predictive point of view (animal, study, severely retarded, institutionalized children), it is not difficult to understand such a conclusion. If one assumes that affective experience is primary and that cognition leads to rationalization and alienation, it is not too much of a leap to rule cognitive experience as less than authentic experience. This latter assumption is a growing affliction in counseling psychology. Most of these assumptions have contributed to the historical neglect of mediational research, however the major problem concerning the status of mediational variables is not theoretical assumptions, but measurement. That is, covert variables by definition are observable by the individual experiencing them and unobservable to others. Thus all measures become indirect. One method used in the past was the introspective approach in which individuals described their subjective experiences. For instance, an individual may be instructed to imagine a particular scene and then may be asked to rate a particular dimension of the imaginal scene (clearness) and/or describe some of its facets (shape, color, and size). Such a methodology has been generally unproductive. Another approach, called neomentalism (Paivio, 1975), appears to have promise. It is based on the traditional theoretical-empirical model in which theoretical ideas about inner events are used to devise specific operational procedures that increase the likelihood that a specific mental process is involved in given task performances. For example, Paivio's research is based on a dual-coding model of information processing that posits two independent yet interconnected symbolic systems. One system is oriented toward imaginal processing of concrete events and objects, while the other system concerns processing verbal material. The dual-coding theory has led to experimental procedures (use of words and pictures varying in imagery value, imagery instructions, reaction-time tasks, use of pictures in associative recall) that permit some confidence in the linkage between hypothetical inner processes and observable performance. This approach is not new, but the growth of experimental psychology, systems science, behavioral methodology, phenomenological analysis, and environmental assessment have added depth and precision. These developments have each contributed to a cognitive-behavioral model of assessment. Let's begin an examination of such a model through a discussion of the contributions of each development.

Experimental Psychology

Experimental psychology provides a general methodology: definition of variables, collection of data, data analysis, and data interpretation. Such an approach provides both the general strategy of counseling adopted in this book and a specific orientation to the assessment process. Unfortunately, assessment and experimental psychology have largely developed along independent paths. In the past, procedures developed in the laboratory to evaluate perception (Bender-Gestalt), memory (Weschsler Memory Scale), conceptual learning (Goldstein-Scheerer Tests of Abstract and Concrete Thinking), and others have served useful functions in applied settings. Recently, there have been renewed efforts to forge a link between psychometrics and experimental psychology, especially cognitive psychology (see Carroll, 1976). For example, Hunt, Frost, and Lunneborg (1973) have sought to demonstrate relationships between psychometric test scores and certain learning tasks used by experimentalists. Their results suggest that psychometric and cognitive theorists could profit from each other's efforts, a suggestion taken seriously by the cognitive-behavioral model. That is, information about relevant cognitive variables may be provided more profitably through the study of cognitive task performances in which such tasks are designed to relate specific external events and cognitive processes.

An example of such a suggestion will help indicate its value. An investigation of depression (Loeb, Beck, & Diggory, 1971) attempted to empirically verify hypotheses derived from Beck's theory of depression (Beck, 1976) through the use of a level of aspiration task. Psychiatric male outpatients were classified on the basis of their scores on the Beck Depression Inventory (Beck, Ward, Mendelson, Mock, and Erbaugh, 1961) and psychiatric ratings. After classification was completed, the depressed and nondepressed groups were randomly assigned to success or failure conditions. These conditions were defined by experimenter control and feedback on the experimental task. The task involved sorting cards (star, cross, and so on) in a limited amount of time. Measures included probability of success estimate (probability of sorting 20 cards in one of seven trials), level of aspiration ("How many cards are you going to sort on this trial?"), actual performance (card-sort time), and evaluation of performance ("How do you feel that you did on this card-sorting task?"). The investigators claimed that the comparatively low estimates of probability of success and poorer ratings of performance by the depressed groups supported Beck's view that depressives consistently and systematically distort their perceptions and consistently maintain a negative view of themselves (poor performance) and the future (probability of success). The other aspect of the depressive constellation (negative view of the world) was not studied.

The importance of this example is not related to the findings or rigor of the study. In fact, the study has many methodological problems (subject selection, control procedures, data interpretation; see Miller, 1975). The importance is in the attempt to use operational procedures (level of aspiration task) that were designed to provide objective data relative to depression. The investigators, while introducing such procedures, do not discuss the evidence or issues involved in the level of aspiration literature (see Atkinson, 1964).

Instead of solely relying on clinical folklore, existing definitions, or untested theories of cognitive-behavioral assessment, objective procedure should be selected on the basis of theoretical interests for purposes of understanding the problematic situation. Such procedures may involve tasks that have shown utility in the laboratory of experimentalists. In this way a cognitive-behavioral assessor can begin to gather evidence on the involvement of cognitive variables that contribute to a client's inadequate performance. After sufficient evidence has accrued, these tasks may be of use in differential diagnosis. As in the previous example, the level of aspiration tasks, after more rigorous examination, may become a useful procedure in discriminating depressed, sad, and normals. Whatever the specifics, experimental psychology has provided a useful strategy and potential tasks in examining the role of client cognitions. It is for researchers and practitioners in applied settings to determine whether such procedures and tasks, which have been developed in laboratories and are largely concerned with static and often meaningless stimuli, are useful in the clinic, hospital, school, or agency primarily involved with multifaceted, dynamic, and meaningful stimuli.

Task Analysis

As stated, task analysis was used extensively by training psychologists in World War II and extended into education and business through systems science. In terms of psychology, task analysis or the study of complex performances in order to reveal the psychological processes involved is not known. Behaviorists have attempted to break down complex arithmetic tasks in terms of specific sets of stimuli and responses (Thorndike, 1922), and Skinner has discussed the importance of "successive approximations" in education (1953). Gestaltists have suggested the necessity of analyzing tasks into perceptual and structural components and relating these components to the whole problem (Wertheimer, 1959). In the 1960s, Gagné's work (1968) on learning hierarchies focused attention on task analysis.

Essentially, task analysis involves procedures, both logical and experimental, in which a complex characteristic is decomposed into its component subcharacteristics and, when possible, arranged into a hierarchy with subordinate and superordinate categories. Such procedures have largely been applied to cognitive and motor tasks. The affective realm has been neglected and may require modifications. A task analysis approach has been used by clinical investigators to identify cognitive deficits in schizophrenia (for example, Price, 1968) and impulsive children (for instance, Cameron, 1976).

What is the typical sequence of events involved in applying task analysis in applied settings? Such an analysis usually begins with identifying a particular competency and specifying the likely components. That is, in the case of characteristic A, the counselor may ask the question, "In order to demonstrate characteristic A, what must the client be able to do, think, and/or feel?" These questions are repeated until all likely components have been identified. As alternatives, counselors may take the tasks related to characteristic A themselves and introspect regarding the strategies involved, or counselors could observe and interview "experts" and "nonexperts" concerning their performances. They could also manipulate task demands (remove prompts, increase time, and so on). All these possibilities are options in understanding the psychological processes involved in a competent response. A few examples may clarify how task analysis can contribute to a more objective approach in understanding client cognitions and their involvement in counseling situations.

The first example comes from the assertiveness literature. In the past, it was generally assumed that unassertiveness was basically a social skills deficit (for example, McFall & Twentyman, 1973). Most treatments have been based upon a skills-deficit model and have been shown to be somewhat effective. Generalization of effects has not been as encouraging (Rich & Schroeder, 1976). Yet the effectiveness of a treatment may not be related to nor indicate the nature of the problem. One need only look to behavioral treatment success with a wide variety of problems, from study skills to obesity, to be convinced. In addition, the general lack of improvement in the natural situation may indicate that such treatment programs are not dealing with other important deficits in nonassertive individuals. Our first example is discussed in this context.

Schwartz and Gottman (1976) investigated the response deficits involved in nonassertive subjects. In following Gagné, the investigators specified the components of a competent response (assertive response) and then tested the extent to which performance of these components differentiated between competent and incompetent groups (low, moderate, and high assertive subjects). The specific components of assertive performance were defined as involving cognitive, physiological, and overt responses. These components were conceptualized in a hierarchial format with assertive performance as the goal. Content knowledge of assertion was seen as a prerequisite for competent performance, with the other assumed components (such as heart rate, self-perceived tension, and cognitive self-statements) serving as possible influence factors in response production. College students were assigned to low, moderate, or high assertive groups on the basis of their scores on a written measure of assertiveness (Conflict Resolution Inventory; McFall & Lillesand, 1971). Assigned subjects were then presented with three sets of situations (knowledge measure, indirect measure, and a direct measure) in which unreasonable requests were made. During these situations, a heart rate measure, a self-perceived tension scale, and a cognitive self-statement questionaire were administered. Results suggested that the most likely source of nonassertiveness may be related to differences in cognitions between the competent and incompetent groups. That is, the low assertive group had a greater number of negative self-statements and fewer positive statements than the other two more competent groups. Important differences between competent and incompetent groups were not found in terms of knowledge, ability to make an assertive response, or heart rate. Yet incompetent groups appeared to lack the ability to respond assertively in situations more similar to the actual situation and rated themselves as more tense.

These findings suggest that traditional, response acquisition treatments may be missing an important ingredient in assertiveness training, namely cognitive interventions aimed at cognitive appraisal and restructuring. Such treatment components may also enhance maintenance and generalization (Derry & Stone, 1979).

Another example is taken from the problem-solving literature (Goor & Sommerfeld, 1975). Creative and noncreative university student groups were formed on the basis of Semantic Divergent Productions (see Guilford, 1967). Following creation of the groups, problem-solving tasks were administered. In order to investigate the creative process, the researchers used the "talking aloud" technique in which the subjects' verbalizations to the problem-solving tasks were recorded and later analyzed. Consistently, high creative subjects spent more time "generating new information," and "in developing or working on a hypothesis" than did the low creative subjects, while low creative subjects spent more time in silence. Moreover, on the abstract tasks, the high creative group spent more time in "self reference or self criticism," while on the concrete task, the low creative group seemed to rapidly decrease in productive work. Such findings may have implications for the understanding of the creative process and for direction in developing developmental programs aimed at fostering creativity in the schools.

Both examples suggest that task analysis procedures may increase our understanding of cognitive processes that underlie complex behavior. Rather then rely on inferences from complex performances or descriptive introspective reports, it is suggested that task analysis offers a more empirical and objective methodology. These suggestions are not without problems, and the studies mentioned are not without limitations (restricted samples, and others). The Schwartz and Gottman study raises a potential problem for task analysis procedures based upon differences between competent and incompetent groups. The procedure is basically correctional and does not necessarily imply that differences between the groups are in any way causative factors, nor does it necessarily imply that deficits revealed by such a strategy lead directly to an effective treatment component. In terms of the latter point, effectiveness of a treatment, as stated earlier, may be unrelated to the nature of the deficit. Such questions are to be determined by appropriately designed empirical investigations. The Goor and Sommerfeld study raises another issue. That is, to what extent do individuals have direct access to their higher order cognitive processes? A recent article by Nisbett and Wilson (1977) has questioned self reports concerning cognitive processes. It may be that self reports merely reflect plausible causes or salient cues rather than the mediating processes involved. Such a concern needs to be addressed when task analytic procedures rely only on self report of cognitive strategies. With such cautions in mind, task analysis appears to be a potentially useful procedure in helping to specify the psychological processes that may be involved in problematic situations.

Behavioral/Phenomenological Analyses

The integration of behavioral and cognitive methodologies appears to be a promising venture. In terms of assessment contributions, the integration focuses attention on the relationship of clients' cognitions and their feelings and behavior. Behavioral assessment emphasized the importance of behavioral tasks and data collection, such as self observation, while phenomenological assessors stressed the value of a client's cognitive appraisals. In bringing these methodologies together, it appears that one fruitful strategy for facilitating increased understanding of problematic situations would be to provide behavioral tasks for clients and then to gather behavioral and phenomenological data. Typically, a client might be asked to perform a behavioral assignment and to record relevant self-statements and images. An example demonstrating a few potential strategies may be helpful.

The example is taken from the general area of anxiety. Individuals engaging in such activities as public speaking, teaching, counseling, and supervision, especially the relatively inexperienced, oftentimes suffer from debilitating anxiety that adversely affects their performance. Generally speaking, these same individuals, after appropriate experience, learn to cope more effectively and do not appear to be maladjusted. Yet there are some individuals who seem to be unable to cope effectively in these situations even after proper experience. One of these individuals is the focus of an example.

Grant, a doctoral student in counseling with no practical counseling experience, presented himself to the psychology counselor as extremely upset over his activities as a supervisor during his initial supervision sessions. He explained that he was supervising five school counselors in a masters program. He indicated that he had not supervised before, but he could not understand how these counselors could be so defensive and so unwilling to appreciate basic counseling skills. Moreover, he was concerned about how anxious and ineffective he felt about these supervisory sessions. It seemed to the cognitive-behavioral counselor that a useful starting point would be to discover how Grant's internal dialogue and images might be contributing to his anxious feelings and interfering with his supervision.

In order to identify such cognitions, the counselor may wish to sensitize Grant to his self talk. That is, it would be unusual if Grant could spontaneously discuss his thinking processes without practice, since a client's beliefs and images often are automatic and habitual. A number of assessment strategies may be useful in bringing such automatic thoughts to a client's awareness through training clients to observe the sequence of external events and their reactions to them.

The counselor may ask Grant to close his eyes and imagine a recent supervisory session. Grant may be asked to describe a specific situation and report a sequence of thoughts and images as he first notices he is becoming upset. Alternatively, supervisory sessions could be videotaped and the counselor could use various modified strategies of Interpersonal Process Recall, a videotape recall procedure developed by Kagan, Krathwohl, Goldberg, Campbell, Schauble, Greenberg, Danish, Resnickoff, Dowes, and Bandy (1967). That is, Grant could be asked to reconstruct his feelings and thoughts as he experienced them during a particular taped segment. Such reconstruction could be facilitated through Grant's selecting the critical incidents or through interrogation by the counselor. In addition, the use of adjunct physiological measures, connected to Grant during a special supervisory session and recorded on videotape, could help pinpoint differences between self-perceived tension and certain physiological reactions and indicate critical incidents for reconstruction. Homework assignments (see Shelton & Ackerman, 1974) could also be devised in which Grant would be asked to analyze supervisory sessions or other related experiences in terms of the ABC sequence described by Ellis (1971). In the Ellisonian analysis, A refers to an objective perceived event (supervisory session); B represents Grant's self-statements (perfectionalistic demands). Negative feelings generated by such self talk are symbolized by C (feelings of anxiety and incompetence). Grant could be asked to use such an analysis by keeping a journal and recording upsetting events in terms of the ABC sequence.

After implementing these strategies, Grant may be able to understand why he feels so anxious during supervision. That is, Grant may be able to notice how intervening thoughts influence his perceptions and performance. For instance, during an early interview Grant indicated that he felt very anxious when one of the school counselors asked him about his past school counseling He reported that he felt very tense ("white knuckles," "dry mouth," and so on) and seemed to ramble on and on. After experiencing some of these cognitive-behavioral strategies, Grant noticed that he did have some intervening thoughts during this interchange ("I am a supervisor," "I am supposed to know everything"). By focusing on these conditions, he was able to understand why he felt anxious. He automatically regarded the role of supervisor as meaning he should be an all-knowing master. Perhaps the school counselors also adopted and conveyed such an expectation. Under these conditions, any cues that might be interpreted as threatening to these beliefs, such as lack of experience, might trigger anxious feelings and a sense of incompetence.

The value of these post hoc reconstruction strategies is not limited to the assessment of the client's cognitions, but can also stimulate a sense of self management (see Meichenbaum, 1977). Implicit in such strategies is the idea that the client is an active contributor to the dilemma, not a helpless victim of uncontrolled thoughts and images. That is, such strategies foster the expectations that clients can do something about their situations by exercising control of their thinking. At the same time, such reconstructions must be viewed with caution. They cannot be assumed to validly represent what the client actually thought and felt during the experience. Moreover, requesting reconstruction may in effect alter the client's thinking patterns and may be representative of the client's internal dialogue about the reconstructed experience. Practitioners and researchers need to be mindful of these restrictions; however, such reconstructed data appear useful for initial assessment questions and seem to be a rich source for research hypotheses.

Other procedures could also be used. Meichenbaum (1977) has discussed a cognitive-behavioral assessment approach and described many potential clinical applications. They include a TAT-like approach in which pictures related to the presenting problem are presented and clients are asked not only to report on what is occurring but to describe what the individual in the picture is thinking and feeling. The talking aloud technique used by Goor and Sommerfeld (1975), in which subjects are asked to verbalize while engaged in a task, could provide useful information on cognitive strategies. A cognitive self-statement Q-sort would provide opportunities for clients to increase their sensitivity to their internal dialogues and implicit valuing processes by asking them to sort a number of positive and negative thoughts about particular targets, such as self. Moreover, a number of tests have been developed that might prove beneficial in aiding the assessment of irrational beliefs (Jones, 1969), self-statements (Schwartz & Gottman, 1974), and problem solving (Spivack & Shure, 1974).

Environmental Assessment

Assessment has primarily been based on the clinical investigation of the individual. The traditional assessment literature has a noticeable tendency to discuss problems in terms of problem individuals (unconscious conflicts). Within the last decade, there has been a growing interest in broadening the individualistic model to include person-environment relationships. Such an interest has been called human ecology (Bruhn, 1974) and environmental psychology (Proshansky, Ittelson, & Rivlin, 1970). Intellectual sources for the development of an ecological approach can be traced back to Lewin's field theory and Murray's exposition of environmental press. Yet these early beginings did not lead to a concern with situational variation. Attention remained focused on the personality variables until empirical research began to question the assumed generality of personality traits (Mischel, 1968). This research (Endler & Hunt, 1968; Mischel, 1968) led to an emphasis on person-environment interactions in which the environment could no longer be neglected. Moreover, recent concern about the environment (pollution, atomic energy, population, health, and others) has undoubtedly abetted the ecological motivation of psychologists. A few ecological approaches are described in order to underscore the potential usefulness of environmental assessment.

One ecological approach has emphasized naturalistic observation and the relationship between people and objects in the environment. Barker (1968) discusses these emphases in terms of a behavioral-setting approach in which the settings of behaviors are observed. From such observations, complex relationships are inferred and implications for intervention are suggested. Studies by Barker and associates have ranged from observing the stream of behavior of an individual for one day in his ecological situation (Barker & Wright, 1951) to the behavior settings in two small towns (Barker, 1960). A finding of the latter study concerned the psychological behavioral impact of the size of the behavior setting relative to the number of people involved in the setting. He suggested that individuals facing less populous settings (undermanned) would be induced to accept more responsibility and to participate more actively. This suggestion was confirmed by Barker and Gump (1964) in their study of small versus large high schools. Thus it may be of some importance for high school guidance personnel to sensitize students to differences between small and large colleges. It should also stimulate personnel in larger colleges to see how they could alter their settings, if deemed appropriate, in order to deal with the problem of density and student passivity.

The environment is not only composed of objects and specific physical arrangements, but is characterized by the participants in that environment and the way the environment is perceived by the participants. Astin (1968) has devised an Inventory of College Activities in order to characterize the environmental press created by one's contemporaries in the college environment. Holland (1962, 1963) has shown that institutional characteristics of a college can influence the stability of vocational choice. College personnel may need to be aware of these influences in order to guide students more effectively. Rudolf Moos has developed an extensive research program (see Moos, 1975a, 1975b) focused around the assessment of the perceived climate of many diverse environments (mental health facilities, prisons, schools, work setting). Moos assumes that environments have unique "personalities," just like people. He further assumes that these environments can be characterized similarly to personality and has developed many scales for such environmental characterization. These instruments, such as the Ward Atmosphere Scale, usually have such subscales as autonomy, insight, control, and others. Moos and associates have found that such perceived social climate indexes of a setting are related to a number of setting-relevant variables. For example, the Family Environment Scale, which assesses the social climate of families, indicates its usefulness by pointing to differences between clinic and matched normal families (for instance, clinic families scored lower on cohesion, intellectual-cultural orientation, and active recreations). That is, identification of psychosocial factors that favor successful families would be an important contribution to the field of family therapy.

Impressive research programs on the effects of the physical environment on human behavior have potential implications for the helping field. The work by Cohen, Glass, and Singer (1973) on the long-term effects of noise indicate that reading difficulties need not always be cast in terms of "reading readiness"; rather, environmental influences such as noise in the child's environment may be contributing to the reading problem. Other problems considered at one time to be a function of the individual may involve the way the environment is constructed. That is, shyness, traditionally thought to be a personality characteristic, may partially result from persons placing themselves in settings in which social contact is inhibited. The setting arrangements may discourage face-to-face contact (for example, a great distance between housing units, lack of common courtyard or meeting area, or a closed off work space).

One of the earliest theoretical works in human ecology concerned the impact of the economy on the community (Park, 1925). Unfortunately, many psychologists, with a few exceptions (G. Katona), have neglected the effects of the economy on human functioning. Studies have shown that an individual's economic situation affects one's health (Midtown Manhattan study; Langer & Michael, 1963), health delivery (Hollinshead & Redlich, 1958), mental hospitalization (Brenner, 1973), and suicide rate (Pierce, 1967). The neglect of economics may be the result of the psychological bias of studying the individual or the political implications of investigating competing economic systems in which rhetoric often replaces a scientific attitude. Whatever the reasons, economic factors should be considered. This is especially true of vocational counseling and career development, which have paid insufficient attention to the marketplace and the importance of an individual's perceptions of economic value in determining vocational decisions.

In the area of therapy, a new view is emerging that shifts the emphasis away from the individual to the family system as a context in which maladaptive behaviors occur. (G. Bateson, D. Jackson, J. Haley, V. Satir, S. Minuchin, L. Wynne, and M. Bower.) Thus another dimension of the environment needs to be considered: the family. Procedures have been developed to tap the interaction patterns of the family (Haley, 1964), family decision making (Ferreira & Winder, 1965), and coalition formations within the family (Haley, 1962). Such procedures proceed from the assumption that the family system influences each family member and an understanding of family dynamics is essential.

From this discussion, it is clear that a human ecological viewpoint affords a rich source of potential perspectives and methods. Moreover, Feshbach (1978) has recently challenged that psychologists need not only be concerned with person-environment interactions, but with the influence of the larger sociocultural environment on such interactions. At the same time that ecological advocates are expanding the awareness of psychologists, it must be remembered that much of the research to date is correlational and that the conceptual linkages and pragmatic procedures needed to relate ecological findings to the principles of human functioning, and such findings to the clinical situation, are just beginning. Yet it is necessary to restate that assessment in the cognitive-behavioral model must concern itself with person-environment interactions. Even though much of this chapter concerns individual assessment of psychological processes, the discussion suggests that a cognitive-behavioral assessor must be concerned with the context in which the individual is enmeshed.

In summary, there appear to be a large number of strategies and methods available to the cognitive-behavioral assessor. They are not without their restrictions, and such procedures are not seen as replacing more traditional methods. It is hoped that these techniques may be integrated with environmental evaluations so as to create a more appropriate systems approach to assessment. With these thoughts in mind, it must be remembered that the purpose of assessment in the cognitive-behavioral model is to help clients conceptualize their problems into a language that fosters understanding, induces a motivation to change, and increases the client's feelings of self efficacy. Such a conceptualization leads the client to want and, more importantly, to feel able, to change. These sentiments also lead to the next chapter in which interventions are described that provide opportunities for the realization of these expectations.

4
INTERVENTIONS

As suggested in earlier chapters, the elaboration of a cognitive-behavioral model leads to a consideration of cognitive processes. The purpose of this chapter is to describe interventions intended to modify aspects of the client's cognitions that are related to behavior change. Each of these interventions is discussed in terms of its antecedents, theoretical conceptualizations, current practice, and empirical support. Examples of the interventions and implications for vocational counseling and prevention are discussed.

GENERAL CONSIDERATIONS

Before each cognitive-behavioral intervention strategy is described, it is important to review some general characteristics that fit most of the cognitive interventions. In contrast to more traditional psychotherapies, cognitive-behavioral counselors are active and direct. That is, such counselors actively structure and participate in the therapeutic enterprise. Clients are also active, carrying out homework assignments and/or graduated performance tasks. In contrast to behavior therapists, cognitively oriented counselors emphasize the role of internal experiences. In contrast to most therapies, cognitive therapy seems designed to train the client in logical and scientific skills. That is, cognitive therapy can be viewed as an apprenticeship in "personal science" (Mahoney, 1974). During the apprenticeship experience, clients are presented with a rational philosophy and problem-solving methods, enabling them to become personal scientists in everyday life. Finally, most cognitive interventions could be subsumed under the category of "insight-oriented therapy." Such insight is usually not associated with intellectual insight alone, but a type of insight that leads to corrective action.

These general considerations may imply a homogeneity of cognitive treatments. However, there are many different ways to conceptualize cognitive processes that are associated with different treatment procedures. The focus of this chapter is on the following therapies: cognitive restructuring, self instruction, self management, attribution, and language.

COGNITIVE RESTRUCTURING

Cognitive restructuring therapies appear to have emerged from an interaction of three factors: clinical experience, philosophy, and psychoanalysis. The main proponents of cognitive restructuring methods have emphasized the importance of their own clinical experience in developing their formulations. In conceptualizing their experiences, Ellis, Beck, and others have relied, to varying degrees, on the ideas of Freud, Adler, and Horney and on the philosophical systems of stoicism, idealism, and general semantics.

The major promise of these therapies concerns a mediational assumption, namely that emotional and behavioral disorders are mediated by an individual's beliefs, cognitive style, and attitudes. That is, inappropriate functioning results from inappropriate thinking. Thus a major therapeutic goal is to alter the client's disordered thinking. The focus of such therapeutic efforts is on ideational content, with various therapies interpreting such content in different ways. Such content can be viewed as irrational beliefs, cognitive distortions, self statements and others. These differing conceptualizations are associated with different programs, which will now be discussed individually.

Antecedents

In terms of popularity and history, the restructuring therapy of Ellis deserves primary consideration (see Dolliver, 1977; Ellis, 1977). Ellis developed his approach mainly through observing his clients and reflecting about these observations within a context of psychoanalytic and stoic ideas. Moreover, Ellis' penchant for active participation and the assertive demands of living in New York City may have influenced his therapeutic style.

Conceptualization and Practice

According to the theory behind rational-emotive therapy (RET), psychological distress is due to the usually overlearned and automatic irrational ways people use to construe their experiences. During the socialization process, individuals naturally tend to adopt a number of ideas that lack empirical support. These unconfirmed ideas are termed irrational by Ellis. Two of the more commonly held irrational beliefs: I must be loved and approved by virtually everybody; I must excel in all possible activities in order to be considered worthwhile. These ideas and others like them (see Ellis, 1970) become automatic and lead to constructions of events that lead to emotional and behavioral reactions. Such reactions may be appropriate to the construction of the event, but not necessarily to the event itself. To paraphrase the stoic philosopher Epictetus (60 A.D.), it is not things that upset individuals, but the views they take of them.

Methodologically, the task for the RET therapist is to somehow provide the conditions through which the client is enabled to think more rationally and logically. Even though Ellis has shared his approach with the public through publications, films, lecture-demonstrations, and so on, little has been done to systematically describe the therapy procedures. Thus the following guidelines, concerned with rationale and orientations, are only suggestive of a useful approach in rationality training (see Goldfried & Davison, 1976).

A basic rationale is given to the client concerning the assumptions underlying treatment. Such a discussion could involve the use of the ABC rational analytic procedure with appropriate examples in which A represents the event, B the intervening self verbalizations, and C the consequences generated by the self-statements. The counselor could point out that there is often nothing intrinsically anxiety-provoking about many situations, but the self generated dialogue about the potential effect of the situation can cause anxiety. For instance, there does not appear to be an inherent danger in making a phone call for a date. Yet different people may have quite varied emotional reactions to such a prospect. One individual may be very relaxed and await making such a call with anticipation. Such an individual may think, "I'm looking forward to this call. I like getting to know people, and this date will give each of us an opportunity to know each other better." In contrast, a second person is distressed. The internal dialogue of such an individual could be, "I wouldn't know what to say. Who would want to go out with me? Ridiculous. It can't be done. The person will probably say no and make me feel worse or, my God, the person may agree and then I wouldn't know what to do except look foolish." Such examples provide an opportunity for exploring the relationship between different emotional reactions and covert self-statements.

A general orientation continues the client's education concerning the general importance of irrational thinking in emotional upsets. It is necessary to sensitize the client to the impact of irrational beliefs because these beliefs are often overlearned and become quite automatic. To facilitate the recognition and untenability of irrational statements, the counselor may use a test (see Jones, 1969) or reading material (*A New Guide to Rational Living*; Ellis & Harper, 1975) for discussion purposes. In addition to helping the client identify such statements, the counselor can aid the client in formulating arguments that refute these irrational beliefs.

After this general orientation, in which irrational thinking is believed to influence emotional reaction, it is time to get specific and analyze the ways in which the particular client may be irrationally construing the world. The preceding chapter on assessment reviewed some of the methods available. These might include homework assignments, rational analysis, interviewing, and recontruction activities in which clients can describe their thoughts about a situation through reconstruction of the event via videotape, imagery, and role playing.

The following description emphasizes the major modification methods, although Ellis (1977) would suggest that such a listing is restrictive and somewhat dated.

In rational self analysis (homework), the client is taught the method of rational analysis (ABC sequence) and the concepts of rational thinking through counselor modeling and reading. The client is asked to practice the method of self training in rational thinking through written homework (see Goodman & Maultsby, 1974). Such homework usually has four sections. In the first, the client is to record only the objective facts of an event that occur at the time of the emotional reaction. The second section deals with the client's self talk about the event. The next section is used to accurately label emotions. That is, "I felt badly about the inability to call for a date" is more accurate as an emotional phrase than "I felt like it was impossible to make that call." The latter quote reflects an expectation that leads to unhappy feelings, not the feeling itself. The last section provides self training in logic and the Socratic method. The client is asked to underline the irrational statements and compare them to previously learned criteria of rationality. The client is to actively refute each irrational statement and to substitute more accurate cognitions. Of course, such homework assignments can become material for discussion, new learning, and feedback within the therapeutic interview.

Rational emotive imagery can be used with clients to increase their awareness of irrational self talk and the experience of the rational reevaluation process (Maultsby & Ellis, 1974). For instance, a person afraid of a specific situation is instructed to imagine such a situation and to note the degree of upset experienced. If the emotional arousal is significant (indicated on a self-rating scale), the individual uses the talking aloud technique to determine the self-generated statements and irrational assumptions that may be contributing to the emotional reaction. After the key irrational cognitions have been identified, the client can reevaluate the situation in more rational terms. Goldfried, Decenteceo, and Weinberg (1974) have developed a systematic rational restructuring procedure that uses this approach. Such a procedure parallels in many respects the self-control version of systematic desensitization. In the restructuring program, rational reevaluation replaces relaxation as the active coping skill with which the imaginal situations in the hierarchy are actively dealt, through logical analysis and refutation, until the emotional reaction is reduced.

Strategies of rational disputing and logical persuasion are the major procedures traditionally associated with Ellis and RET. During a consultation, the rational-emotive therapist may confront a client's statements and beliefs. It is made clear to the client that one of the objectives of RET is to challenge irrational ideas, not the individual that holds them. The therapist may challenge, use humor, and educate by means of a Socratic dialogue and logical analysis in order to persuade the client that maladaptive behavior reflects maladaptive thinking.

Increasingly, rational therapy groups are developing and providing opportunities for individuals to learn to challenge their irrational beliefs while experiencing social support and different views of experience. Such group settings afford excellent laboratories in which to practice rational living, especially along interpersonal dimensions (for example, shyness, dating).

Since RET has become widely available through numerous publications, workshops, films, and personal demonstrations, a therapist could use bibliotherapy and modeling as adjunct methods to educate the client in logical self examination.

Evaluation

From an evaluation viewpoint, RET appears to have generated a large amount of empirical research (see Ellis, 1977; DiGuiseppe, Miller, & Trexler, 1977; Mahoney, 1974). Unfortunately, there is some disagreement over the nature of the evidence, which is not unique in psychotherapy research. On one hand, Ellis (1977) states that the research support for RET is "immense—indeed almost awesome." On the other, most recent reviews (DiGiuseppe et al., 1977; Mahoney, 1974) suggest cautious optimism. That is, there appears to be some degree of promise (see Smith & Glass, 1977), but the evidence is far from conclusive.

One issue concerns the definition of RET. According to Ellis, RET has undergone change and development (maybe 50 to 60 new procedures) and through such growth has become synonymous with cognitive-behavior therapy. This current inflation of RET causes concern in many of the critics. It appears that any evidence suggesting the influence of cognitive processes is accepted by Ellis as supporting RET. Moreover, the critics suggest that Ellis has not been sufficiently sensitive to the inadequacies of many of the supporting studies and has neglected disconfirmatory investigations. Of course, these critics need to remember that selective attention and biases in psychotherapy and counseling are not unique to Ellis nor are critics immune to such tendencies. On the other hand, self proclamations by proponents of particular theories that define and delimit the appropriateness of evidence need to be carefully evaluated by scientific criteria and understood in the context of those making the declarations.

At this point, it might be helpful to critically examine one of the stronger studies that offers supportive evidence of RET. In a recent review, the DiLoreto study (1971) was described as one of the most advanced comparative studies to date in psychotherapy (DiGiuseppe et al., 1977). The study also received favorable comment from Bergin and Strupp (1972). The DiLoreto study attempted to deal directly with the relationship of relative treatment outcome (systematic desensitization, client-centered therapy, rational-emotive therapy, attention placebo, and no-contact control) and personality type (extrovert and introvert) of university students concerned about interpersonal anxiety. Generally, the findings were a) that all three treatment groups were more effective than the control procedures; b) that client-centered therapy (affective group counseling), rational-emotive therapy (cognitive group counseling), and systematic desensitization (behavioral group counseling) were more effective with extroverts, introverts, and both personality types, respectively; c) that some of the outcome variance was attributable to a counselor effect; and d) that while systematic desensitization was more effective in reducing anxiety, rational-emotive therapy produced larger increases, at least for introverts, in self-reported interpersonal activity outside treatment. Such findings are gratifying to RET adherents because it appears that introverted clients, assumed to be more common in therapeutic counseling, reduced their anxiety as much as they did with systematic desensitization and demonstrated a greater increase in self-reported interpersonal activity outside of treatment. The results and conclusions, nevertheless, are limited due to questions of treatment validity and to the nature of the study (for example, subjects, therapists, measures, and analysis). It is uncertain whether the treatments were representative of the respective therapies, that is, whether the treatments were implemented appropriately and/or accurately based on updated procedures. Independent ratings of the interviews and protocols in terms of relevant dimensions would have been helpful. Expectations do not appear to be empirically determined. Expectation findings may be relevant to the inferior performance of the placebo group compared with the active treatments. Counselor effects suggest some caution in determining the meaningfulness of general treatment effects. There is some question whether interpersonally anxious, university-student clients and graduate-student therapists can be considered equivalent to therapeutic clients and experienced therapists. In terms of the results, the study would have been strengthened if it had included performance measures gathered outside of treatment. Finally, the unit of analysis was the individual subject even though treatment was administered in a group setting. It could be argued that a larger aggregate (group) should be the unit since subjects in the group may influence each other, which would question the statistical assumption of independence.

In sum, the DiLoreto study is limited and does not warrant uncritical acceptance as supportive evidence of RET. Of course, this is only one study, but it is supposedly better than most. The evaluation of the DiLoreto study is similar to the general empirical evaluation of RET, namely, that existing experimental evidence on RET is limited and such limitations do not permit a conclusion on the clinical effectiveness of RET from a scientific perspective. The evidence may be promising, but "awesome" support is a premature conclusion.

Other Restructuring Programs

The other major restructuring therapies, Beck's cognitive therapy (Beck, Rush, & Kovacs, 1976) and Meichenbaum's self-statement therapy (Meichenbaum, 1973), are similar to RET. All three share rationale and procedural orientations which emphasize the role of cognitions in psychological distress, training in observation and discrimination of relevant cognitive processes, reliance on behavior therapy procedures and performance assignments, and explicit instruction, modeling, rehearsal, and feedback that selectively emphasize the importance of cognitive factors in maladaptive behavior. In terms of Beck's rationale and therapeutic focus, the emphasis on dysfunctional beliefs in RET is supplemented by a concentration on distortions of logical thinking. For example, common errors in depressed thinking include arbitrary inference, selective abstraction, overgeneralization, magnification (minimization), and personalization (Beck, 1976). Some examples:

> An instructor who arbitrarily infers that students who do not use office hours are evidence of student rejection. Such arbitrary inference involves the drawing of a conclusion in the absence of supportive data or in the presence of contradictory evidence.
> Employees who attend only to the negative comments from a supervisor, even though the more frequent and salient feedback is positive. Moreover, on the basis of such selective attention, employees come to believe in their incompetence. The selective focus on a part (negative comments) while ignoring other more salient aspects of the context (positive feedback) and then conceptualizing the whole (competence) in terms of the selective focus is what Beck describes as selective abstraction.
> A female client who concludes that since her male counselor shows sex bias, all male counselors are biased. This overgeneralization is based on drawing a general conclusion on the basis of a single situation.
> A business executive who interprets a slight reduction in work due to illness as a complete personal failure with consequent feelings of worthlessness and anticipation of excommunication from the business community. Such a gross error constitutes a magnification distortion not unlike Ellis' "castastrophizing."
> A minority person who takes responsibility for being unable to live in a restricted neighborhood: "I do not deserve to live there because of my inferior status." Individuals relate an external circumstance (institutional bias) to themselves when there is no basis for the relationship. Such a tendency is called personalization.

These distortions of thinking are treated in Beck's cognitive therapy by a multitude of cognitive-behavioral methods. The cognitive strategies are based on epistemological principles and include distancing (objective thinking), decentering (reduction in personalization), changing the rules, reality testing, and authenticating the validity of one's thoughts. Moreover, behavioral methods of activity schedules, graded task assignments, and homework provide the situational context and behavioral data by which clients can test the validity of their assertions and in which cognitive reappraisal can occur.

In terms of research, Beck's therapy has primarily been associated with the alleviation of depression. Most of the research has been correlational and consequently provides little substantive validation of a cognitive model of depression. That is, the negative phenomenology of depressed patients may or may not have etiological significance. Moreover, the translation of the contruct depression into appropriate measures has been problematic. The use of self-report checklists and clinical ratings with analogue subjects (induced depression, sadness) appears questionable and susceptible to pathological bias.

A recent comparative study on depression by Shaw (1977) has received favorable comment (Beck, 1976). Shaw evaluated the effectiveness of three types of group therapy in the treatment of university students indentified as depressed. The treatments included Beck's cognitive treatment, nondirective treatment, and a waiting list control. Results indicated support for the cognitive modification procedure. This study attempted to correct some of the inadequacies previously outlined. Shaw used multiple criteria, such as self report, Beck Depression Inventory, and clinical ratings, to identify depressed subjects. Such a multi-stage assessment procedure appears useful for future depression research. Moreover, the use of a comparative study potentially provides more control and more information than depression studies using correlational or treatment/no-treatment strategies. While the study has many positive attributes, it also has problems. Age of clients and severity of depression are restricted in this study to a moderately depressed, predominately female, university population. Experimenter effects cannot be ruled out since the author was the only therapist. Nonspecific influences (for example, expectations of clients and therapist, treatment credibility, and demand) do not appear to be adequately controlled. The group format raises questions of the independence of the group members' observations and the appropriateness of the unit of analysis. Larger sample sizes could provide replications of the different groups. With these contraints in mind, Shaw's investigation as a representative study has presented evidence concerning Beck's approach and demonstrated that such a procedure has promise with moderately depressed individuals.

Meichenbaum's self-statement therapy has been derived principally from RET. It should be noted that Meichenbaum's approach is more comprehensive than indicated here and is covered more extensively under self-instructional therapy. The following represents only one application of self-instructional training, but this application appears to be more logically related to Ellis and Beck than to other self-instructional applications. Meichenbaum's treatment rationale emphasizes self verbalizations and internalized sentences as mediators in maladaptive behavior. That is, Meichenbaum suggests that clients talk to themselves inappropriately. Clients arouse themselves, depress themselves, put themselves down, and worry themselves inappropriately through their private monologues. Typically in Meichenbaum's approach of cognitive behavior modification (CBM), clients work to increase their awareness of their self-defeating verbalizations and images that are emitted in specific problematic situations. This can usually be accomplished by the activities described earlier, such as role playing, instructions, videotape, task performances, and homework. In addition, clients are trained to produce more positive self verbalizations that lead to performance facilitation.

Procedurally, RET and Meichenbaum's approach (1973) are very similar. Distinctions focus on the role of logical analysis of the so called irrational belief system and the use of coping skills. In comparison with Ellis, Meichenbaum relies less on rational analysis while emphasizing the importance of clients learning various problem-solving strategies. Moreover, it has been suggested that RET is more authoritarian and directive than CBM. Whether this suggestion is of substance depends on how one compares the assertive style of Ellis in doing logical analysis versus Meichenbaum guiding clients to institute more adaptive self-statements.

The research on CBM is growing and appears promising (see Mahoney, 1974; Meichenbaum, 1977). One such application of CBM has been in the treatment of speech anxiety. Meichenbaum, Gilmore, and Fedoravicius (1971) developed a group insight-oriented therapy in which subjects (mainly university students) were to become aware of their anxiety-producing self instructions emitted during interpersonal situations and to produce more adaptive self instructions and behavior. The effects of such group insight training were compared to other group treatments: desensitization, desensitization plus self instruction, attention placebo, and a no-treatment control. Two measures of behavioral performance and four measures of self-reported anxiety were used to assess outcome. Results indicated that the group insight treatment was consistently effective in reducing anxiety as reflected by behavioral, cognitive, and self-report measures. Such effectiveness was maintained at a three month follow-up assessment and was comparable with the group desensitization treatment. Moreover, it appeared that the group desensitization treatment was more effective with participants with specific speech anxieties whereas the group insight treatment was more effective with subjects suffering from generalized social anxiety.

The study contains many positive features including the use of appropriate control groups (waiting list, placebo, social comparison), diverse measures, multiple therapists, and the investigation of patient X treatment interactions. Again, questions of treatment validity, credibility, expectations, unit of analysis in group studies, and others could be raised. Perhaps a more serious issue has to do with the relative effects of cognitive and behavioral treatments (see Ledwidge, 1978). In this study and in the cognitive restructuring literature generally, Ledwidge suggests that there is little evidence of the superiority of the cognitively oriented treatment compared with behavioral treatments. The issue is whether there is sufficient data to warrant the current enthusiasm for such cognitive therapies. It appears to be too early to resolve the issue since such therapies have demonstrated promise, but have not yet proven to be more consistently effective than behavior modification nor as widely investigated.

In sum, cognitive restructuring seems promising, but its empirical and theoretical adequacy cannot rely on enthusiasm alone. The question of empirical soundness has been addressed. In terms of theoretical adequacy, the variety of cognitive restructuring strategies raises theoretical and practical questions—that is, to adopt and modify the useful phrase of Paul (1969), what conceptualization and/or approach is most effective for what specific problem. Perhaps it is not the differences among therapeutic approaches that should be salient, but the commonalities of helping individuals reconstrue their problems into problem-solving situations in which they have a sense of impact and self control. The specific content of the various reconstruction models may not be of great import except that they be credible and systematically associated with task performances. Whatever the hypothesis it appears that such theoretical and practical questions deserve systematic inquiry.

SELF INSTRUCTION

Antecedents

Meichenbaum's self-instructional treatment methodology appears to be primarily based on the developmental perspectives of language in the Russian psychological literature (for example, Luria, 1961; Vygotsky, 1962). This literature emphasizes the function of self verbalization in the control of nonverbal behavior. These perspectives became salient when Meichenbaum serendipitously discovered during his dissertation study (Meichenbaum, 1969) that a number of hospitalized schizophrenic patients operantly trained to emit "healthy talk" appeared to spontaneously repeat the experimental instructions ("give healthy talk; be coherent and relevant") while emitting "healthy talk" in other, nontrained situations. This spontaneous self instruction seemed to mediate generalization and led Meichenbaum to search the self-verbalization literature. There he found the importance of instructions and the internalization of such instructions as a crucial step in a child's development of voluntary control of behavior (Vygotsky, 1962). Moreover, he discovered in Luria (1961) a stage model of the internalized control of behavior that could serve as a training paradigm for future cognitive self-guidance training. It should also be mentioned that the literature concerned with covert verbal mediation (S. L. Bem, 1967; Kohlberg, Yaeger, & Hjertholm, 1968; Palkes, Stewart, & Kahana, 1968), the popular self-improvement press (Bain, 1928; Carnegie, 1948; Coué, 1922; Maltz, 1960; Peale, 1960), and the writings of cognitive therapists (Frank,

Kelly, Ellis) provide additional support concerning the role of internalized speech in behavioral regulation.

Conceptualization and Practice

The self-instructional methodology focuses on verbalizations that prompt behavior and guide performance. Much of the inspiration for the methodology and procedural sequences is traceable to Luria's three stages of interiorization of behavioral control. Luria (1961) has stressed that the speech from external sources, such as parents, initially guides a child's behavior. Over time children begin to direct their own behavior through overt speech, and only later will interiorization of language occur in which such speech becomes internalized and expands its guidance function. Specifically, self-instructional methodology proceeds as follows (Meichenbaum, 1977).

> An adult model performs a task while talking aloud (cognitive modeling).
> The child performs the same task under the direction of the model's instructions (external guided practice).
> The child performs the task while self instructing aloud (overt self-guided practice).
> The child whispers self instructions throughout the task performance (faded overt self-guided practice).
> The child performs the task while guiding the task performance via private speech (covert self-guided practice).

It may be helpful to supplement instructions with vivid imagery ("I will not go faster than a slow turtle, slow turtle . . ."), especially for young children. In addition, such cognitive guidance programs would do well to use a developmental perspective in terms of its own training components. That is, training might be more productive if it began with tasks at which the trainee was already somewhat successful and with simple self-statements ("Stop," "Think before I answer"), evolving into more complex self-statements through a series of successive approximations. An example of more complex self instructions follows, initially modeled by an external source and subsequently used by the trainee (overtly, then covertly).

> Okay, what is it I have to do? You want me to copy the picture with the different lines. I have to go slow and be careful. Okay, draw the line down, down, good; then to the right, that's it; now down some more and to the left. Good, I'm doing fine so far. Remember, go slow. Now back up again. No, I was supposed to go down. That's okay. Just erase the line carefully . . . Good. Even if I make an error I can go on slowly and carefully. Okay, I have to go down now. Finished. I did it. (Meichenbaum & Goodman, 1971, p. 117)

The model indicates several performance-relevant skills: a) problem definition ("What is it I have to do?"), b) focused attention plus response guidance ("be careful . . . draw the line down"), c) self reinforcement ("Good, I'm doing fine . . ."), and d) self-evaluative coping skills plus error-correcting options ("That's okay . . . even if I make an error I can go on slowly").

Evaluation

Self instruction, first explored with impulsive children by Meichenbaum and Goodman (1971), has been subsequently investigated by Meichenbaum and his colleagues in such diverse areas as test anxiety, animal fears, public speaking, creativity, anxiety relief, geriatrics, worrying, and on schizophrenic perceptual and verbal behavior (see Meichenbaum, 1975, 1977).

In their work with impulsive children, Meichenbaum and Goodman (1971) noted that these children tended to work rapidly and make many errors. The effectiveness of self instruction in improving task performances of second-graders identified as having problems with behavioral impulsivity and/or having low scores on school administered IQ tests was investigated. Fifteen second-graders so identified were assigned to one of three groups: cognitive training, attention control, and assessment control. Effectiveness was evaluated in terms of various performance measures (Porteus Maze, Kagans MFF). The half-hour training sessions were administered individually over a two-week period. Training consisted of the stages in the internalization of behavioral control. Essentially, the experimenter modeled thinking aloud as he performed several tasks, using behavioral control verbalizations (for instance, "work slowly," "be useful"). This led to self verbalization by the elementary school children (first overt, then covert). Participants in the attention control were untutored but received the same number of sessions as the cognitive training group, were exposed to identical materials, and engaged in similar activities, but did not receive any self-instructional training. The other contact control group served as a no-contact control. Results indicate that the self-instructional group obtained superior performance on the Porteus Maze test, on Performance IQ (WISC), and on a measure of cognitive impulsivity (MFF test).

These results are encouraging, but must be viewed within the context of certain restraints, including small sample size, possible experimenter effects, questionable methods of subject assignment, treatment credibility (for example, attention control), and the lack of generalization to the classroom. At the same time, it should be remembered that this was primarily a demonstration study that initiated more sophisticated inquiries (see Meichenbaum, 1977) and replications by other researchers (e.g., Hartig & Kanfer, 1973).

Several issues emerge in the discussion of self instruction. They involve the component analysis of self-instruction training (for instance, Horan, Hackett, Buchanan, Stone, & Demchik-Stone, 1977), repetitions as a confound self instruction (Bender, 1976), generalization (Meichenbaum & Goodman, 1971), population differences such as normals versus impulsives (Denney, 1975), and the necessity of inferring internal constructs. In terms of the latter issue, it appears necessary to delineate the alternative paradigms available to interpret the psychological processes involved in self instruction. Such a therapy could be interpreted from an information-processing, conditioning, or cognitive perspective. Can self instruction be most usefully conceptualized as rules for encoding information? What about the importance of stimulus control features to self instructions? In terms of a cognitive perspective, what types of private events (images, verbal codes) are investigated by self instructions? It may be necessary to reflect and design experimentation addressed to such theoretical questions before self instruction is given a more prominent role in cognitive-behavior modification.

SELF MANAGEMENT

The emergence of self management as a central focus in the clinical literature needs to be understood in the context of behavior modification. Early behavior modification practice and research relied heavily on environmental control and concentrated on discrete, situation-specific responses. Most would agree that such procedures have been effective. However, as critics will enthusiastically attest and adherents reluctantly admit, problems have been encountered. These include 1) the difficulties associated with the treatment of private events that may not be sufficiently public for adequate modification by others, 2) the problem of treatment generalization, 3) the obstacles in moving from a therapist-aided and situation-specific therapeutic experience to the ultimate goal of helping: the provision of resources to the client for coping independently with a broad range of everyday problems. These limitations have stimulated therapeutic innovations that focus on broad-based coping skills that supplement other behavioral change methods. It is assumed that most of the problems encountered by clients occur in the natural environment and that clients are often in the best position to observe and alter their behavior. A common belief in self management is that clients must assume responsibility for changing and maintaining their behavior. Typically, the therapist is a consultant to the client and therapy is conceptualized as providing training in appropriate self-management skills for use in the natural environment, rather than providing an insight experience or deconditioning process in the consultation office. Self management clearly emphasizes the importance of what occurs between consulation sessions as well as what occurs within them.

Historically, such a self-management perspective gained prominence through the early behavioral applications of self contol (see Goldiamond, 1965; Ferster, Nurnberger, & Lewitt, 1962; Fox, 1962). Self-control methods now contribute a major treatment methodology within behavior modification. The more important techniques include stimulus control, self observation, and self-administered contingencies. Stimulus-control treatments enable clients to identify controlling stimuli and to help clients eliminate or enhance the controlling function of specific stimuli. Self-observation training can help clients increase awareness of their behavior and initiate action to change undesired behavior. The self administration of contingencies is a common self-control strategy. A client can be taught to self reinforce or to self punish in order to modify maladaptive behaviors.

Each of these techniques falls within the realm of clinical applications of self control and, to a lesser or greater extent, is representative of operant-conditioning formulations of behavior change. These methods are important precursors of a more mediational perspective and are often included in more cognitively oriented treatments. For purposes of this chapter, the various forms of self management will be limited to coping skills and problem solving.

Coping Skills

The most frequent application of a coping-skill perspective has been in the control of anxiety. Three self-control variations of relaxation training have been developed and investigated. These variations include coping skills (Goldfried, 1971), anxiety management training (Suinn & Richardson, 1971), and cue-controlled relaxation (Paul, 1966; Russell & Sipich, 1973). Common sources involved in the emergence of these perspectives include the realization of deficiencies associated with traditional desensitization practices and the influence of self control in behavior modification. In terms of the latter, Homme's (1965) suggestion that clients can be enabled to detect aversive private events and to alter such events has stimulated these self-control variations. In addition, Skinner's (1953) discussion of controlling behavior and the autogenic training recommendations of Schultz and Luthe (1959) are influential.

Conceptually, each of these perspectives has recast, in varying degrees, traditional systematic desensitization into a coping-skill process. According to these investigators, traditional desensitization (Wolpe, 1958) is time-consuming and aspects of desensitization procedures are problematic (for example, individual hierarchy construction, presentation and timing of hierarchy items, validity and imaginal process). Moreover, traditional desensitization does not appear to provide sufficient competence for the client to deal effectively with future stressful life events. In reaction to these several deficiencies, the passive counterconditioning experience traditionally associated with the systematic desensitization process has been reconceptualized into an active process of acquiring general relaxation skills. Methodologically, all three self-control variations involve client training in developing competing responses such as relaxation. Such alternate response training emphasizes a coping orientation in which the client is taught to actively relax away anxious feelings. Specific procedures of the three programs vary. Coping skills and anxiety-management practices emphasize the use of heterogenous arousal scenes and the use of relaxation as a coping strategy. While these two programs stress the arousal and removal of anxiety, the cue-controlled approach involves the pairing of relaxation and a specific self-produced cue word ("calm"). Such systematic pairing over time is hypothesized to enable the client to use the cue word to elicit relaxation feelings in anxiety arousing situations. The following procedural guidelines are suggestive of a self-management program concerned with anxiety.

> Rationale. The rationale is described in terms of generalized skill training. Goldfried (1971) has presented a useful example of such a rationale. In elaborating the orientation, a counselor discusses how anxiety reactions are learned and how to reduce anxiety by learning to relax. The client is told that learning to relax is like most other skill learning. That is, given opportunities to practice relaxation skills will be provided so that the client will be able to use such skills when appropriate.
> Skill training. The client is trained in deep muscle relaxation (Jacobson, 1938). Moreover, the client can be taught additional skills including self instructions (cue words) and stimulus-labeling strategies (Goldfried, 1973). In the cue-controlled procedure, cue words are systematically paired with feelings of relaxation and deep breathing.
> Discrimination training. The client is taught to identify and experience internal anxiety cues through the use of heterogenous arousal scenes and/or the use of fantasy readings and music.
> Behavioral rehearsal. Opportunities are provided to relax away scene-induced anxiety. In addition, homework assignments are given through which clients can practice these skills in typical anxiety arousing situations.

The theoretical foundation for many of these self-management procedures (for instance, Russell & Sipich, 1973; Suinn & Richardson, 1971) is a conditioning model. In these procedures, it is assumed that internal anxiety responses can be viewed as discriminative stimuli and that clients can be conditioned to respond to these stimuli with responses that effectively interfere with anxiety and consequently reduce stress. Goldfried (1971) would emphasize a mediational interpretation, rather than a conditioning model, in which the client is enabled through practice to identify internal cues of muscular tension, to voluntarily relax it away, and to relabel the consequent emotional state. Whatever the specific interpretation, each of these programs favors an internal and generalized skill perspective in terms of how relaxation responses are triggered rather than the externalism of traditional desensitization whereby relaxation responses are conditioned to specific situations.

All three coping-skill programs began with case studies (Goldfried, 1973; Russell & Sipich, 1972) and have involved controlled investigations. The programs have demonstrated at least equivalent effectiveness when compared with standard desensitization procedures (Goldfried & Trier, 1974; Russell &

Wise, 1976; Suinn & Richardson, 1970). But the cumulative evidence from well-controlled studies and recent critiques of systematic desensitization (for example, Kazdin & Wilcoxon, 1976) suggest that support for coping-skill programs is premature. Evidential support is promising, but inadequate. These programs have typically been employed with a rather restricted range of anxiety responses (for instance, speech anxiety, test anxiety), but there is evidence that researchers are beginning to investigate other areas (such as Beck, Kaul, & Russell, 1978).

A more recent treatment program developed from a coping-skills perspective is stress-innoculation training (see Meichenbaum, 1977). This program relies on Meichenbaum's self-instructional research. It was stimulated by the coping-skills model (for example, Goldfried, 1971) and the stress literature (Janis, R. Lazarus, Orne, Epstein). From such antecedents, heavy emphasis was given to cognitive training, in the form of self instructions, imagery, rehearsal, and body-relaxing exercises. Conceptually, these antecedents highlighted the importance of generalized skills, which can be applied across situations and problems, and the complexity of the coping process. This latter highlight, response complexity, suggested a need for a multifaceted training package that included many behavioral and cognitive strategies.

In response to these suggestions, Meichenbaum and his colleagues developed a stress-innoculation procedure. It was designed to be a preventive intervention approach in which a client is enabled to tolerate greater intensities of stress. This approach is described by Meichenbaum (1977) as a behavioral analogue of the immunization model in biology.

Procedurally, stress-innoculation training consists of three phases. The first phase describes the educational nature of the treatment in which the client is provided a conceptual framework in order to understand the nature of stress. It is important that the educational program be understandable to a layperson, be plausible, and facilitate the client's acceptance of the therapeutic work to be done. Such conceptualizations do not require conclusive scientific validity, but face validity is much more crucial. In treating phobias and experimentally induced pain, the conceptualizations of Schachter's (1966) theory of emotion and Melzack and Wall's (1965) theory of pain have been offered, respectively. For instance, a client's anxiety response could be viewed in terms of a Schachterian model in which such responses are conceptualized as stress reactions consisting of two components, psychological arousal and anxiety-inducing cognitions. Moreover, it can be pointed out that one's cognitions play an important role in stress reactions. Such a conceptualization can easily translate into treatment procedures that help the client control physiological responses and alter the anxiety-inducing self-statements. Thus the educational phase can offer a new way of viewing one's problem and can inspire a sense of being able to do something rather than being overcome with acute anxiety and feelings of impotence.

In phase two, the client is introduced to a number of skills that can be emphasized during the coping process. The coping skills involve both behavioral and cognitive strategies. Included among the behavioral strategies are information-seeking skills, physical relaxation, and breathing-control exercises. That is, the client would gather reliable and valid information about the stressor, the relevant environmental factors, and about his or her competence in the stressful situation. In addition, the client could obtain the coping skills of relaxation. Cognitive coping strategies are encouraged by indicating to the client the importance of self-statements in mediating adaptive and maladaptive behavior. Procedures for monitoring self-defeating statements are used to set the occasion for producing self-generated coping self-statements. These statements can reflect such dimensions as appraisal, expectancy, attribution, and self perception. Such self-experiencing is used to help the client to prepare, confront, and cope with the stressor. Moreover, the client can be reinforced for coping attempts by using positive sets of self-statements.

In phase three, the application phase, the client tests the skills acquired during the previous phases. These applications are typically conducted with laboratory stressors, such as unpredictable electric shock, cold pressor test, and stress-inducing films).

In summary, stress innoculation training is based upon a "learn-practice-test" model. That is, clients learn about the nature of their emotional reactions, practice a variety of coping skills, and test these skills under stressful conditions. Stress-innoculation training has received empirical support in the area of phobias (Meichenbaum & Cameron, 1973), anger (Novaco, 1976), and pain (Meichenbaum & Turk, 1976), but the evidence is too tenuous to argue the program's effectiveness with any degree of confidence. Component analyses of the multicomponent training are beginning (Horan et al., 1977), but a clear understanding of the factors contributing to the program's effects is not discernible. In fact, it can be argued that component analyses may be premature. That is, more work is needed at the outcome stage in order to demonstrate a reliable effect for the training package rather than assuming such a state of affairs and too quickly moving into the engineering arena of dismantling the program for purposes of isolating significant contributing components. Furthermore, such outcome data are needed with more clinically relevant measures. Many of the laboratory stressors (for example, cold pressor), at least in the area of pain research, appear susceptible to demand characteristics and are somewhat questionable as adequate analogues for clinical problems (for instance, Weisenberg, 1977).

Conceptually, many questions emerge from broad-based coping-skill strategies. Is there a necessary relationship between response complexity and the number of strategies used in therapy? Which is a more appropriate explanation of coping-skill training: overlearning? distraction? expectation? generalized problem-solving skills? There needs to be more evidence and discussion of conceptual issues before coping-skills training can be advanced beyond the stage of preliminary support.

Problem-solving Skills

Problem solving has been an area of concern for some time in education and psychology. One can point to James (1895), Thorndike (1911), and Dewey (1916) as focusing attention on the problem-solving process. Some of the pioneer work in problem solving emerged from the controversy surrounding the work of Gestalt psychologists in animal learning. Wolfgang Köhler (1925) investigated a wide range of problems concerned with primates using objects to obtain various foodstuffs. He recorded many occasions when solutions appeared suddenly in the apparent absence of previous learning. Such experiences led Köhler to speculate about insight as a fundamental process in solving problems. Thorndike (1911) and others, including more recent writers (Gagné, 1964; Skinner, 1974), argue that past experience is the key variable. The controversy has continued and left its mark on subsequent learning theories. In subsequent investigations, laboratory studies in problem solving increasingly drifted to the study of human learning (see Davis, 1966). Areas of study have included anagram solutions, computer simulations, probability estimation, and creativity. Other antecedents include industrial research of problem-solving training (see Davis, 1973). One such program was brainstorming, developed by Osborn (1963), that emphasized the generation of ideas while suspending critical judgment.

As indicated, problem solving has a lengthy history, but the therapeutic relevance of problem solving from the psychological and industrial literature is not apparent. More direct clinical relevance of problem solving has been evidenced in vocational counseling (Williamson, 1965) and behavior modification (D'Zurilla & Goldfried, 1971).

Although there is an extensive problem-solving literature, the process by which people solve problems is still unclear. There are many explanatory models, but these models are generally developed for purposes of organizing the process for evaluation and training or are highly plausible descriptions of problem-solving operations without necessarily accurately reflecting the actual or ideal operations. The absence of a consensually validated model has not hampered the development of contemporary applications of problem solving. Most of the models and practices to be discussed closely resemble Dewey's prescriptions. In his book, *How We Think* (1933), Dewey outlined five phases: recognizing the problem, defining or specifying the difficulty, suggesting possible solutions, selecting an optimal solution from the suggestion, and executing the solution.

As discussed, Williamson clearly articulated a Dewey-inspired problem-solving approach to vocational decision making. He stressed the importance of Dewey's problem-solving phases in his model of the counseling process (analysis, synthesis, diagnosis, counseling, and follow-up). Moreover, the trait and factor approach advocated the teaching of appropriate instrumental skills for future adaptive behavior. The impact of the trait and factor approach has been to establish the decision-making process as a fundamental aspect of counseling psychology (Horan, 1979).

But it is D'Zurilla and Goldfried (1971) who have most clearly articulated the therapeutic relevance and process of problem solving. Conceptually, the problem-solving therapy of D'Zurilla and Goldfried is based on assumptions from the social learning and self-control literature. First, the problem-solving approach adopts a social learning conceptualization of maladaptive behavior. In accounting for ineffective behavior, the traditional medical approach emphasizes specifying symptoms and syndromes of some underlying disease process (for example, syphilis) whereas social learning stresses the importance of ineffective learned responses. To overcome possible learning deficits, problem-solving therapy relies heavily on a self-control perspective. In the past, training in symbolic skills with broad generality has been neglected in behavior modification. It is assumed that a focus on such complex responses would be a promising approach.

Procedurally, D'Zurilla and Goldfried (1971) have relied on a stage-sequence conceptualization of the problem-solving process. After reviewing the extensive problem-solving literature, the authors suggest the following five stages: general orientation, problem definition, generation of alternatives, decision making, and verification.

General orientation is regarded as establishing a set in approaching problematic situations. It has many similarities to a cognitive organizer in which a person learns an attitude toward situations to make problem situations meaningful, that is, it mobilizes effective resources for solving problems.

At least three processes are involved in establishing an effective set: attitude change, stimulus discrimination, and response inhibition. Clients need to actively adopt a coping attitude. Such an attitude recognizes that problem situations are part of everyday existence and that it is possible to cope with most of these situations effectively. A second class of orientation behaviors is concerned with facilitating the client's ability to discriminate problem situations. That is, the client would need to identify external and internal stimuli and label them appropriately in order for other problem-solving activities to be cued. A final class of orienting behaviors concerns the inhibition of impulsive and self-defeating behaviors.

In terms of facilitating the orienting process, little explicit guidance is available. A rationale could be presented in which problem situations are rationally discussed and the importance of carefully thinking things through, as opposed to automatic responding, could be stressed. Moreover, a self-management expectation can be made explicit and reinforced, suggesting that clients can learn to cope independently with many problem situations. Clients can become more sensitive and discriminating through homework assignments in which they record problem situations. Counselors could adopt a methodology similar to Ellis and Beck in which clients are first taught the nature of problem situations and emotional reactions. After clients are made sufficiently aware of their personal reactions and the contributing external variables, they can attend to and record such factors between consultation sessions. Once clients make explicit their internal dialogue in problem situations, opportunities for modifying self-defeating statements and replacing them with coping statements are afforded through rational-emotive or self-instructional methodology.

The second stage focuses on defining the problem. Problem definition and formulation consist of information gathering, operationalization, concept learning, and information processing. That is, consider all possible bits of information, define all aspects of the situation into concrete terms, identify relevant concepts and rules, and process information in a meaningful way.

Given these requisite operations, how does a counselor help a client to define the problem? Several possibilities suggest themselves. The client can be aided in gathering information through counselor reflection and probing. These methods can stimulate clients to attend to their experiences and to stimulate further exploration and processing of self-relevant information. Moreover, information-seeking skills can be directly taught to clients. Clients can be made aware of types of information (self information, interpersonal information, environmental information), sources of information (experienced others, actual situations, books, media) and information-seeking strategies (interrogatory strategies, observation skills).

Once the information is gathered, it is often ambiguous and often inadequate in terms of suggesting the next appropriate steps in the problem-solving process. Thus all informational terms need to be defined concretely. Counselors can help clients define vague terms by using interview skills (Eisenberg & Delaney, 1977; Stone, 1975), based on Skinner's discussion of verbal acts (1957). Such skills aid clients in translating abstract language into behavioral terms. In addition, self-monitoring behavior and homework assignments can provide clients with specific concrete examples for their verbal referents.

In the previous discussion, the emphasis was upon the provision of comprehensive and usable information. The next step in defining the problem involves the processing of this information in a meaningful way. Meaningful processing often requires the development and elaboration of highly organized conceptual processes. Such processes are related to such terms as rules, schemata, hierarchialized skills, heuristic rules, and concept formation. These processes share a common mediational perspective and classification function. That is, the role of conceptual processes is based on the assumption that individuals experiencing problems do not only respond to the physical situation, but are also responding to mediational processes that have more or less transformed external stimuli and related the consequent information to other bits of information. Thus individuals are dealing with concepts and meaning as well as physical objects and situations. In addition, the information conveyed by concepts is often the product of classification operations in which the information about a problem situation is subdivided into more manageable chunks, and these informational chunks are related to other chunks within a category that the individual has experienced in the past. In order to help clients expand their processing capabilities, the counselor can serve as a surrogate information-processor by modeling and stimulating elaboration of experience through empathic communication (Wexler & Rice, 1976). As discussed, empathy can be conceptualized as providing new perspectives and elaborations of the client's problem situation that may enable the client to process more experiential In addition, clients can be taught more directly how to elaborate information through semantic processing (Craik & Lockhart, 1972) and self processing (Rogers, Kuiper, & Kirker, 1977), in which clients are instructed and given (Rogers, Kuiper, & Kirker, 1977). in which clients are instructed and given practice in encoding information semantically and self-referentially. For example, in discussing a problem situation clients often externalize their descriptions. In response, counselors attempt to have clients examine what contribution they are making to the situation. In today's jargon, counselors want clients to "own their feelings" and be responsible for their actions. From a depth or spread of processing perspective, external description is a rather weak encoding process whereas self reference ("own your feelings") enriches the input by relating the vast amount of personal data represented by the self to the new input. Such deep encoding procedures may produce a semantically rich memory from which additional cues become available for processing.

The major task in the third phase is to generate alternative solutions. Logically, it would appear that the alternatives stage is dependent on the previous stage. That is, more and better solutions are proposed when the information about a situation is clear, specific, meaningful, and usable. When these tasks have been accomplished, it is necessary to generate as great a variety of response solutions as possible. Much in the area of idea production is from the work on brainstorming by Osborn (1963). From his discussion of brainstorming rules (for instance, criticism is ruled out, "free wheeling" is welcomed, and quantity, combination, and improvement are sought), two principles appear important (D'Zurilla & Goldfried, 1971): deferment of judgment and quantity breeds quality. It is assumed that more effective responses will be generated when one defers evaluation and generates as many alternatives as possible. There does appear to be empirical support (such as Parnes & Meadow, 1959) for these methods, especially for the quantity breeds quality procedure. Whether these principles enjoy universal effectiveness across problem situations (for example, convergent tasks, divergent tasks) is unclear, but the evidence seems supportive.

In alternative training, clients can be instructed in the rules of response generation. Opportunities for rehearsal with actual problem situations can be provided in which clients can practice generation strategies. Clients can be taught to talk aloud about their strategy use in order to discover incompatible behaviors (emotional reactions, fixated response patterns, restrictive cognitive rules). If such incompatible responses appear, adjunct procedures such as relaxation training, self-statement methods, and/or perceptual altering exercises (guided fantasy, analogies) can be implemented. Moreover, prompt and partial solutions can be offered to maintain attention and interest.

The fourth stage involves decision making, which includes probability learning, evaluation of consequences, selection, and specification. Since little data are available on this particular stage, the following discussion relies on decision theory and probability learning. In contrast to describing the decision-making process as practiced, which is of questionable validity (see Nisbett & Wilson, 1977), guidelines are specified that attempt to provide an optimal model of decision making.

Procedurally, the strategy alternatives generated earlier need to be screened, subjective estimates of consequence probability recorded, consequences evaluated, optimal strategy selected, and behavioral alternatives specified (see D'Zurilla & Goldfried, 1971). A client can be asked to generate and list significant consequences. In estimating the likelihood of occurrence of these various alternative-consequence events, the client can be directed to consider information on the relative frequency of a specific alternative resulting in various outcomes. After this information is recorded, consequences are judged in the context of the client's value system and values are assigned to the various outcomes. It is probably more accurate to describe the predictive and evaluative components as reciprocal, rather than sequential, processes. Following prediction and evaluation of consequences, the client makes a judgment as to the best strategy. In addition, the decision-making stage feeds back to the preceding stage of alternative generation. That is, the selected strategy is often vague. Thus clients are requested to state their selected strategies in terms of specific alternative behaviors, and the resulting alternative actions are fed forward to repeat the decision-making process. The decision-making processes involved with general strategies, on one hand, and specific behaviors, on the other, are very similar. One difference concerns the criteria involved in the evaluation process, namely, specific behaviors, in addition to being judged within a value context and resolving the problem, must also be judged by how effective the general strategy is when implemented.

Are there counseling practices relevant to this stage? D'Zurilla and Goldfried (1971) suggest the use of simple checklists in order to process the alternatives. Consequences of each alternative can be listed by categories (personal, social, short-term, long-term) and rated for frequency (very frequent, frequent, infrequent) and value (goal-scaling procedure of most satisfactory to least satisfactory).

The literature in probability learning (Estes, 1976) may suggest potential practices. Specifically, Estes (1976) suggests that individuals encode the relative frequency of event outcomes, rather than probabilities, and frequently such information is encoded selectively, which results in decisions that can be widely discrepant from actual probabilities. Thus inadequate decisions can result from bias in encoding events in memory. In order to improve probability learning, the individual can be helped to attend to and encode occurrences that may have been selectively ignored in the past. A counselor may facilitate a more accurate assessment of probabilities by requesting clients to seek additional information about the occurrences of alternative events and the opportunity of such events to occur in the client's environment. Clients can be questioned, given homework assignments to record positive and negative events, and exposed to various perception-altering experiences (role playing) in order to effect a change and/or reevaluation of their previous probability estimates.

In coming to terms with the selection of the optimal strategy, three aspects need to be mentioned. First, the chosen strategy needs to be translated into specific alternative actions and such actions assessed through the decision-making phases previously described. Counselor/client activities have already been discussed in relation to this aspect. The second aspect involves an appraisal of personal capability and environmental opportunity. It may be that a client is incapable (for example, skill deficient, inhibited) of implementing the selected plan and/or that the environment would be unduly punitive (loss of job) if such a course of action was instituted. Such appraisals can be facilitated by accurate assessment, role playing, and gathering additional information. Additional treatment may be indicated before problem-solving activities can be completed successfully.

In helping clients make decisions, the value dimension cannot be overlooked. In training a person to solve problems, the decision-making process occurs within the context of an individual's value system. Counselors can help clients become aware of their own values through various value-clarification exercises (Simon, Howe, & Kirschenbaum, 1972) and help clients to see the positive relationship between evaluation of an activity and performance.

The final stage provides an opportunity for clients to verify their decisions. Up to this point, the problem-solving process has been discussed in terms of cognitive operations. In translating plans into actions, Miller, Galanter, and Pribram (1960) have proposed a test-operate-test-exit (TOTE) routine. The TOTE routine serves as a feedback loop in which individuals guide their activities. An individual's problem-solving activities are guided by the match between a standard and the outcome of such activities. A congruence between a standard and a selected course of action is evidence to discontinue current problem-solving operations until successful progress is indicated by future testing.

Self evaluation plays a central role in this last stage. From a social-learning perspective (Bandura, 1977), self-regulatory mechanisms such as self evaluation involve at least three activities: self-monitoring, comparison operations, and self reinforcement. Such activities suggest that counselors could be helpful to clients during this final stage by focusing on the development of self-evaluation skills. (Self monitoring has been mentioned frequently before and will not be elaborated on here.) Comparison operations entail a rather complex judgmental process with several components. One such component involves setting a standard against which clients can compare the actions of problem-solving activities. One guide to such standards is Goal Attainment

Scaling (Kiresuk & Sherman, 1968) in which clients can be directed to list expectations ranging from the worst possible outcome to the expected outcome to the best possible outcome. Moreover, such clients can be directed to consider standards from many vantage points: previous experience (self-evaluation), observed performance of others (social comparison), and ideal performance criteria. It is not clear that these three referents, self, vicarious, and ideal, are as separate as implied, but clients may observe which referents predominate in their comparison operations and the scale may suggest some alteration if standards are unrealistic.

Once a personal standard has been established and comparisons between performances and reference standards are being made, it is necessary for people to produce self-generated consequences in order to maintain their performances and to derive personal satisfaction.

In reviewing the problem-solving sequence, a problem-solving set has been established, the nature of the problem situation has been analyzed, different strategies have been generated, a decision based on predictions about the potential and value of each option has been made, and a specific plan of action has been tested. Suggested counseling practices for each phase have been discussed.

Problem solving has been investigated in many contexts: animal laboratory (Riopelli, 1967), human laboratory (Davis, 1966), industrial settings (Davis, 1973), schools (Ojemann, 1969), enrichment-program centers (Stanley, 1972), and counseling settings (Evans & Cody, 1969). In addition, the problem-solving approach has become an important component in preventive-program development (see Cowen, 1977). No attempt is made to review this vast amount of literature. Rather, the therapeutic applications of problem solving and decision making are selectively discussed and some generalizations tentatively made. These two focuses appear to be the most relevant to counseling psychology.

Recently Spivack and his colleagues have added evidence concerning the therapeutic relevance of problem solving. Based on prior investigations with normal and clinical samples, it was concluded that there are consistent differences in social problem-solving skills (Platt & Spivack, 1972, 1974; Shure & Spivack, 1972) and that there is a strong relationship between such skills and various indexes of adjustment (Shure, Spivack, & Jaeger, 1971). On the basis of such findings, Spivack and others have developed a social problem-solving curriculum for young children and have demonstrated that such skills can be taught and that the gains are maintained during the next year (Shure & Spivack, 1975). Moreover, gains in such skills were related to a decrease in maladjustment ratings.

In addition to the work of Spivack and his colleagues, a number of recent applications illustrate the therapeutic value of teaching clients problem-solving skills. These applications have included the use of problem solving in marital therapy (Weiss, Hops, & Patterson, 1973), with emotionally disturbed boys (Giebink, Stover, & Fahl, 1968), in crisis clinics (McGuire & Sifneos, 1970), and with adolescents dealing with interpersonal anxiety (Christensen, 1974).

In the area of decision making, many authors have described models (Gelatt, 1962; Horan, 1979; Krumboltz, 1966b; Stewart & Winborn, 1973) and have used case studies and experimental investigations to demonstrate that these skills can be taught (Evans & Cody, 1969; Russell & Thoresen, 1976; Smith & Evans, 1973; Yabroff, 1969). An issue in the decision-making literature is the lack of data supporting the relationship between problem-solving skills and making better decisions. A criterion problem can always complicate this issue (What is the definition of a "better decision?"), but even in the area of vocational indecision it is not clear that problem-solving skills distinguish between decisive and indecisive students (see Holland & Holland, 1977). It appears that problem-solving training is not a sufficient treatment condition alone, but may make an important contribution when combined with other treatment approaches. This hypothesis received support in one of the initial studies of the effectiveness of various counseling methods for indecisiveness (Mendonca & Siess, 1976).

The study by Mendonca and Siess is an illustrative study of self management since it compares coping skills with problem-solving treatments in alleviating vocational indecision. Thirty-five students were chosen on the basis of their scores on an experimenter-developed inventory concerned with anxiety in decision making. These identified subjects were randomly assigned to five conditions: anxiety management, problem solving, anxiety management plus problem solving, a placebo procedure, and a no-treatment condition. In a repeated measures design, seven dependent measures were used, including two outcome variables (awareness of career plans and exploratory behavior) and five process variables (anxiety and problem solving). The major finding was that combined training is more effective than either method alone and more effective than the control procedures in vocational exploratory behavior and problem solving.

The study has many positive features. Students were prescreened in order to ensure the relevance of vocational decision making. Control procedures were designed to assess the impact of expectancies and other nonspecific factors. Multiple measures were used and a precise analysis of change scores (analysis of covariance) was done. At the same time, many potential problems are raised. The study would benefit from an increased sample size and extension to other types of populations (for example, female, nonuniversity). One counselor administered all treatments. Such a restricted counselor sample raises questions about generality and counselor expectancy. The authors also use many measures that they developed. These measures may not possess the psychometric properties necessary to provide a valid assessment. Finally, some of the gains reported in problem solving were made on analogue measures that do not necessarily imply improved ability in the students' actual decision-making concerns. Finally, a conceptual issue is raised by this study. It is assumed that university students who are anxious about pending career decisions need treatment. In an age of rapid change and economic instability, it is not entirely clear when anxiety and vocational indecisiveness become dysfunctional.

In summary, a self-management perspective emerged from behavior modification and has begun to move from discrete responses toward more general strategies. Self-management techniques are considered cognitive behavior-modification methods because they are directed toward building styles of reaction to various problems. That is, common to each of these self-management methods are cognitive reappraisal based on a reconceptualization of the problem, self observation, discrimination, and problem formulation; skill training that includes training in broad and effective coping skills; and behavioral experimentation through which individuals rehearse and test their skills. The approach is a broad social-competence model that includes multifaceted treatment programs. In closing, it should be emphasized that most of the coping-skills programs are not simply cognitive treatments, but are conducted with a close association to task performance and are generally used as adjunct treatment procedures. Coping-skills programs have shown promise, but the role of external factors and behavioral experimentation should not lack emphasis in order to promote a mediational model.

ADDITIONAL INTERVENTIONS

The number of interventions encompassed by cognitive-behavior modification is not rigidly codified nor consistently defined. The interventions discussed to this point were selected on the basis of their clinical utility and empirical evidence. The following interventions are not given extended discussion because of questions of clinical significance and/or weak empirical documentation. It would, however, be premature to entirely disregard their potential contributions. Many other strategies are not individually reviewed because they are included within other interventions. For instance, the imagery-based procedures of desensitization and covert modeling have been reconceptualized as a self-control procedure and as symbolic practice, respectively, and included with coping skills. Other mental imagery methods await conceptual development and empirical investigation (see Singer, 1974). Attribution therapy and language therapy are now briefly mentioned.

Attribution Therapy

Attribution has become one of the most heavily researched areas in social psychology (Nelson & Hendrick, 1974). Despite its current relevance, definitions have varied considerably. Attribution generally refers to the conditions associated with individuals' attempts to explain their behavior and the behavior of others. In essence, attributional approaches assume that individuals act like scientists, obtaining information and trying to discern the causes and consequences of behavior and environmental events.

These approaches have been nourished by the cognitive emphasis in psychology. Major empirical traditions associated with attributional approaches include person perception, social comparison, attitude change, and social perception. In terms of individual contributions, Heider's (1944, 1958) work on naive causal analysis deserves special recognition in stimulating the growth of attribution research. Other major theoretical contributors include Jones and Davis (1965), Kelley (1967), Schachter and Singer (1962), Rotter, Chance, and Phares (1972), D. J. Bem (1967, 1972), and Weiner (1974b).

These diverse theoretical contributions have been brought together in a collected book (Jones, Kanouse, Kelley, Nisbett, Valins, & Weiner, 1971) and are currently being extended (Harvey, Ickes, & Kidd, 1976). Thus the attributional style continues to be a widespread phenomenon.

As an indication of its expansiveness, many psychological researchers and clinical investigators have pondered the clinical significance of causal attribution (for example, Ross, Rodin, & Zimbardo, 1969). Initial investigations concerned the relationship of causal perceptions and emotionality. In a classic study, Schachter and Singer (1962) revealed that the arousal of drug-injected individuals did not increase when they were provided with a nonemotional stimulus source (epinephrine). However, drug injected individuals experiencing similar symtoms and who were provided emotional stimuli (euphoric or angry models) experienced heightened emotionality, congruent with the presented stimuli. It appears that a nonemotional attribution is likely to occur when physiological arousal is associated with an emotionally neutral stimulus (drug information), while emotionality and associated attributions occur more readily when arousal is associated with an emotionally charged source (angry or euphoric model). This research suggests that emotional disorders may be influenced by the attributions a client makes about the causes of his or her maladaptive behavior, and that it may be of value to provide an alternative nonemotional source to which the client can misattribute his or her aroused state. In fact, early laboratory research indicated that an individual's emotionality could be decreased by the individual misattributing emotional behaviors to such nonemotional sources as a placebo pill (Nisbett and Schachter, 1966) or noise (Ross et al., 1969). More recent research has systematically investigated misattribution with snake phobics (Valins & Ray, 1967) and insomniacs (Davison, Tsujimoto, & Glaros, 1973; Storms & Nisbett, 1970).

Another clinical area in which the role of cognitive labeling may be important concerns the common predisposition to attribute abnormal and inadequate interpretations to ourselves and others. Such a predisposition is often seen in new psychology students as they obsessively scan their personalities and the personalities of other for indications of pathology. This predisposition is not restricted to the campus, but is encouraged by cocktail party humor and is constantly reinforced in television soap operas and by magazine articles and newspapers featuring self-administered tests of psychological adequacy. Attributions resulting from such experiences are relatively harmless and can be illuminating. But there are times when individuals obsessively monitor their behavior in light of the therapeutic culture and are prone to interpret common and normal behaviors as abnormal.

Consider the following. A male athlete went to see a counselor, complaining of vague feelings of anxiety. As the first session progressed, it was revealed that the client was 20 years old, unmarried, and had come for counseling because he thought he was inadequate with women. His inadequacy attributions were based on several recent failures to complete intercourse satisfactorily. In discussing these experiences, it became apparent that the client believed he was insufficiently endowed and that his partner would think him inadequate. These beliefs made him feel anxious and led to unsatisfactory sexual experiences, thus confirming his beliefs. The client was asked about his "inadequate penis" belief. The client indicated that his friends showed him some magazines of "well-hung incredible hulks" and later how his friends kidded him in the shower as being the "missing dink." Counseling was initiated by explaining the issue of penis length (for example, normal range when erect) and how he should view his penis in a mirror instead of from above (shorter from above). The counselor explained how the sexual revolution may be causing anxiety and that social comparison and humor are natural consequences. In addition, it was pointed out how the client's beliefs had exacerbated sexual performance through increasing anxiety that interfered with sexual activity and how such experiences led to a vicious circle of reconfirming his beliefs of inadequacy. Such reeducation appeared to help the client reduce his inadequacy beliefs and enabled him to improve his sexual experiences.

The promise of these misattribution therapies and cognitive-labeling procedures has been limited by the failure to replicate findings (see Kent, Wilson, & Nelson, 1972). There has also been some question about the clinical usefulness of such methods (see Bandura, 1969). That is, it is rather optimistic, if not absurd, to believe that a simple cognitive induction (misattribution to an erroneous source) can eliminate strong fears and inhibitions. Of course, most attributionally oriented clinicians would point to attribution as only one factor in the therapeutic experience and they would suggest that it was never to be used in isolation. Finally, the issue of deception has been raised. A case can be made for the counselor to emphasize those aspects of the perceived problem situation most likely to be helpful and to withhold information that could be harmful. In terms of an attributional approach, it can be argued that certain nonemotional or extrinsic factors are possible contributors to the client's problems. To the extent that such a possibility has merit, the issue of deception appears less troublesome.

Another attributional approach has to do with locus of control (Rotter, 1966). Recent evidence suggests that whether an individual perceives him- or herself as an active agent or a passive pawn subject to external influences has substantial clinical relevance (Strickland, 1978). That is, there is good evidence for a relationship between feelings of personal control and physical well-being.

On the other hand, feelings of helplessness are increasingly associated with various types of disease onset and bodily deterioration (American Psychological Association, 1976). A number of investigations have suggested that individuals with previous experience and perceptions of personal control tend to exhibit less distress when confronted with aversive situations (for instance, Glass, Singer, & Friedman, 1969). Moreover, there is some evidence to indicate the importance of self attributions in the maintenance of behavior change. Davison and Valins (1969) found that individuals (placebo group) who attributed increased shock tolerance to themselves subsequently tolerated more shock than individuals (drug group) who made drug attributions. Overall, the reported research focuses on the importance of internal expectancies and an active coping orientation in facilitating adaptive behavior.

The promise of personal control attributions is moderated by theoretical and methodological concerns. Methodologically, there are concerns with the literature on locus of control and health. Most of the research is univariate and correlational while behavior change is multifaceted and interactive with many variables. The area of measurement of control attributions is a major problem. Various self-report assessments are typically used with different item content and are susceptible in varying degrees to social desirability and cultural, racial, and sexual bias. Theoretically, Storms and McCaul (1976) have questioned the universal value of self attributions. In the locus of control literature, there has been a strong tendency to associate internal control attributions with desirable qualities and external attributions with negative characteristics. In contrast, Storms and McCaul propose that self attributions of unwanted behavior can elicit increases in anxiety and self-defeating cognitions that exacerbate maladaptive behavior. For example, many therapy programs encourage the alcoholic to become aware of his or her undesirable drunken behavior. Such awareness often leads to self attributions ("I am an alcoholic") and increases anxiety. Regrettably, an alcoholic usually responds to increases in anxiety with increases in drinking. Storms and McCaul (1975) have investigated this exacerbation model with stuttering and found support for the model. That is, attribution of maladaptive behaviors (stuttering, insomnia, excessive drinking) to the self (stutterer, insomniac, alcoholic) creates anxiety and this anxiety subsequently increases dysfunctional behaviors. Thus it would seem necessary for mental health professionals to be sensitive to the inferences clients make about their maladaptive behavior and to clearly discriminate the conditions under which self attributions may be appropriate and when they may exacerbate the problem.

One of the conditions in which self attributions may be therapeutic is maintenance of behavior change. Recent work by Bandura (1977) and D. J. Bem (1972) has suggested the development of procedures aimed at encouraging the self attribution of therapeutic improvement. From this perspective, behavior change procedures appear to have more enduring effects if they are associated with self attribution. Yet most therapies rely on a professional expert and an extensive repertoire of therapeutic aids. Under these conditions, most therapeutic interventions encourage the client to ascribe changes in behavior to external factors, which often reduces the generalization of specific changes learned in the consultation office to everyday life. In order to enhance self attributions, Bandura (1977) recommends that clients be given opportunities for self-directed performance after the desired behavior has been established. Recent work with adult phobics (Bandura et al., 1977) indicates that providing an opportunity for self-directed performance after the desired behavior has been established enhances self-efficacy expectations and, in turn, increases in efficacy expectations were positively associated with increments in desired behavior changes. The preliminary evidence suggests that varied mastery experiences arising from effective performance enhance self attributions and that self attributions facilitate therapeutic maintenance. It would appear that such a performance-based induction is a more powerful method than the persuasion-induction used in misattribution and cognitive labeling.

In summary, it is proposed that attributional processes have clinical relevance. It has been suggested that therapy may be used to induce less debilitating situational attributions when clients persist in dysfunctional dispositional explanations for their problems. On other occasions, it is often valuable to induce clients to attibute their reactions to intrinsic factors when such attributions are likely to lead to an attitude of personal competence. Moreover, performance-based induction methods appear to be more powerful in altering attributional processes than verbal persuasion techniques. Although these suggestions appear to support the clinical usefulness of attributional processes, the validity of such a proposal awaits empirical investigation with diverse clinical populations.

Language Therapy

Bandler and Grinder (1975, 1976) have proposed that linguistics serve as a base for understanding human interaction and as a tool for therapy. They suggest that the transformational model of language (Chomsky, 1965) provides an important model for counseling and psychotherapy. A central aspect of this model concerns the deep structure/surface structure distinction.

The deep structure/surface distinction emerged within linguistics, but appears to have similarities to the philosophy of idealism. In linguistics, the deep structure refers to the abstract, structural, and complete semantic representation of an experience from which actual words and phrases of surface structures are generated. For, example, "reading this chapter is an experience" and "it is an experience to read this chapter" have the same deep structure meaning, but the different word orders (transformation) represent different surface structures. Thus deep structure rules determine the meaning of surface structure, while more than one surface structure may represent the same meaning. Similarly, in philosophy, Plato speaks of two worlds, the supersensible world of eternal essences (ideas) that consists of forms and patterns and the temporal world of sights, sounds, and individual things. The ideas in the first realm serves as standards for the things we perceive, while the individual things in the second realm are mere shadows of the reality of the forms of the first realm. Plato's two worlds, the world of eternal essences and the world of perception, seemingly correspond to the linguist's categories of deep structure and surface structure, respectively.

Bandler and Grinder have applied this distinction to psychotherapy and have labeled their application a Meta-model. In describing their conceptualization, deep structure represents the semantic representations or models of human experiences. Verbal transactions are surface structures that communicate such models. Basically, Bandler and Grinder believe that individuals suffer psychological distress because people create and communicate impoverished definitions of the world. Such inadequate semantic representations limit choices and foster defeatist attitudes. That is, people suffering anguish are not necessarily sick or crazy. They simply do not have enough choices available. The problem is not wrong choices, but limited choices due to our creation of impoverished models and our mistaken identification of such limited models with the richness of reality. Three processes contribute to the incongruence between semantic structures and reality: generalization, deletion, and distortion.

In generalization, part of experience is taken for the whole experience. Suppose that the first few times a female job applicant applies for a job she is rejected. She might develop a rule for herself that she can never be gainfully employed and refuse to ever try again. Another female applicant creates a model that includes rejection as a possibility, but distinguishes between rejection for some jobs and all other kinds of employment opportunities. Such a model has more choices.

In deletion, we selectively attend to certain aspects of our experience and exclude others. For example, a woman who was convinced that she was a bad mother often blocked herself from hearing positive messages from her husband and children. Such a reduction of messages reduces the richness of the world and sacrifices numerous choices.

Distortion allows us to misinterpret events, which can reduce the richness of a person's experience. For example, the "bad mother" client could also distort, as well as delete, positive messages in order to maintain her generalization. That is, she could reinterpret these positive messages as insincere ("You are just saying that . . . you don't mean it . . . if you only knew me better . . . ").

It should be pointed out that these are the same human processes that lead us to our more unique and creative human experiences. They allow us to create models of experience that reflect the richness of the human condition as well as ones that are improverished and limited.

One way we model our experiences is through language. The use of language in communication and creating deep structures involves these processes and determines to a large degree what we experience, how we perceive the world, and what choices we see available. Such reasoning led Bandler and Grinder to their work on the language analysis of therapy. That is, a therapist can come to understand a client through language analysis (transformational grammar). Based on the processes of modeling (generalization, deletion, distortion), Bandler and Grinder suggest two major therapeutic tasks: to help the client recover the deep structure through changing surface utterances to make them more representative of deep structure and to challenge the deep structure in order to make it reflect more meaningfully the client's experience.

Procedurally, work on surface structures involves recovering the missing material in order to reconnect surface structure with a fuller semantic representation. The recovery process involves the use of guidelines derived from transformational grammar (for example, intuitions about well-formed sentences, sentence structure, and logical relations). These guidelines help the therapist determine the completeness of the surface structures. For example:

Client: Everyone expects too much of me.

The counselor would now check his or her guidelines to examine the completeness of the client's surface structure. That is, the counselor could conclude that the surface structure utterance is incomplete since it violates a guideline of a well-formed sentence; the noun, everyone, does not specify a referent.

The counselor can now use verbal interventions in conjunction with this impoverished utterance. The counselor could challenge the utterance by using a form of reflective/confrontive communication in which the voice quality emphasizes the nonspecific nature of the referent (everyone). For example:

Client: Everyone expects too much of me.
Counselor: *Everyone* (pause). They all expect so much of you.

Such an intervention can lead the client to attend to and verify his or her utterance. Moreover, continued reflective and confrontive responses of the counselor stimulate the client's sense of responsibility in recovering the lost information. These nondirective interventions are common in the client-centered tradition with its emphasis on self exploration and client responsibility.

A more direct intervention may be more efficient, such as simply asking the client for the missing bit of information. That is:

Client: Everyone expects too much from me.
Counselor: Who is everyone?

This probe may help the client correct the surface structure utterance. The client immediately can supply the deleted information or, through stimulating a process of self expansion, the client is enabled to fill in the missing part of the deep structure.

Another intervention strategy is to use interpretation. The counselor may guess at or interpret the missing information. Based on the counselor's experience, educated intuitions, and observation of the client, the counselor may have a hypothesis that the client is the central factor in creating these excessive expectations.

> Client: Everyone expects too much of me.
> Counselor: I want you to say this and see whether it makes sense to you: "I expect too much of me."

As a safeguard, the counselor statement requests the client to "try on" this statement. That is, the counselor could be wrong. As a precaution, Bandler and Grinder suggest that the client "try on" the interpretation in order to see if it resonates with the client's semantic representation. Moreover, it makes good sense from an information-processing point of view. That is, self-referenced communications provide a powerful method of encoding information and enriching and elaborating deep structure (Rogers, Kuiper, & Kirber, 1977).

These surface structure interventions are not new nor do they exhaust all the possibilities. For instance, the counselor could accept or ignore the surface structure utterances of the client. The preceding interventions are focused on the first therapeutic task: involving the client in recovering the deep structure.

Once the client's surface structures begin to reflect the full semantic model of the deep structure, the next therapeutic task is for the counselor to challenge the deep structure so as to enrich it. Many interventions are available. Traditional psychotherapy procedures can be seen as challenging the client's impoverished model. For instance, role enactment strategies enable clients to re-experience problematic situations and, in so doing, the counselor can help clients give fuller linguistic representations of their experiences. For instance, the client who believes she is a bad mother could be involved in the following interchange.

> Client: The basic problem is that I am a bad mother.
> Counselor: To help me understand better, I want you to act like a bad mother next week.

This paradoxical task could reduce resistance ("act like a good mother") and stimulate the client to initiate changes in her deep structure. Such nonverbal interventions as psychodrama, performance tasks, homework assignments, and paradoxical intentions can also be seen from the Meta-model perspective. That is, these behavioral interventions can help clients reconnect their linguistic model with their world of experience.

Although the Meta-model can be generalized to behavioral interventions, Bandler and Grinder focus on verbal interventions. In challenging deep structure, the counselor has numerous verbal strategies. The counselor may choose to ask clients to be concrete or may use confrontation and metaphorical language in assisting clients to challenge their models. Language is involved in each of these procedures. The value of concreteness in helping clients recover missing information has been shown. Confrontation can be used to directly challenge the assumptions of a client. For example:

Client: My teacher makes me feel incompetent.
Counselor: How can someone *make* you feel any emotion?

The client's verbal expression is semantically inappropriate. The client has assigned responsibility for her emotions to external factors rather than understanding that emotions are generated from one's model. The client's mistake has been to interpret an act of the teacher as causing her emotional response. It simply is not semantically appropriate to state that one person can create an emotion in another person. Thus the counselor attempts to assist the client in accepting responsibility for her response.

The use of rich language can help the client process information more meaningfully by expanding the client's model and shifting the pattern of deep structural relations. Metaphorical language is one way of enriching the client's experience. For example:

Client: I feel so alone . . . unfulfilled . . .
Counselor: The loneliness of a long distance runner . . .

This evocative language can be effective in communicating this person's sense of aloneness, but also suggests other possibilities of dedication, hunger for achievement and acceptance, even fear of failure. Such evocative messages can evoke powerful client experiences that can stretch an individual's characteristic model of the world.

In summary, the Meta-model, adapted from transformational grammar, provides explicit strategies for understanding and inducing change in impoverished client models. Bandler and Grinder have suggested that certain grammatical conditions are appropriate for the therapeutic encounter and that these conditions can help enrich the client's experience. While they have concentrated on the verbal system, they have made suggestions on how Meta-model processes can be generalized to other forms of human behavior.

In terms of evaluation, there is not a well-developed and programmatic research literature concerned with the Meta-model. Some preliminary evidence indicates promise about the impact of therapist expressiveness on the richness of client verbal expressions (Wexler & Butler, 1976) and about such enriched client self exploration and therapeutic outcome (Rice & Wagstaff, 1967).

While the evidence is thin, the issues that surround the Meta-model are potentially great. The surface structure–deep structure distinction closely resembles a language equivalent of the intrapsychic model (symptom/pathology distinction). Such an analogy does not necessarily impugn the medical or language model, but points to the potential problems of using such models in understanding psychological distress. That is, one can be so concerned with deep structures (intrapsychic processes) as to ignore what the client is saying and doing (symptoms).

Another issue is the way Bandler and Grinder label their books: *The Structure of Magic*. No matter how useful the concept of magic may be to therapeutic work, the authors should have been aware of how susceptible the public, including some helping professionals, are to the tendency to mystify therapy and to the tendency to associate unrealistic expectations and magic qualities with therapy. Their approach carries a heavy enough burden, translating grammatical rules into therapeutic methods. The addition of a magic milieu does not lessen its burden or enhance its effectiveness.

Researchers in this area need to demonstrate that their conceptualization is not simply a redefinition of traditional psychotherapy into transformational grammar terms. Such a program needs to be more. That is, it needs to be a basis for developing explicit therapeutic methods and for establishing independent measurement of its constructs. Moreover, systematic empirical evaluation of its methods is needed before such a program is indiscriminately put before the public.

SUMMARY

Interventions in the field of cognitive-behavior modification are developing and changing so rapidly that it is difficult to describe them comprehensively or accurately. In attempting to summarize these diverse interventions, the following statements are warranted. One is that all of these psychological interventions are mediational in the sense that human behavior change is formulated in terms of cognitive processes. A second statement is that these so called cognitive methods rely on behavior tasks as a major means to induce change in cognitive events. Finally, most of these interventions reinforce a self-management perspective. Specifically, behavior change is not portrayed as an external and peripheral process, but as a central process in which the person can have a great impact.

As stated repeatedly, the evidence does not warrant unambiguous support for any of these interventions. Some procedures have more evidential support than others, but all raise issues for clarification and empirical evaluation.

IMPLICATIONS FOR VOCATIONAL PSYCHOLOGY AND PREVENTION

Vocational Psychology

Most of the cognitive-behavioral literature focuses on the misconceptions associated with personal-social concerns. Although little work has been done with these methods in vocational counseling, it would not be surprising to find cognitive processes involved in vocational concerns. Thompson (1976) has suggested that many clients in vocational counseling exacerbate their concerns by holding faulty beliefs about career decision making. Perfectionistic ideas can lead clients to chronic indecision. Clients may expect a perfect decision to be made at a specific point in time. They may assume that there is invariably a right decision to be made and that the expert counselor and vocational tests will ensure an accurate choice and guarantee job success and satisfaction. These expectations may be overstated here, but experience suggests that a client's thinking about vocational goals is often characterized by such extremes. To the degree that these expectations are operative, the counselor can expect increased anxiety about decision making, procrastination in career planning, and a reduction in client responsibility. That is, a client that continually indoctrinates him or herself with such irrational vocational statements is likely to be fearful of making a mistake, since it would be a catastrophe if a perfect solution was not found. Consequently, the client may become overly cautious and reluctant to formulate any concrete action plan or engage in meaningful career planning that may be perceived as bringing the client closer to making a decision. Moreover, the reciprocal interaction of anxiety and catastrophizing inner dialogues would seemingly strengthen the client's reliance on testing and the advice of the counselor and weaken the client's sense of responsibility. Unfortunately, such tendencies would reinforce the attitudes of many professionals and consumers who continue to overestimate the value of testing and expert opinion.

In addition to faulty assumptions, clients may lack relevant skills. They may not be able to think logically, to problem-solve, and/or to reduce anxiety. For example, a client may not be aware of some of the common errors of logic described by Beck and Bandler and Grinder when assessing the relevance of vocational information. For example, information traditionally used by counselors often contains distortions: A female client interested in becoming a dentist is presented with information about dentistry that contains sex-biased language and illustrations of male dentists and female dental assistants. Such information can be misleading.

It appears that the interventions discussed earlier can contribute to the vocational development of clients. The cognitive-structuring methods provide ways of assessing and altering irrational vocational talk. It would seem important that such misconceptions be dealt with and the more vocationally relevant assumptions of client responsibility and career development be clarified. Coping-skill interventions can help clients reduce anxiety and learn relevant problem-solving skills (see Mendonca & Siess, 1976). Moreover, a cognitive-behavioral model suggests implications for vocational counseling research and theory development. The following issues appear important. Do vocationally indecisive clients differ from decisive individuals in terms of internal verbalizations, skill competence, and/or anxiety level? If such differences emerge, what type of vocational counseling experiences appear more relevant? Are there developmental changes in cognitions and vocational self talk that parallel other postulated changes in vocational behavior (Super, 1957)? How important are vocational verbalizations and images in facilitating or hindering effective career planning? Theoretically speaking, vocational theorists such as Vroom (1964) have been interested in explaining vocational motivation in terms of the attractiveness of outcomes (valence) and subjective probability (expectancy). It would appear that such cognitive factors as appraisal (see Lazarus, 1966) and self efficacy (see Bandura, 1977) could enrich such theoretical accounts by providing understanding of the processes that underlie vocational interests and expectancies. That is, self appraisals (rational and irrational self-statements), goal setting, and self evaluation may play an important role in self judgments about the attractiveness of job-related outcomes and job expectancies. Some of these issues have been touched upon in vocational research, but the influence of cognitive psychology can give renewed cogency to the understanding of cognitive processes and vocational development.

Prevention

Although prevention has become a terribly major topic in mental health circles, a cognitive-behavioral perspective shares a remedial emphasis with other clinical theories. As is the case with other clinical methods, cognitively oriented interventions have been primarily concerned with maladaptive behavior. Consequently, the implications of a cognitive-learning perspective for normal development and prevention are rather rudimentary in comparison with the implications for therapeutic work. Preventive applications of cognitive and problem-solving therapies to school children have yielded promising results (Allen, Chinsky, Larcen, Lochman, & Selinger, 1976; Spivack & Shure, 1974; Stone, Hinds, & Schmidt, 1975). Such exploratory efforts need to be enlarged in order to address the preventive implications of cognitive therapies. What would happen if an expanded package of coping skills (for example, restructuring methods, anxiety management, problem solving, self instructions), became part of the educational curriculum? Would the incidence of maladjustment be reduced? Would normal development be accelerated? Would there be important secondary effects in terms of an impact on the teaching staff and parents? These questions can help enlarge the focus of cognitive-behavioral interventions.

Although such chronological studies have not been reported, the following guidelines for preventive program development are offered.

A major obstacle in the area of prevention has been a lack of specific goals. Although personal adjustment has long been of concern to the helping professions and many have talked about self-actualization goals, little attention has been paid to what personal adjustment or self actualization means behaviorally or to the means of developing such goals. Since mental health goals are generally vague and poorly defined, helping professionals are often at a loss in selecting appropriate interventions and evaluating their efforts.

The literature in cognitive-behavior modification may help practitioners translate global mental health goals into specific response strategies. D'Zurilla and Goldfried (1971) provide a useful example in their conceptualization of the problem-solving process. Research (for example, Larcen, Spivack, & Shure, 1972) can suggest goals through the establishment of relationships between certain competencies and indexes of adjustment. Another strategy is to use a task-analytic approach. Identify individuals exhibiting desirable behaviors, put them under a cognitive-behavioral microscope, and observe what they say and do while performing specific tasks. Talk-aloud strategies and performance measures can be used to sample an individual's cognitive functioning. Comparison groups can be used for purposes of evaluation. This approach would require some careful consideration of the reliability and validity of procedures used for identification, observation, and evaluation.

As described earlier, numerous cognitive interventions appear to be congruent with a preventive perspective. Coping skills seem to be easily translatable into a preventive program. In implementing a coping-skills program, it would be important to ascertain whether individuals lack these skills. It may be inefficient to offer skill programs indiscriminately without conducting a deficit analysis of the target group. For example, self-instructional methods may be important with impulsive children because such methods help these children focus on the task. On the other hand, self instruction may be redundant for nonimpulsive children who experience little difficulty in attentiveness (see Stone & Noce, 1980). Careful analyses of individual differences and treatment programs are required in order to enhance treatment effectiveness and consumer satisfaction.

Once broad adjustment goals have been adequately defined and interventions sufficiently articulated and differentiated for different consumers, an opportunity for evaluating a program's effectiveness and efficiency is provided.

In summary, it is fitting that evaluation is the last component mentioned in a chapter on interventions. Such a discussion focuses on a major issue in determining the future impact of cognitive psychology on the helping process. That is, implications of a cognitive-learning model for the helping process are useful to the degree that the adequacy of derived interventions and concepts are empirically evaluated. Thus the importance of proper evaluation to the elaboration of cognitive-behavioral methods of treatment is evident.

5
RESEARCH

POINT OF VIEW

Expression of a personal perspective seems to be an appropriate way to introduce this chapter. After reading and digesting material on counseling research, it is apparent that it tends to discuss research in terms of a dichotomy. There currently seems to be great importance attached to the distinction between action research (Goldman, 1978) and laboratory research. This debate concerning merits of basic and applied research has a long history in science. In recent discussions of counseling (Goldman, 1978; Krumboltz, 1967), action research is clearly preferred because it is assumed to provide answers to practical questions, while laboratory research is seen as having limited impact on practice. On the other hand, some researchers in other contexts (Kerlinger, 1977) suggest that greater practical benefit can be expected from basic research than from applied research. Such categorization of research fosters a limited perspective that often results in misguided debates of the white knight/black knight variety (for example, science versus nonscience, relevance versus irrelevance) and in research that is often rigorous or relevant, but seldom adequate conceptually. Moreover, the basic/applied debate leads to extreme positions that are clearly questionable and possibly detrimental to the development and growth of scientific research in counseling psychology.

Specifically, Goldman (1978), an action research advocate, has stated that "much or most of the research published in the counseling field has made little contribution to practice in the field" (p. 3). Goldman's position has at least two problems, including lack of evidence and inadequate conceptualization of science and practice and their relationship. In terms of evidential support, Goldman appears to corroborate his position by citing other authors and review articles. Review articles are far from being "the best single kind of evidence of the value or lack of value of research" (Goldman, 1976, p. 543). They are usually written by authors who must examine hundreds of published studies on a certain topic, studies that often report conflicting results and have used widely different populations, instruments, treatments, and settings. As a result, authors are usually free to see what they want to see in the collected results. Even the selected studies to be reviewed are often so noncomparable that so called firm conclusions are unobtainable.

If one wants to summarize applied research on a topic it would be more appropriate to use methods that may reduce reviewer bias for intergrating the data. Such an approach, called meta-analysis or the analysis of analyses, has been proposed by Glass (1976). Meta-analysis means the statistical analysis of a large collection of results from prescreened individual studies. The goal is to reach an overall conclusion, based on all the relevant findings in the literature, about the size of an experimental effect, using a common metric for estimating such effects. This objective distinguishes meta-analysis from conventional review articles that focus on individual findings, differences among studies, a box score listing of studies supporting hypotheses, and the usual litany that more research is needed. A meta-analysis would seem more appropriate for Goldman's position, but even this support or nonsupport from meta-analysis appears indirect. It would seem more appropriate to obtain direct and clear evidence about the sources of advances in counseling practice. One way would be to collect descriptions from practitioners of the advances in counseling practice they consider to be the most important to their clients. This list could be further reduced by having a panel of practitioners vote on the ten most important advances within a certain time period. A panel of experts would be asked to identify the essential bodies of knowledge that had to be available so that such advances could be made. This expert panel would then be requested to identify the key research articles that were important to the development of these essential bodies of knowledge and to classify such articles into basic research or applied research. In a biomedical context, such a study was done by Comroe and Dripps (1976), who found that basic research has been more important than applied research in influencing clinical practice. In another context, such as weapons development in the military, it might be found that nonbasic, mission-oriented, and targeted research strategies were superior. Such direct evidence may not be easily transferable to a counseling context, but it does suggest that research into research, proposed by Glass and conducted by Comroe and Dripps, is needed in counseling psychology if well-founded conclusions about the relative effectiveness of various types of investigation are to be drawn.

In addition, the traditional concern of translating the outcomes of counseling research into a plan of counselor action is an excessively narrow viewpoint. Conventionally, the linkage between practitioners and researchers in counseling has been practice. In this perspective, the practitioner is seen as a person who applies knowledge and skills in helping clients to resolve problems in living. Consequently, counseling researchers are to influence the counseling actions of helping practitioners. Such a view obscures how a practitioner changes and what else might need to be changed other than the practitioner's way of doing things. First, practitioner change is rarely direct and simple. It can be assumed that many counselors have changed and improved their practices as a result of reading research. Quite often, however, the changes in practice are more complex, emerging out of complex interactions between public demand, administrative policy, scholarly works, political expediency, personal needs, and practical necessity.

Secondly, the traditional view neglects other practitioners perspectives. An obsessive focus on counseling actions neglects the way counselors think about their actions. Included in such a perspective would be such global cognitions, as beliefs about reality and the future. In terms of the counseling context, such cognitions influence the counselor in formulating a rationale for practice, in developing goals (what is important and obtainable), and in making commitments to implement procedures. These kinds of effects are overlooked by researchers who give exclusive attention to improving counseling practice. Researchers who become so absorbed with the goal of improving practice also neglect the possibility of the appropriateness of much of what counselors are already doing and forget the importance of theory-relevant research in providing a firmer rationale for counseling practice. Such a rationale and external confirmation of ongoing practices may be of greater help in sustaining a sense of mission for the practitioner than recommendations about how simply to perform tasks better. This is not to suggest that all counselor action is inspired by noble theories, but the practitioner is not simply a person performing a task. It is to suggest that the connections between research and practice are manifold; that is, theory-relevant research has potential in altering practitioner beliefs and offering an improved rationale for counseling practice as well as providing better ways of working with clients.

The other extreme is represented by Kerlinger (1977), who believes that the "basic purpose of scientific research is theory." Here the researcher eschews any concern for practical questions and relegates questions of practical objectives to technology. Such a narrow definition of science has logical problems and unfortunate consequences for counseling research. Logically, most attempts to set science apart from nonscience have not been successful. That is, attempts to erect a criterion of demarcation have failed (see Weimer, 1976; Mahoney, 1976). The separation of theory and practice and their assignment to science and technology, respectively, is artificial. The pure researcher, who believes that there is little direct connection between recent developments in research (for example, energy) and practical consequences, holds a difficult position. Past history (for instance, atomic bomb, Jensen's genetic-intelligence studies) would suggest that basic research cannot be so easily separated from its practical consequences. Moreover, there appears to be no logical or practical reason why research conducted by those interested in applied inquiry cannot be scientific and theory-relevant (see Cook & Campbell, 1979).

A most unfortunate consequence of Kerlinger's views is to further encourage counseling researchers, especially graduate students, to view their research as less than scientific and to promote atheoretical investigations. Kerlinger's attempt to isolate applied researchers from science will aggravate the problems in counseling research. Too many faculty and graduate students in counseling programs act as though Kerlinger's position is accurate. Thus the dissertation is a hurdle to overcome rather than an opportunity to learn how to be a productive researcher and contribute to scientific knowledge. The review of the literature becomes a selective list of studies on the topic with little conceptualization, critical thinking, or relation of the topic literature to broader areas of psychology. The design is selected from a Campbell and Stanley catalog, with little thought of how the questions can be best addressed. Statistical analyses are selected from available canned programs without living with the data in terms of exploratory data analysis (see Tukey, 1977). Rarely are these activities construed in the context of science nor do they lead to programmatic research that has practical import, much less theoretical relevance. It would be unfortunate if Kerlinger's view continued to enhance such an approach to counseling research.

This discussion emphasizes the difficulties and problems of most applied fields, such as counseling psychology, in separating analytic and technological functions. A broad approach to science is recommended in which both basic and applied research are valued as scientific enterprises. That is, counseling researchers need to be concerned with the usefulness of counseling research to building and testing theory as well as to assessing the effectiveness of counseling practices. The crucial question does not appear to be whether the research can offer immediate solutions to practical problems, but whether it is conceptually and methodologically adequate. It is doubtful that conceptually and methodologically weak research can offer useful recommendations to counseling practice. It is this point that many action researchers seem to forget. In their legitimate protests against scientism, many of the problems they raise are not limited to experimental studies. Threats to validity also arise in less formal and more humanistic approaches to knowledge. The problem is which approach offers the more plausible results. The experimental method is not being suggested as removing ambiguity from counseling research, but it is preferred because the results of experimental methodology appear to be more interpretable than the results of the more subjective and qualitative approaches.

The emphasis on experimental science and theory relevance have been given renewed importance through the growth of cognitive science. The purpose of this chapter is to outline an experimental approach to counseling research. Many topics are not covered. Practical topics, including how to develop and check the theoretical and clinical relevance of one's research questions, how to construct and validate measures, and how to collect data, are not directly addressed. Moreover, technical discussions of philosophy of science, including examination of prediction, causation, and explanation, are not offered here. Theoretical relevance is mentioned, since one theme of the entire book is the conceptual implications of cognitive science for professional psychology. In addition, selected topics of experimental methodology and various experimental strategies are examined. Illustrations from counseling research will be used in the discussion of these topics and strategies.

Some of the many methodological concerns of counseling researchers are discussed in this section. These concerns are grouped under four headings: Internal Validity, Construct Validity, Statistical Conclusion Validity, and External Validity. Much of the following discussion is based on Cook and Campbell (1979) and the recent issue on methodology in the *Journal of Consulting and Clinical Psychology* (1978).

INTERNAL VALIDITY

Internal validity refers to the approximate validity (logical warrant) with which a given set of research procedures allows one to infer a causal relationship between two variables as manipulated and measured in an experiment. The major task of internal validity is to decide whether a causal relationship exists between two variables once it has been established that these two measured or manipulated variables covary.

Many counseling researchers have been guided by Campbell and Stanley (1963) and their descriptions of internal and external validity. Thus many of the threats to internal validity are well-known (history, maturation, testing, instrumentation, regression, selection, mortality, selection interactions), and many research studies have adopted randomization to take care of many of these threats. Of course, much applied research lacks randomization and the applied researcher must explicitly state and rule out each threat. The emphasis of this chapter is on true experiments because randomized experiments make causal inference easier. Thus the focus of this section will be on methodological concerns that are not ruled out by randomization. Other sources are available for quasiexperimentation (Cook & Campbell, 1979). Borrowing from Cook and Campbell (1979), the following threats to internal validity are not ruled out by randomization: diffferential mortality and various reactive conditions to awareness of treatment (imitation of treatments, compensatory equalization, compensatory rivalry, demoralization, and testing). These threats can lead to spurious differences, especially within research designs containing no-treatment control groups.

Differential Mortality

Differential mortality is a methodological concern when a treatment effect may be due to treatment-related attrition. While differential attrition can offer important information about the consequences of various treatments, it can also lead to the possibility of a selection artifact and the obscuring of the interpretation of the results. These undesirable consequences occur when different kinds of research participants drop out of a specific treatment group, leaving it composed of kinds of persons at posttest that may not be comparable to those in the other treatment groups. Thus, if there were differential attrition from a counseling treatment study, say an experiment on the effect of including the spouse in the behavioral treatment of obesity, it would be difficult to determine whether a relationship between spouse participation and weight reduction was a function of spouse participation or of the selection differences resulting from the kinds of participants who remained in each treatment condition during the investigation. In counseling research, difficulties of maintaining group comparability are often encountered in studies that last a substantial amount of time and/or in studies in which treatments differ in perceived desirability. In addition to the usual practical difficulties, differential attrition between experimentals and controls may occur because of the experiencing of differential pull of the experiment by experimentals and controls in responding to follow-up efforts, that is, greater implicit obligation of experimentals. Differential attention of experimenters to experimentals and controls during follow-up data collection could have a similar effect. In terms of desirability, participants who perceive that they are missing out by experiencing a less desirable treatment may drop out prematurely. Such an effect can arise if potential clients of a counseling center are assigned to experimental and control groups (waiting list control) for purposes of improving interpersonal skills. Control participants could drop out because they perceive their control experience as less than satisfactory or they may drop out to find help elsewhere. Experimentals may also drop out due to the undesirability of treatment (for example, time). Moreover, attrition of experimentals may be of practical significance since dropping out may indicate that experimentals have improved their interpersonal relationships.

This example raises some important points. First, attrition itself may be a treatment effect. That is, dropping out of a developmental program in a counseling center or out of individual therapy may be an indicator of positive significance—that a person has obtained his or her personal goals—but any other posttest differences between groups would be difficult to interpret. Secondly, the counseling center example indicated that dropouts could occur in both groups. The problem is not dropouts but the differential attrition across groups that renders the groups noncomparable.

There does not appear to be any satisfactory way to deal with differential attrition since it violates the assumption of randomness. Procedurally, an experimenter should empirically assess for the selection confound in attrition. Assessment could involve the rate of attrition to see whether attrition rates were comparable across groups. Moreover, the experimenter could use preexperimental data (for example, reason for dropping out, background data, pretest results) in testing whether the remaining experimentals and controls were comparable.

If a comparative bias existed, one could attempt to reduce the importance of this violation due to a plausible hypothesis (for instance, college students who drop out of control groups are usually more able students who find alternative resources) or replicate the study using a preexperimental review of the last study and past research and explicating the possible reasons for attrition. After the review, the study could attempt to take those reasons into account and plan the investigation in such a way as to reduce the attrition bias. This latter point is a good place to start before undertaking any experiment.

Reactive Conditions

Knowledge of treatment content can be communicated between experimental and control groups in situations in which participants are in close proximity to each other. Thus the planned differences between experimental and control groups living in the same residence hall may be invalid due to their close proximity and communication patterns. The same phenomenon can occur when treatment-relevant information is handed out to experimentals in a situation in which the controls can have access to the information through physical closeness.

Knowledge of treatment content can also be communicated through repeated testing and/or by using tests that have a special relationship to treatment. A greater threat of repeated testing and treatment-specific tests is that they offer alternative explanations for treatment effects. That is, performance may be enhanced due to familiarity with the tests or to the use of treatment-biased measures.

Most of the other concerns accompany the inevitable social comparison processes elicited from experimentation in the form of specific people being identified as receiving one treatment and others as receiving different treatments or no treatment at all. When the experimental group is perceived to be receiving desirable treatment and the assignment to experimental and control conditions is common knowledge, certain patterns of reactions that reduce the interpretability of the results can emerge. Reaction of no-treatment control respondents or respondents receiving less desirable treatments can be associated with compensatory rivalry or demoralization. Compensatory rivalry occurs when control group participants are motivated to outperform their experimental colleagues due to stimulation by social competition. On the other hand, control group respondents could become angry or demoralized and retaliate by reducing efforts. These reactions are not restricted to the participants in the experiment. Responses from administrators who are responsible for the administration of the organization in which the experiment is being conducted can also reduce the planned differences between experimental and control groups. These responses can lead to compensatory equalization, in which administrators respond to the demand for equal treatment by no-treatment control constituents, which removes the logic and content of the planned contrast. As an example, imagine that an experimenter wishes to assess the contribution of a group experience to a counselor's interview behavior. In conducting the experiment, a first-year class on interviewing is used in which students are randomly assigned to experimental treatment or no-treatment control. Those assigned to the experimental treatment are exposed to an encounter group experience in addition to their classroom experience, while the control group only receives the classroom experience. The groups would undoubtedly learn of their assignments through the procedure of informed consent and rumor. Such public knowledge would inevitably focus on the differences that accompany treatment/no-treatment designs, especially when conducted within an intact unit (classroom). Such differences can lead to the perception of desirable services being restricted to the experimental group, since the treatment and its impact may be seen as directly related to the respondents' goals of increasing effective interpersonal skills and, as a result, obtaining a better grade in the interviewing class. Moreover, the group experience may be perceived as valuable in terms of receiving feedback and enhancing self development. Such perceptions could lead the control participants to demand the class instructor include more experiential exercises in the classroom activity (compensatory equalization). In addition, these perceptions could stimulate demoralized and angry feelings (demoralization), leading to atypical behavior during the posttest, or the stimulation may generate a sense of competition in which the control group gains a sense of solidarity and attempts to reverse the expected differences and show the experimenter how effective it can become (compensatory rivalry). This latter phenomenon is more likely if the group experience is perceived as having an impact on grades.

The effects of these various reactive conditions lead to atypical performance of the no-treatment control respondents or respondents that receive less desirable treatments. Diffusion of treatment and compensatory equalization usually lead to weak experimental effects since the planned differences have been obscured. Compensatory rivalry leads to similar weak effects, but the atypical increase in the control group's performance is a function of the competitive conditions experienced by respondents of the less desirable treatments, while compensatory equalization and diffusion are a response of administrators and a response to treatment information intended for others, respectively. Demoralization can lead to an atypical suppression of the control group's performance, resulting in spurious differences, while treatment-specific tests or repeated testing may result in inflated treatment effects.

In determining the possibility of these threats, direct and indirect measures of all treatment and control groups are essential. In the preceding example, the classroom activities (hopefully audiotaped) should be reviewed and the instructor questioned about the possibility of diffusion of experiential learning among the controls. Control participants could be requested to participate in a think-aloud procedure in which an individual respondent is questioned about his or her experience and feelings about the experiment. Such evidence may be helpful in explaining ambiguous findings and atypical behavior of control group participants. As stated, the most appropriate procedure is to consider these possibilities before experimentation and take appropriate action to reduce their plausibility.

CONSTRUCT VALIDITY

The impact of cognitive science on counseling research is to view construct validity as importantly as internal validity. Construct validity has to do with the relationship between the treatment and measure specifications used in an experiment and their referent constructs. This validity category involves confounding when the experimenter's operations are designed to reflect particular cause or effect constructs, yet can be construed in terms of alternative constructs. The problem is the confounding of rival explanations, and the task of researchers is to ensure that their cause and effect operations reflect their research constructs. The following discussion of theoretical context, stimulus sampling, method bias, nonspecific effects, and treatment validity concerns this task.

Theoretical Context

As discussed before, much counseling research is atheoretical, with experiments providing little impact on theory development. As a result, many constructs remain unclear and many operations used in counseling studies are inadequately related to their referent constructs. For instance, in consulting the client-centered literature, one finds that the therapeutic conditions related to client growth must be communicated by the counselor and experienced by the client. Such an analysis suggests the inadequacy of only measuring counselor verbal behavior as an index of the therapeutic climate. Another example concerns the conceptual confusion surrounding attitudes and beliefs (for example, expectancies). Attitudes are usually defined as a stable predisposition to respond. In many studies, written preferences for particular targets (for instance, counselor style, client characteristics) are elicited at a single time and called attitudes. Such operations appear questionable when attitude-behavior consistency or attitude consistency over time are not tapped. Moreover, attitudes appear to rely on a heavy affective component, while expectancy seems more related to a cognitive mode of responding (for example, probability learning). Yet many researchers interchange these concepts and measure them using similar procedures.

In order to enhance construct validity, the selection and labeling of treatments and measures should be undertaken within a well-defined theoretical context. The specific operations to be used can then emerge after a useful conceptual analysis of the salient constructs. Such an analysis will clarify constructs and permit the development of treatments and measures that clearly reflect their referent constructs. These procedures will more likely be adopted when counseling researchers recognize the value of theory-relevant research and attempt to relate their research questions to other bodies of psychological knowledge.

Stimulus Sampling

Many studies use unrepresentative designs in which the cause and effect constructs are represented by single operations. These single operations contain many irrelevant and idiosyncratic attributes and rarely include all the relevant construct dimensions of interest.

These concerns are germane to counseling research because such research often uses a human stimulus. For instance, the studies examining sex effects or clinical judgments would need to consider the value of sampling the stimuli, that is, the use of many examples of the sex or client constructs, respectively, in order to provide a more representative design. Such a consideration would also be indicated in the use of many counselors and clients in process studies and in treatment-outcome investigations.

Single operations are not restricted to the cause construct in counseling studies, but often occur when assessment of effects is limited to one measure. The earlier discussion of the singular focus on counselor verbal behavior in some client-centered investigations is an example.

Thus an appropriate approach to counseling research is to use representative designs that include multiple manipulations and measures. If small sample size prohibits separate analysis by source in factorial designs, the use of different manipulations can still be used in a design sense and combined for purposes of analysis in order to test the effect despite heterogeneous sources.

Method Bias

Counseling research often uses many manipulations or measures, but the problem of a single-stimulus sample occurs at the method level at which manipulations are presented the same way or all the measures use the same method of recording responses. In an experiment on dependency and counselor style, an experimenter divided participants into independent and dependent groupings on the basis of a paper-and-pencil questionnaire. The groupings were randomly assigned to different counseling style conditions presented via written examples. Self-report measures were collected in which respondents had to respond to instruments assessing the counselor's attractiveness, expertness, and ability to deal with various problem types. The problem is that the possible experimental effects may be attributable to the method (written simulation, self report) as well as to the experimental factors. In this example, the use of a single method precludes the separation of experimental factors and methodology.

As discussed earlier, multiple operations appear to reduce these problems. Thus the use of other forms of manipulations and methods of recording data (for example, written, performance, self report, raters) is recommended. Moreover, multiple operationalism has implications for the microlevel as well as for the macrolevel of experimental design. On the microlevel, assessment instruments need to reflect systematic variation in their formats (such as alternating positively and negatively valenced items and varying the valence of the end points of response scales) in order to reduce response bias.

Nonspecific Effects

The question of nonspecific effects has a long history in medical and psychological therapies, commonly referred to as placebo effects (see Shapiro & Morris, 1978). Debates in counseling and psychotherapy research often concern whether the effects of a treatment are solely attributable to specific therapeutic processes beyond nonspecific factors. In addressing this question, a key task in psychological treatment is to be able to separate specific from nonspecific actions. The task is an empirical question requiring controlled research (Kazdin & Wilcoxon, 1976). For purposes of the present discussion, specific activity is conceptualized as the therapeutic influence attributable solely to the theoretically relevant ingredients of concern to the research.

Many nonspecific factors have been identified (see Shapiro & Morris, 1978). Two nonspecific processes will be examined: social influence and expectancy. Social influence processes may be facilitated in the experimental situation. Role demands may influence participants to reflect the role of a good subject. In performing the good subject role, the participant may attempt to satisfy the experimenter by guessing what the experimenter wants to happen and then attempting to act in a way to confirm the hypothesis. Even during the final debriefing session, subjects may not include their awareness of the experimental hypothesis in an effort to satisfy the experimenters.

Recent research on research (Rosenthal & Rosnow, 1969; Chaves & Barber, 1974) indicates the potential influence of role demands. These role demands become more viable as rival explanations in reactive research in which the experimenter's hypothesis is obvious. For instance, subjects asked to rate the effectiveness of various counseling styles may be presented with such extremes that the nature of the hypothesis is only too clear. To give a more specific example, male subjects asked to rate the attractiveness and other characteristics (for example, intelligence) of various females representing different levels of attractiveness via videotape may react to the transparent hypothesis by giving atypical responses. That is, the attractiveness manipulation, even if extreme, may not hold for males due to their attempts to receive a favorable personal evaluation in the cultural context of changing attitudes toward women, especially if the experimenter is a female. It would seem that most research dealing with attitudes about race, sex, and the handicapped would have to be careful of the potentially reactive nature of their investigations.

In addition to social influence, the participants' perception of treatment and their expectancy of improvement can prove to be viable alternative explanations. To give an example, various short-term treatments, including attention placebo, are administered by one counselor (the experimenter). The possibility exists that these treatments are not equally credible and that participants will pick up expectations from the counselor or rely on their own ideas. Such expectations and credibility perceptions can influence posttest performance and lead to confounding.

Expectations and perceptions of credibility are often serious factors in outcome studies. Nonspecific control conditions used in treatment studies, such as systematic desensitization, appear to generate lower expectations for improvement and credibility than does treatment (see Borkovec & Nau, 1972). These same findings may occur in counseling research in which different treatments are compared with attention-placebo control groups. Such control groups may be exposed to nondirective group discussion, films, reading material, or other media programs. It would certainly seem possible that these control procedures, in comparison with various counseling interventions, would elicit differential expectations and treatment credibility ratings. Such findings would not rule out previously documented treatment effects, but they would suggest that nonspecific factors could not be ruled out as a rival hypothesis.

In responding to nonspecific influences, researchers should plan to incorporate various design and data analysis strategies in order to ensure high construct validity. In terms of social influence, role demands can be assessed by using naive confederates instead of the experimenter to obtain postexperimental perceptions. Simulation control groups can be used in preexperimental studies in which subjects are provided a brief exposure to the treatment rationale and content and asked to simulate the effects they believe the experimenter desires, while other groups are asked to simulate the opposite. The use of simulator effects does not rule out treatment effects, but can suggest the reactive nature of the research. Such information may be helpful in deciding to use naive experimenters, intentionally using fake expectations, or masking the experimental purpose.

Nonspecific control conditions have been increasingly used in outcome studies in order to control for nonspecific influences. Unfortunately, the vast majority of outcome studies have not adequately dealt with treatment credibility and client expectancy. Future investigations must include appropriate controls, such as active placebo groups, that can demonstrate empirically their credibility and ability to influence client expectations.

Multioperational strategies appear useful in addressing the issue of treatment credibility and expectancy. Both should be assessed at different points and use different methods. For instance, treatment credibility could be assessed after presentation of the treatment rationale, in the middle of treatment, and at the conclusion of treatment. Assessment could include self report as well as unobtrusive measures, such as bogus measures that are suggested to the participants as reflecting treatment effects. Expectancy assessment could follow the same procedure, namely the use of multiple operations over time.

Treatment Validity

Treatment validity can be conceptualized as part of construct validity. That is, while construct validity concerns the fit between planned constructs and the operations, treatment validity concerns the fit between the planned operation as described by the researcher and the actual implementation of the operation. Most often, little direct data is collected in the assessment of the independent variable. In counseling research, the evidence is usually the word of the researcher. In outcome research, such counseling methods as client-centered or rationale-emotive interventions are described as various treatments. Such research often lacks the data from experts in these respective areas on their assessment of randomly selected protocols. Independent variable assessment in analogue research is not much better. Researchers' statements about the components of independent variables, such as "failure feedback," "good examples," "structured interview," "nonverbal condition," "assertive responses," and "high self-disclosing interview," often fail to reflect empirical validation. Research descriptions are not infallible. Thus it is always better to monitor and conduct several check analyses on the experimental procedures as implemented in order to ensure reasonable approximation between operations as planned and operations as implemented.

A more basic issue may be that such empirical checking is impossible due to inadequate specification of the independent variables. Too often the description of the independent variable is inadequate for analysis or replication. The problem of inadequate specification of the independent variable is considered in more detail as a concern of external validity.

The discussion of construct validity has highlighted a number of themes: planning, design considerations, and data analyses. In terms of planning, the researcher was encouraged to relate the research questions to a theoretical context, to critically analyze relevant constructs, and to tailor the manipulations and measures to the relevant constructs. In addition, preexperimental testing of the possibility of nonspecific influences was recommended. Design considerations focused on multiple operations of independent and dependent variables and the inclusion of relevant and empirically determined control groups, while data analyses were discussed as important in the determination of construct validity. Data analyses do not ensure high construct validity, but they would suggest the viability of rival explanations and the degree of fit between treatment as implemented and treatment as planned.

STATISTICAL CONCLUSION VALIDITY

Statistical conclusion validity is concerned with the appropriate use of statistics and precision, such as reducing random error, in determining whether a presumed cause and effect covary. The issue of precision is discussed first.

Precision

One cause of inflated error is the low reliability of measures. In counseling research, paper-and-pencil measures (often constructed by the experimenter) may not have enough items or items may not have been selected according to a sound psychometric procedure (for example, strategies using covergent and discriminant validity). One-item tests can lead to instability, especially if the attitude measure is assessing other than salient attitudes. To ensure reliability, it is generally wise to include multiple items carefully selected for high intercorrelations.

In process studies, raters are often needed for analyzing the content of interviews. In these situations, the use of multiple raters, extensive rater training and appropriate indexes of interrater reliability (see Tinsley & Weiss, 1975) are suggested. One-rater situations are similar to one-item tests. That is, instability can easily occur in such situations and raise questions about the generalization of results. Incorporating multiple raters represents an increase in reliability since a subject's score is represented by a mean (aggregate of ratings across raters), which is more stable than an individual rating. Moreover, the use of multiple raters can reduce contamination when more than one measure is being used by assigning different raters to different measures.

Extensive rater training, based on a specified procedure including manuals, protocols, and established criterion responses, is required if other researchers are to replicate the procedure. Too often, rater training depends on ambiguous content and processes that are difficult to replicate. After didactic training, sample protocols can be rated independently and discussed in relation to criterion samples in order to elaborate a common written understanding of the criterion. Preliminary interrater data can be gathered to see whether further training is required. In addition, raters can be informed that their ratings will be reviewed. This information often increases rater attention and fosters a greater degree of accuracy.

Appropriate indexes of interrater agreement and reliability need to be reported in order to achieve an accurate assessment of the reliability issue. These indexes should be based on the ratings by the different raters of the data reported in the study. Specific information about the rating procedure (portion of interview, rating intervals, number of protocols included in the reliability estimate, sex of rater, and so on) and the strategy for estimating agreement (for example, number of categories, base rates for categories, estimate of chance agreement) and reliability (for example, interrater variance included or excluded in the error variance) can be helpful to other researchers. For instance, many studies have adopted a percentage of rater agreement. Such an agreement index can be misleading unless the researcher provides data on the base rate for rating categories and an estimate of chance agreements. Tinsley and Weiss (1975) have described the advisability of using an index of agreement (corrected for chance) and an index of reliability (intraclass correlation). Their article should be consulted when attempting to decide on an appropriate assessment of interrater reliability.

Treatment implementation can be an additional source of variation. Differences can occur because of different persons administering treatment or from differences arising from occasion to occasion by the same person. Such differences can be reduced by standardization of treatment content and procedures. For example, the experimental setting or procedure may be an uncontrolled source of variation. Many investigators using video treatments have found that problems with the picture and/or sound can affect the participants' attention. In these studies, investigators need to ensure the quality of the video presentation and assess the respondents' attention to the presentation through a content assessment of the treatment. However, in most cases, despite standardization, treatments will contribute to error variance. Thus it is necessary to monitor and measure treatment implementation in order to assess the degree of unplanned variability.

Another potential source of variation has to do with individual differences. Error variance is inflated when subjects differ on factors related to outcome measures. In order to reduce such error variance, a homogeneous population can be selected or the relevant subject variables can be reliably assessed and, under the proper conditions, used as covariates. These procedures involve some cost, including potential limitations on external validity or meeting the assumptions of analysis of covariance. It is also worth noting that these procedures assign individual differences of error. It may be more important to consider particular dimensions of the respondent to be of substantive value, rather than error, and to cross these relevant subject variables with treatment variables in factorial designs. The information from such designs appears to be potentially theory-rich and practically relevant. This last procedure is elaborated upon in the section on experimental strategies.

Use of Statistics

The concerns listed here are not exhaustive, but are representative of statistical problems encountered in counseling research that can lead to spurious inferences. Researchers interested in more detailed exposition should consult basic design and statistical texts. Two general statistical issues are briefly discussed here, followed by a discussion of three specific concerns.

One of the basic questions a researcher must ask concerns the assumptions of the statistical tests he or she plans to use. For example, in the analysis of covariance, the regression of the posttest on the pretest covariate should be homogeneous. Examination of scatterplots will reveal whether such an assumption has been met (see Glass, Peckham, & Sanders, 1972). Most regression techniques, including analysis of variance, are robust to certain assumptive violations (for example, normality), but the violations of correlated errors and incomplete data sets with heterogeneous variances become threats to meaningful statistical interpretations. From these examples, it should be clear how important it is to consult standard statistical references about assumptions of a selected statistical procedure in order to see what problems might arise in using the the selected procedure with a specific set of data.

A general problem in counseling research has to do with the number of statistical comparisons researchers do per experiment. In some cases, researchers do so many comparisons that they fail to realize the inflationary impact of multiple comparisons on Type 1 error. There are methods available for adjusting the error rate per experiment. In terms of multiple comparisons, a new statistic can be obtained by dividing the desired level of significance by the number of experimental comparisons or by establishing different levels of significance for different comparisons based on theoretical relevance. These adjusted values reflect a more conservative strategy when multiple comparisons are being made. Another method for controlling the error rate problem is to use conservative multiple comparison tests (for instance, Tukey or Scheffé tests). When there are multiple dependent variables and these variables are empirically and conceptually related, it would seem prudent to adopt a multivariate analysis of variance in order to control for chance effects among numerous univariate tests.

There are many other concerns, including the use of inferential statistics itself (Weimer, 1977). Among these varied concerns, three specific concerns are relevant to counseling research. They include the appropriate choice of a statistical test (such as variance or covariance analysis), appropriate form of dependent variables (such as transformed data), and the difference between statistical and clinical significance. Each of these issues could easily lead to a prolonged and technical discussion. For our purposes, each issue is briefly addressed and the reader is directed to additional readings.

Growth and change are processes relevant to the helping field. Unfortunately, the measurement of these processes is not straightforward (Cronbach & Furby, 1970). Several approaches have been used in the analysis of change. When a pretest/posttest design is used, some researchers use a repeated-measures analysis of variance, while others use a gain-score approach (posttest minus pretest). Recently researchers have been advised to bypass these strategies in favor of a covariance approach (Huck & McLean, 1975). It appears the covariance analysis is a powerful strategy, but the decision of which to choose should reflect the researcher's questions and the adequacy of the data.

Another specific issue has to do with the form of the dependent variable. This issue becomes important in interview-process studies concerned with a content-analysis methodology. In this methodology, raters usually work independently in identifying and scoring various counselor and/or client verbal behaviors into relevant categories. The subjection of the resulting raw category scores for analysis may reflect an uncontrolled source of variance, namely, loquacity rate. That is, the potential differences in talk time may be reflected in spurious differences of the verbal categories due to differences in opportunity to use the category. In order to control for loquacity rate, many researchers use ratio scores in which proportion scores of category responses to total verbal responses are determined. In addition, these ratio scores can be passed through an arcsin transformation if there is serious question about the nature of the ratio scores. Whatever the dependent variable happens to be, the form of the dependent variable must meet the requirements of additivity, normality, and homogeneity.

A major issue in counseling research has to do with the criteria for evaluating effects. One way of evaluating treatment effects is through statistical significance. Traditionally, a conservative decision about covariation is made based on the comparison of covariation and random error within the context of an a priori specified risk of being wrong (that is, inferring covariation when it is not present). The risk is usually set at 0.05, reflecting a greater concern about incorrect assertions. The five percent level is arbitrary, but, once the probability level has been set, observed relationships below the specified level are treated as though they are effects while those above it are treated as non-effects. If the researcher chooses to rely on inferential statistics, researchers should explicitly state their significance level and, if different from the traditional level, should also provide a rationale.

Other researchers claim that an estimate of the amount of covariation is also needed in evaluating treatment effects. These researchers suggest that magnitude estimates are less dependent on sample size than estimates of statistical significance. A significant F ratio for treatment effects only indicates that there is an association between two variables. This F ratio does not indicate whether the effects are large or small, information provided by magnitude estimates. A rough estimate of the strength of effects in analysis of variance can be provided in using a ratio of the variance of any treatment divided by the total variance. A more precise estimate based on expected values is the omega squared $(\omega^2)^2$ estimate (see Hays, 1963). These variance component analyses enable the researcher to estimate the proportion of variance in the dependent measure that can be accounted for by the independent variable.

A focus on magnitude estimates has some implications for counseling research. In large-sample counseling research, many analyses and significant effects are reported. For instance, it is often difficult to sort out important from trivial correlations in matrices with a large sample, since trivial associations among variables may achieve statistical significance if the sample is sufficiently large. Thus researchers should report magnitude estimates along with statistical significance for large-sample research. In terms of small-sample research, the question of magnitude estimates becomes a question of power. In recent writings (Cohen, 1969 Haase, 1974), researchers have been encouraged to conduct power analyses. Such recommendations suggest that many investigations in counseling research lack sufficient power to detect expected effects. In order to conduct power analyses properly, the investigator must know valid variance estimates and an estimate of the size of the expected effect prior to the study in order to determine the appropriate sample size. These estimates are usually not available before a study, but it is still possible to gather information retrospectively about sample sizes and variances in order to calculate the size of any effect that could have been detected with 95 percent confidence. Such information can be useful to the researcher and reader in evaluating whether the research endeavors are worth pursuing with more powerful designs. When research results in a no-difference conclusion based on a small sample, it seems worthwhile to conduct a retrospective analysis as outlined.

Recently, a major issue in evaluating change has concerned clinical significance, which refers to the value or importance of the change (for example, impact on client functioning). On the other hand, statistical significance can only show a reliable treatment effect that may or may not be clinically important. The clinical criterion is often difficult to specify because it involves decisions about acceptable and unacceptable levels of behavior. Kazdin (1978) has discussed two procedures for assessing clinical significance: social comparison and self report. The social comparison method involves the comparison of pretreatment and posttreatment client behavior with the behavior of nondeviant peers. It is assumed that the client differs markedly in the target behavior from his or her identified peer group prior to treatment. After treatment, a clinically significant change should be reflected in the comparison of client and peer group. That is, the comparison of the client's posttreatment behavior with peer behavior should demonstrate that the client's behavior has moved within the acceptable range of functioning.

A problem with this methodology is in identifying normative criteria and appropriate peer groups for evaluating treatment effects. It does not appear that counseling has developed empirically established criteria by which investigators can easily decide whether their levels of significant treatment effects are of practical significance. For instance, how would an investigator evaluate the practical significance of obtaining different levels of client self disclosure as a function of counselor reinforcement? Are there empirically established levels of self disclosure that clearly indicate a range of client self-disclosure production necessary for an effective counseling session? It would seem that normative information has to be gathered. Moreover, the question of whether such information can serve as appropriate criteria would have to be decided before the question of clinical significance could be addressed within a social-comparison methodology.

A self report usually relies on the client or significant others, who are in a special position to observe the client's behavior, to make judgments about how well the client is functioning. These global judgments provide an evaluation of the impact of specific treatment-related changes on how the client and others view the client's behavior. Such global ratings can be helpful in identifying behaviors for treatment as well as highlighting qualitative improvements associated with behavior change. Of course, these global assessments may reflect bias, but such ratings coupled with specific performance measures can provide an alternative evaluative dimension that may help in assessing the practical significance of behavior change as experienced in day-to-day interaction.

In addition to social-comparison and self-report methodologies, it appears that generalization and maintenance of treatment effects should constitute important factors in judging the practical significance of results. Too often, adjustment studies rely on demonstrating short-term therapeutic improvements without considering whether these effects are maintained over time or generalize from the consultation office to the family and work settings. These concerns are elaborated upon in the section on external validity.

In closing, it should be noted that the emphasis given to inferential statistics here constitutes neither a sacred view of statistical significance nor a positivistic view of science. All of the previous statements should reflect a great deal of caution, tentativeness, and concern about approximation rather than concern about finding and declaring the truth. Naive quantifiers tend to rely on computer printouts and forget about ordinary perception and qualitative judgment. The problems with the uncritical use of statistics have been pointed out by critics and their criticism is useful, but their advocacy of other methods (for example, uncontrolled case studies) would suggest that the search for objective and verifiable knowledge has been abandoned. It would seem better to use statistics in a cautious manner as an approach in dealing with the problem of covariation than to substitute other so called humanistic methods that seem to have greater weaknesses.

EXTERNAL VALIDITY

External validity refers to the generalizability of a presumed causal relationship across persons, settings, and times. Most counseling research adopts a two-stage process in terms of external validity: a target population of persons, settings, and times is defined, then samples are drawn to represent these populations. Typically, convenient samples are drawn and representativeness entails class membership (for example, undergraduate) and intuitive appeals for representatives. Rarely are samples drawn systematically from populations with known probabilities. Occasionally, accidental sampling (for example, a subset of clients in a counseling center) is used. Often these achieved populations are inaccurately declared to be representative of target populations of which they are members.

Several examples of the various limitations to external validity that are often encountered in counseling research could be cited. In terms of person categories, most analogue counseling research uses a specific target class: the ubiquitous undergraduate student. Even when participants are all undergraduate volunteers, systematic recruitment factors lead to limiting generalizations to volunteers who receive pay or experimental course credit, or to those volunteers who are interested in interpersonal relationships or who have nothing else to do.

Sometimes an experiment coincides with particular historical changes and causes a researcher to question whether a causal relationship will hold in the future. For instance, the research procedures that have been used in the past to document sex bias in career counseling may not be applicable to a situation in which a great deal of attention has been focused on women through the women's movement. The findings may or may not still be applicable, but the use of ratings of written protocols identified by sex may be so transparent as to lead to response bias. Thus the concern of generalizing procedures as well as findings across time periods becomes problematic.

Another external validity problem has to do with the nature of the setting in which an experiment takes place. It has become a common criticism of analogue research that its experimental setting is too different from the typical organizational environment of the so called real world. It is not necessary to repeat these helpful criticisms of analogue research because they are well-known and reported elsewhere. It should be noted that field experiments suffer limitations of external validity as well. This should not be surprising since all human research efforts (except research on research), whether laboratory or field experiments, are analogue studies. Field studies are subject to many of the same biases as discussed in the critical literature about analogue studies. For example, university counseling centers have been surveyed on numerous topics (such as counseling-center models, functions, services, roles, training). Such survey studies are subject to a volunteer bias. The refusal rate encountered in obtaining the cooperation of counseling centers is often high, especially if one includes those that were never contacted because of practical limitations or because it was decided that the center would not cooperate. The volunteering centers will often be the most progressive, proud, and institutionally strong. Is it legitimate to extrapolate from these centers to centers in which morale, pride, and institutional stability are low?

Different approaches have been suggested to increase external validity. The most powerful mode is to use random sampling of a target population. Such a method is likely to be impossible for settings and time and probably feasible, but unlikely, for people. A second approach is to adopt replication within a single experiment. Covenient samples across types of people and settings can be used. This heterogeneity inflates the error term, but it also provides a test of whether treatment effects hold despite differences between kinds of people and kinds of settings.

Consecutive replications can be planned to see whether the causal relationship holds over time. Perhaps of more importance is the systematic replication by independent investigators. If independent replication procedures are to be adopted, researchers must be explicit about their procedures and share specific information about these procedures in their written reports (Cornfield & Tukey, 1956). Such specific information enables practitioners and researchers to evaluate the usefulness of the findings for their settings and to replicate the experiment with fidelity.

An example of using replication procedures is demonstrated in a recent study by Helms (1978). Helms attempted to extend the external validity of an earlier analogue study (Hill, Tanney, Leonard, & Reiss, 1977) concerned with the treatment of female clients. She partially replicated the study, using parallel measures obtained in a naturalistic counseling setting. Results of the naturalistic extension were similar to the analogue investigation (for example, relative importance of personal-interpersonal problems and number of sessions required to resolve the problem). Such findings suggest the relevance of using replication procedures in translating analogue studies into naturalistic ones. In addition, it may provide a counterpoint to action advocates who have difficulty seeing the relevance of analogue research.

PRIORITIES

It should be apparent that the previous discussion does not exhaust the potential methodological concerns involved in conducting research. In addition, the list of validity types and the subdivision of specific concerns within each type are not meant to result in exclusive categories. The purpose was simply to provide a practical scheme in which methodological issues could be discussed. For this purpose, Cook and Campbell's (1979) scheme was adopted and modified. Such an approach is entirely practical, thus many of the validity types may appear arbitrary or the concerns may seem to overlap with other validity types.

Given the limitations of the scheme, the relative importance of various validity types can be based on the kind of research being conducted. In this book, the explication of a cognitive science paradigm in terms of the counseling process has been a major theme. Such a preference has inevitable consequences for research. One implication of the cognitive paradigm is an increased interest in theory-relevant research. For investigators with theoretical priorities, the listing of validity types in this chapter (internal, construct, statistical conclusion, and external) appears appropriate. For these investigators, the priorities are on demonstrating that a relationship between variables is causal and that the variables involved in the research are theoretically relevant.

Applied researchers may have a different set of priorities. Their interests may be more concerned with solving practical problems. Consequently, their studies would be undertaken in field settings that might permit wide generalization (external validity). Such research efforts are less concerned with causal constructs (construct validity) than with the effectiveness of complex treatment packages.

Discussions of research priorities often neglect the trade-offs between validity types that may be required. For instance, internal validity may be best served by isolated settings, randomized experiments, and standardized procedures, but the issue of generalization becomes less important. Consequently, many critics of counseling research are willing to abandon internal validity for the sake of external validity. Such a procedure seems to risk the possibility of making causal statements for the benefit of appearing professionally relevant. It appears that internal validity must be a primary concern in laboratory and field research if causal hypotheses are to be tested and a body of knowledge developed. As discussed earlier, research strategies that emphasize theory (construct validity) and practice (external validity) are both necessary and important. At the same time, a preference for theory-relevant research and design is clearly seen here. Such a preference is not absolute in the sense of appropriating science and identifying it with this preference, but is made as a reflection of a commitment to a particular paradigm: cognitive science. These commitments do not reflect the basic truth, but are relative commitments that enable researchers to identify problems, select variables for investigation, and choose appropriate designs. In conclusion, it is suggested that counseling research can ill afford to be solely preoccupied with its immediate practical payoff, but should recognize the reciprocal relationships between conceptualization, experimentation, and application. Although the latter two traditions have been of central focus in counseling research, the analytical tradition appears to be less salient and therefore should receive renewed attention.

ILLUSTRATION

For purposes of clarification, a recent study by Stein and Stone (1978), published in the *Journal of Counseling Psychology*, is evaluated in the light of the preceding methodological discussion.

Effects of Conceptual Level and
Structure on Initial Interview Behavior[*]

Marsha Lomis Stein and Gerald L. Stone
University of Western Ontario, London, Canada

This study assessed the impact of the conceptual level matching model within a counseling situation. A 2 x 2 x 2 randomized block

---

[*]From M. L. Stein and G. L. Stone, Effects of Conceptual Level and Structure on Initial Interview Behavior. *Journal of Counseling Psychology*, 1978, 25, 96-102. Reprinted by permission of the publisher, American Psychological Association, Inc.

design was used to compare the effects of matching counselee conceptual level (CL) to counselor-offered degree of structure in a 40-min. initial interview analogue. Two treatment levels of counselor structure (low structure and high structure) were crossed with two blocks of subjects (24 low-CL students and 24 high-CL students) and two interviewers. We predicted that matched persons (low CL, high structure; high CL, low structure) would respond better than mismatched persons (low CL, low structure; high CL, high structure). The high-CL matching predictions were supported in expressions of self-awareness ($p < .01$) and satisfaction ($p < .05$). The low-CL matching predictions were supported in the areas of satisfaction ($p < .01$). Use of different behavioral outcomes and a flexible counseling style are stressed.

Researchers have emphasized the importance of using matching models in psychological research (e.g., Strupp & Bergin, 1969). One such paradigm used in educational research is the conceptual level (CL) matching model (Hunt & Sullivan, 1974) involving coordination of a personal characteristic (CL) and an environmental dimension (degree of structure). The CL matching model generally predicts an inverse relation between CL and degree of structure. That is, low-CL persons profit more from a highly structured environment and high–CL persons profit more from a low-structured environment, or, in some cases, are less affected by variations in structure.

Conceptual level has been described as a dimension of personality development indexing both cognitive complexity (differentiation, discrimination, and integration) and interpersonal maturity (self-responsibility; Harvey, Hunt & Schroder, 1961). Basically, low-CL persons are relatively dependent on external standards, stimulus bound, and categorical thinkers. High-CL persons are generally characterized as being relatively independent and capable of generating new concepts. In counseling, Bordin (1955) has identified the environment dimension of structure as the ambiguity dimension, encompassing all levels of counselor control and interview direction. When ambiguity is greatest, the counselor gives minimal structure to the client; as the counselor gives progressively more structure to the client, the ambiguity of the interview concomitantly decreases.

The Cl matching principle has been confirmed in several studies in education (summarized by Hunt & Sullivan, 1974). Preliminary evidence suggests the usefulness of a CL matching approach in counseling (e.g., Posthuma & Carr, 1975).

This study compared the effects of matching counselee CL to counselor-offered degree of structure during a 40-min. initial interview analogue concerning adjustment to university. In the present study, counselors used two different interviewing styles in an effort to match counseling style with client characteristics. The following hypotheses were tested:

1. High-CL persons receiving low-interview structure (Group A)

respond better than high-CL persons receiving high-interview structure (Group B).
2. Low-CL persons receiving high-interview structure (Group D) respond better than low-CL persons receiving low-interview structure (Group C).
3. Differences between high-CL and low-CL persons are greater under low than under high structure.
4. Under low structure, high-CL persons respond better than low-CL persons.

In the context of this study, "responding better" was viewed in terms of the clients' talking longer, producing more meaningful self-disclosure, expressing greater satisfaction with the interview, perceiving the interviewer as more understanding and more helpful, showing a greater degree of goal attainment, and showing a higher return rate for a second interview.

In terms of our methodological discussion, this introduction does establish a theoretical context (conceptual level, ambiguity) and a methodological perspective (matching models, factorial design). In addition, specific methodological procedures are introduced and experimental hypotheses are specified (last two paragraphs). On the other hand, explicit discussion of the similarities and differences between different formulations of conceptual level (for example, Hunt, Kelly, Bieri, Harvey) and specification of the multiple dimensions of structure might help readers clarify the theoretical constructs.

Method

Subjects

Subjects were 48 male and female students at the University of Western Ontario representing the top and bottom quartiles of CL scorers from an original sample of 98 introductory psychology students. The quartiles were equivalent in distribution of age (18-25 years) and sex (one third male, two thirds female).

Interviewers

Two experienced counselors, one 29-year-old male and one 26-year-old female, served as interviewers. Ratings by two judges on scales of empathy and global facilitativeness (Carkhuff, 1969) indicated that the counselors were functioning at or beyond Level 3 on both scales.

Instruments

Assessment of CL was accomplished by using the Paragraph Completion Method (Hunt, Greenwood, Noy, & Watson, Note 1). This is a semiprojective procedure that consists of six sentence stems, each of which must be completed in 3 min., for example, "What I think about rules . . ." and "When I am criticized. . . ." Each paragraph was rated independently by two trained raters; raters' scores were averaged for each protocol. Reliability coefficients were .72 for the mean of the three highest paragraph scores and .77 for the mean of the six paragraphs (intraclass correlation).

For rating client participation and self-disclosure, two raters independently rated 10-min., tape-recorded excerpts, randomly selected from the middle 20-min. portion of each interview.

Client participation was defined as total talk time over a 10-min. excerpt, excluding silences of more than 3-sec. duration. Interrater reliability on a random sample of 19 excerpts was .97 (Pearson r); because of the high reliability coefficient, analyses were performed using one rater's ratings.

As a behavioral measure of meaningful self-disclosure, the Haymes method (Jourard, 1971) was used. This method controls for verbal productivity, uses four rating categories (emotions, needs, fantasies, and self-awareness), and weights scores (e.g., 2 points = first-person referent). Reliability coefficients (intraclass correlation) on category ratings (unweighted frequencies) were lower than that for the total self-disclosure scores ($r = .88$); while reliability was moderate for self-awareness ($r = .57$) and emotion ($r = .51$), it was relatively low for needs ($r = .20$) and fantasies ($r = .28$).

A modified form of the Patient's Therapy Session Report (Orlinsky & Howard, Note 2) was used to assess counselee satisfaction and perceptions of counselor helpfulness and understanding. The satisfaction section contained 10 items, each rated on a 5-point scale, tapping factors of catharsis, insight, encouragement, and so on, for example, "I feel that I got a chance to let go and get things off my chest" scored "no" (1 point) through "A lot" (5 points). This section was administered as a pretest with the items phrased in terms of expectations, to control for possible response biases. The experimenter presented it in counterbalanced order with an open-ended, goal-attainment measure: "What do you want, or hope to get out of this session?" After the interview, students rated satisfaction obtained, extent of goal attainment, counselor helpfulness, and counselor understanding on 5-point ratings scales similar to the one above. As a measure of convergent validity, a 7-point, global rating scale of satisfaction was also administered at posttreatment only.

Students were given a written statement offering the opportunity for a second interview. Individuals who scheduled and participated in a second interview were considered to have returned. Students were also given a written definition of the ambiguity dimension in which low, moderate, and high levels of counselor topic control and interview direction were described. Students rated on a 9-point scale how much structure they perceived in the interview.

Procedure

Students were solicited by written announcement for experimental credit. The first session was devoted to CL assessment on the Paragraph Completion Method (Hunt et al., Note 1). Students were rank ordered on the basis of the mean of their three highest paragraph scores (primary CL score); when ties occurred, students were subranked according to the mean of the six paragraph scores (secondary CL score). The extreme-groups approach was used to select 24 students for the high-CL group and 24 students for the low-CL group. For the high-CL group, primary CL scores ranged from 2.17 to 2.83 on a scale of 0 to 3. Secondary CL scores ranged from 1.67 to 2.46. For the low-CL group, primary CL scores ranged from .67 to 1.67. Secondary CL scores ranged from .46 to 1.30.

Analyses (t ratios) indicated that the CL groups differed significantly ($p<.001$) from each other on both the primary scores and on the secondary scores. Participants in the high- and low-CL groups were randomly assigned to counselor and treatment conditions for a 2 x 2 x 2 randomized block design with six students in each cell.

Treatment administration. Two levels along the ambiguity dimension that Stein (1973) used were chosen for treatment conditions, as follows: (a) a moderately low-structured interview with counselors allowing and encouraging participants to determine interview direction by using minimal encouragements to talk and reflection responses (counselors avoided introducing topics to discuss) and (b) a moderately high-structured interview with counselors determining interview direction by asking specific open- and/or closed-ended questions about topics related to school adjustment (participants were allowed approximately a minute to respond to a question or longer if the information was directly relevant).

Counselors were given written copies of the two interview roles and participated in a 2-hour training session. For the purpose of clarity, the interview conditions are referred to as low structure and high structure, respectively. The topic for both conditions was "Adjustment to University."

Interviews were scheduled across a 4-week period for both counselors. Students were asked to complete the expectations and goal-attainment forms prior to the interview. Each student was then introduced to a counselor. Interviews were tape recorded with students' permission. After 40-mins., the counselor directed the participant to the experimenter-investigator, who administered four posttreatment measures in counterbalanced order over participants in each cell. The four measures were (a) Goal Attainment Scale, with preinterview goal statement attached; (b) Therapy Session Report; (c) Option for a Second Interview; and (d) Structure Scale.

Students indicating a desire for a second interview were contacted within 2 days of treatment by the investigator. An appointment was arranged with their assigned counselor for 1 week following the date of the initial interview.

Analyses

Three-factor analyses of variance or covariance were performed on all dependent variables. The interviewer factor, though not of direct interest, was included in the factorial analyses for precision, but interviewer means were combined for all planned comparisons across each CL X Treatment group, following the procedure in Kirk (1968). Thus, four group means were used in planned comparisons (one-tailed t test): Group A - high CL, low structure (matched); Group B - high CL, high structure (mismatched); Group C - low CL, low structure (mismatched); Group D - low CL, high structure (matched). Four contrasts, with predictions, were carried out as follows: Hypothesis 1, Contrast 1-A $>$ B; Hypothesis 2, Contrast 2-D $>$ C; Hypothesis 3, Contrast 3-A-C $>$ | D-B |; Hypothesis 4, Contrast 4-A $>$ C.

Methodologically, the study appears to have reduced many of the threats discussed previously. Randomization has ruled out many of the threats to internal validity. The other internal validity threats of differential mortality and reactive conditions did not occur or lack plausibility (that is, absence of a no-treatment control group). Multiple operations were used to define interviewer and dependent variables. In terms of the dependent variables, more than one method of obtaining data was used. Moreover, some of these measures attempted to address nonspecific effects (for example, expectancies, satisfaction). Numerous strategies were used for purposes of precision such as blocking, inclusion of the interviewer factor, interrater reliabilities, covariance analysis.

Although one could probably go on listing positive methodological points, it might be more useful to concentrate on a few aspects of contrast validity that may be adequately addressed. It should be noted that this study is restricted to treatment manipulations presented through one modality: the interview. Also, the assessment of conceptual level is based on written responses and appears to be heavily influenced by verbal productivity (see Hurndon, Pepinsky, & Meara, 1979). These new findings and method bias in this study raise the question of whether verbalization can be disassociated from conceptual level. It might even suggest that verbalization may be a more appropriate label for the construct than conceptual level. A related question could be raised about the dimension of structure. That is, the structure dimension appears to be directly related to the talk time of the counselor. Such a dimension may be central to the construct of structure in an interview setting, but it does highlight how closely this study's manipulations and, possibly, its measures are associated with verbalization.

Results

Treatment Check

Raters. Two raters used a definition of the ambiguity dimension

(Stein, 1973), and independently rated randomized 5-min. excerpts from all interviews, with an obtained reliability of .87 (intraclass correlation). Excerpts were rated for degree of structure on a 9-point scale, with higher values indicating increasing structure. Means were ordered as expected: low structure = 4.00; high structure = 6.85. A three-way analysis of variance indicated the treatments were significantly different from each other ($p < .0001$); all other effects were nonsignificant.

Participants. Participants' mean ratings of degree of structure on a 9-point scale were as follows: low structure = 3.04; high structure = 7.42. A three-way analysis of variance indicated the treatments were significantly different from each other ($p<.0001$). All other effects were nonsignificant.

Dependent Variables

A summary table of analyses is presented in Table 1[5.1].

Client participation. Results of client participation, as indexed by total talk time (seconds), are depicted in Figure 1[5.1].

Planned comparisons indicated that neither Hypothesis 1 nor 2 was confirmed, while Hypothesis 3 was confirmed. Differences between CL groups' talk times were significantly greater under low structure (difference = 53.6) than under high structure (difference = 27.2), $t(40) = 2.07$, $p < .025$. Hypothesis 4 was confirmed, that is, under low structure, the high-CL talk time ($M = 490.4$) was significantly longer than low-CL talk time ($M = 436.9$), $t(40) = 2.03$, $p < .025$.

Self-disclosure. None of the hypotheses were confirmed for total self-disclosure scores. However, a multivariate analysis of variance of the four category ratings indicated qualitative differences in the types of disclosures made. Univariate analyses indicated that CL and treatment effects occurred for self-awareness, as graphically presented in Figure 2[5.2].

Planned comparisons were carried out on the self-awareness scores. Hypotheses 1 was confirmed. The high-CL, low-structure, group gave significantly more expressions of self-awareness ($M = 7.58$) than the high-CL, high-structure group ($M = 5.25$), $t(40) = 2.74$, $p<.01$. Hypothesis 2 was not confirmed. Hypothesis 3 was confirmed; that is, the difference between CL groups' self-awareness expressions emerged significantly more prominently under low structure (difference = 3.29) than under high structure (difference = 1.17), $t(40) = 3.72$, $p<.0005$. Hypothesis 4 was confirmed, that is, high-CL persons gave significantly more expressions of self-awareness ($M = 7.58$) than low-CL persons ($M = 4.29$), $t(40) = 3.87$, $p < .0005$.

Satisfaction. Satisfaction data, adjusted for the pretest (expectation) covariate, are presented graphically in Figure 3[5.3]. Because there was a main interviewer effect, the means for both interviewers are displayed; however, interviewer means were combined for the planned comparisons on satisfaction, as in all other measures.

TABLE 5.1 Summary table for F ratios.

EFFECTS OF CONCEPTUAL LEVEL AND STRUCTURE

Measure	Interviewer (A)	Conceptual level (B)	Treatment (C)	A×B	A×C	B×C	A×B×C
Verbal behavior							
Talk time	.33	4.69*	1.24	1.64	1.68	.50	1.19
Self-disclosure							
Total score	.03	1.03	.16	.19	.95	.04	1.76
Overall category effects[a]	.37	3.35*	2.96*	.67	.19	.96	.77
Emotions	.11	.65	.65	2.74	.06	1.18	2.44
Needs	.43	1.00	3.87	.00	.15	.62	.07
Fantasies	.24	.79	.48	.01	.09	.24	1.18
Self-awareness	1.01	13.81**	4.49*	.10	.64	3.14	.01
Self-report							
Satisfaction[b]	6.19*	.78	.009	.12	.004	7.36**	1.49
Understanding	.31	.00	.00	.31	.31	.00	.31
Helpfulness	2.31	.37	2.31	.09	.00	4.54*	3.33
Goal attainment	.43	.02	.17	1.54	.17	2.30	.02

Note. Table represents summary of analysis of variance except where indicated.
[a] Multivariate analysis of variance.
[b] Analysis of covariance.
* $p < .05$.
** $p < .01$.

Source: Reprinted from Stein, M. L. & Stone, G. L. Effects of conceptual level and structure on initial interview behavior. *Journal of Counseling Psychology*, 1978, 25, 96-102, with the kind permission of the American Psychological Association.

FIGURE 5.1 Counselee perception of counselor helpfulness as a function of interview structure and counselee conceptual level(CL). (Stein & Stone, 1978)

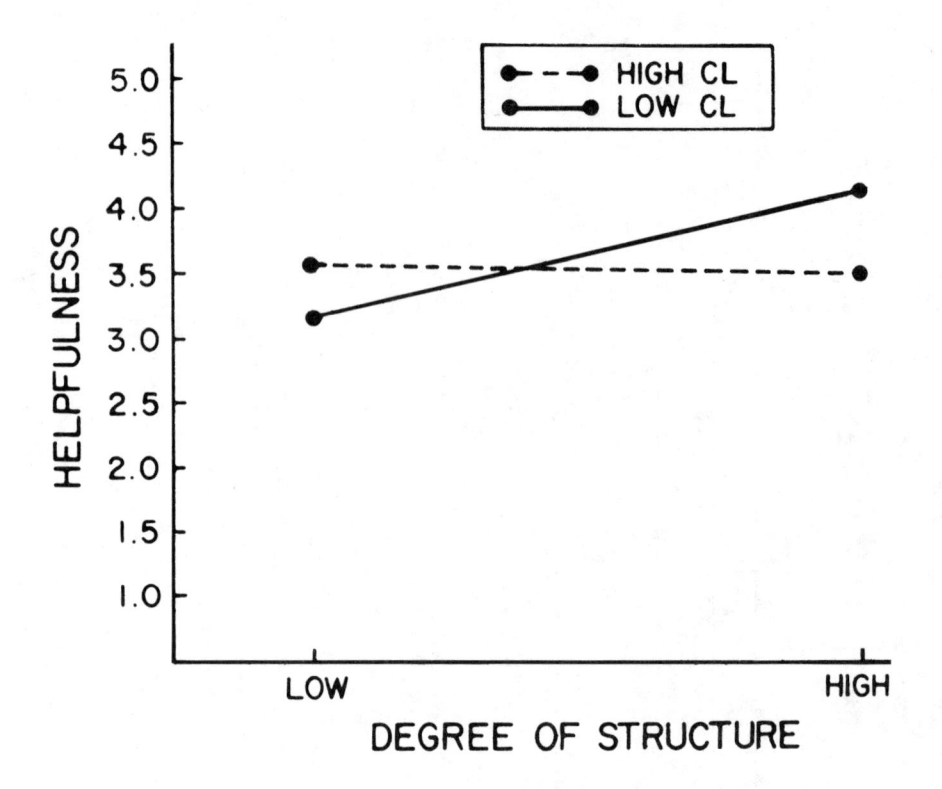

Source: This figure and following figures (5.1 through 5.4) are reprinted from Stein, M. L. & Stone, G. L. Effects of conceptual level and structure on initial interview behavior. *Journal of Counseling Psychology* 1978, *25*, 96-102, with the kind permission of the American Psychological Association.

FIGURE 5.2 Satisfaction as a function of counselor interview structure and counselee conceptual level (CL). (Stein & Stone, 1978)

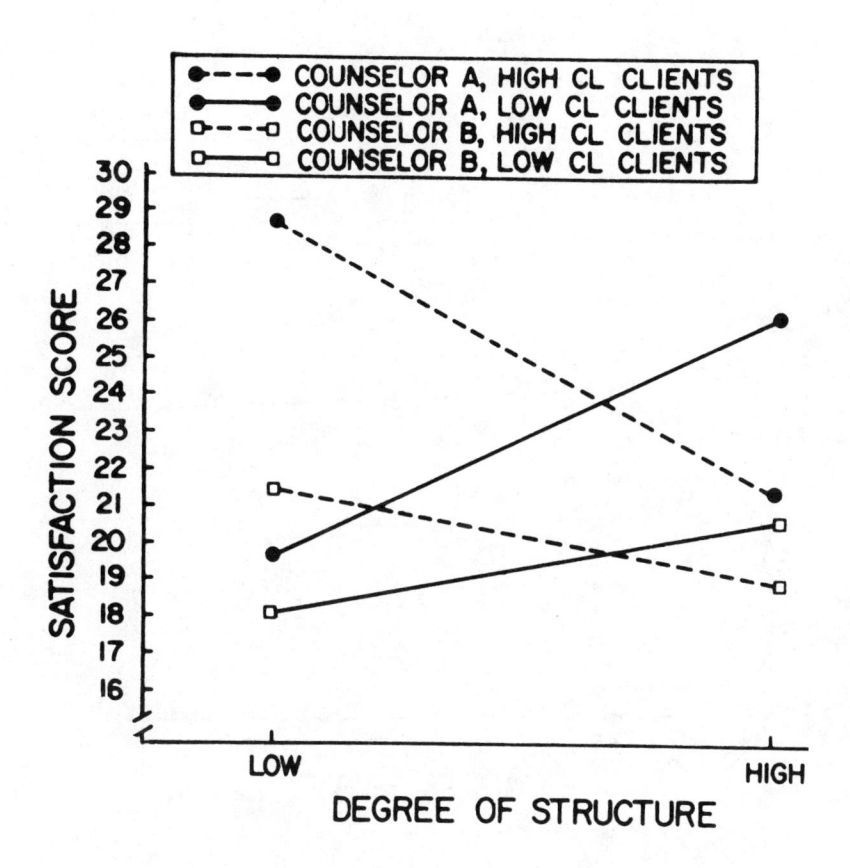

Source: See Figure 5.1

118 / *A Cognitive-Behavioral Approach to Counseling*

FIGURE 5.3 Expressions of self awareness as a function of counselee conceptual level (CL) and degree of counselor-offered structure. (Stein & Stone, 1978)

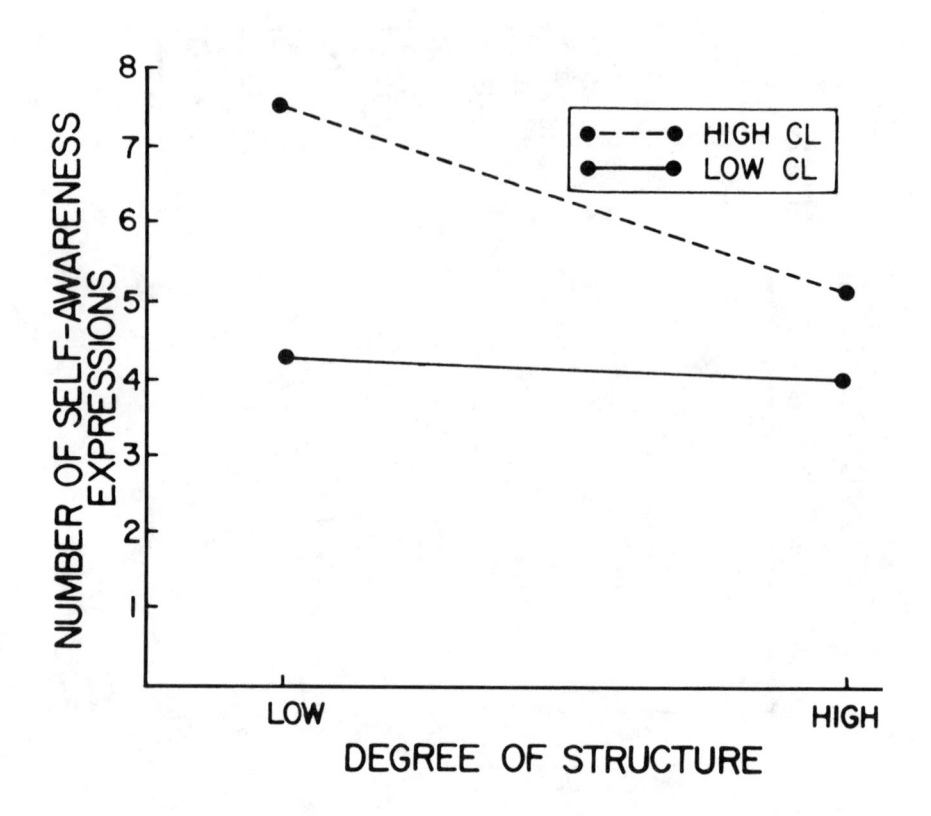

Source: See Figure 5.1

FIGURE 5.4 Counselee talk time as a function of interview structure and counselee conceptual level (CL).

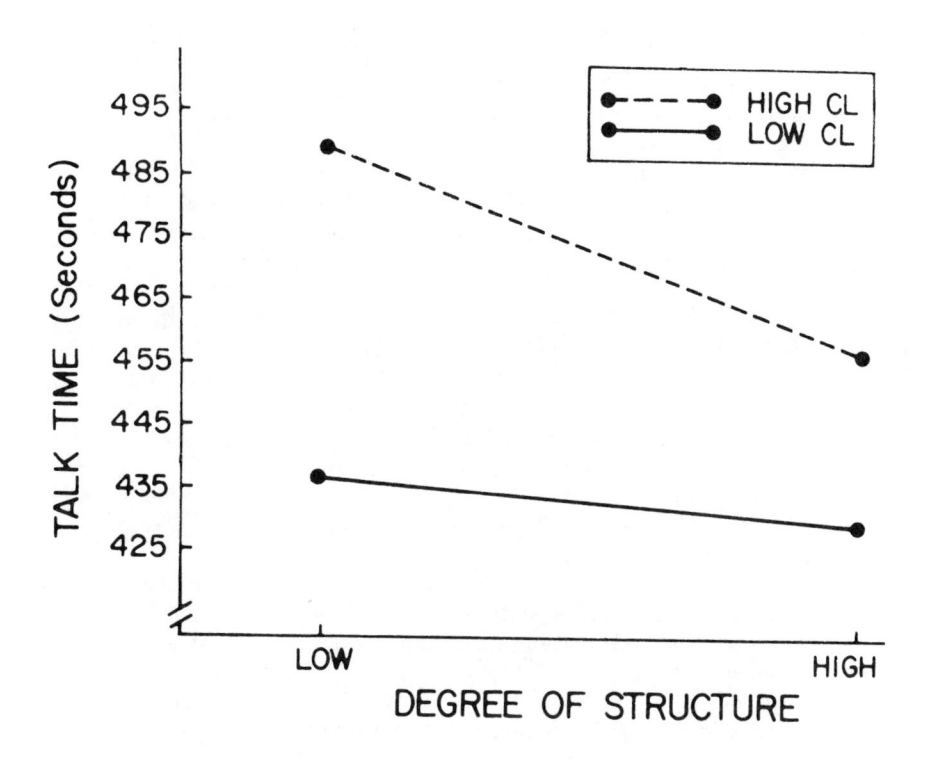

Source: See Figure 5.1

Planned comparisons indicated the following results. Hypothesis 1 was confirmed. The high-CL, low-structure group was significantly more satisfied (M = 25.26) than the high-CL, high-structure group (M = 20.41), t(39) = 2.02, p<.05. Hypothesis 2 was confirmed. The low-CL, high-structure group was significantly more satisfied (M = 23.59) than the low-CL, low structure group (M = 19.07), t(39) = 1.88, p < .05. Hypothesis 3 was not confirmed. Hypothesis 4 was confirmed; that is, under low structure, the high-CL group was significantly more satisfied (M = 25.26) than the low-CL group (M = 19.07), t(39) = 2.57, p < .01.

The pattern of means on the 7-point, global satisfaction item of the Therapy Session Report was consistent with the disordinal, CL X Treatment interaction reported above, although the analysis of variance indicated that the CL X Treatment interaction did not attain the traditional level of satistical significance (p <.056).

Counselor understanding. There were no significant differences among CL and treatment means on this variable.

Counselor helpfulness. Results of counselee ratings of counselor helpfulness are graphically depicted in Figure 4[5.4].

Planned comparisons indicated that Hypotheses 1, 3, and 4 were not confirmed. Hypothesis 2 was confirmed. The low-CL, high-structure group perceived the counselors as significantly more helpful (M = 4.17) than the low-CL, low-structure group (M = 3.17), t(40) = 2.56, p < .01.

Client goal. Planned comparisons indicated that the hypotheses were not confirmed at a statistically significant level, nor did an analysis of variance reveal any significant effects. Descriptively, goal attainment means were higher for matched conditions than for mismatched conditions. Means were as follows, with a higher score indicating greater goal attainment: low-CL, high-structure group (matched) = 3.25; high-Cl, low-structure group (matched) = 3.17; high-CL, high-structure group (mismatched) = 2.83; low-CL, low-structure group (mismatched) = 2.67.

Counselor goal. Only two subjects participated in a second interview; therefore, no statistical analyses were performed.

The results section indicates that treatment validity was ensured through the use of evaluation by multiple sources (raters, participants). The use of statistics appears appropriate (analysis of covariance for change scores, multivariate analysis of variance for related measures of self disclosure, planned comparisons). Figures and a table are presented to clarify the results. Unfortunately, the only estimate of clinical significance is in terms of client self report (goals, satisfaction). It might be helpful to the readers if the data could be summarized using magnitude estimates.

Discussion

Ratings of counselor-offered structure by judges and participants indicated that the treatments were validly administered by counselors to represent moderately low and moderately high degrees of structure.

The major question of the current research was, "What counseling procedure would be most effective for what type of individual?" Hypothesis 1 predicted that a low-structured counseling approach is more effective for high-CL persons; Hypothesis 2 predicted that a high-structured counseling approach is more effective for low-CL persons.

Results from the verbal-behavioral measures of participation and self-disclosure did not give strong evidence to support the matching model; however, there were some significant differences between the CL groups that emerged under low structure, indicating that differences in verbal-expressive behaviors of the CL groups may reflect differences in the way they process information. It appears these differences may be masked by the degree of task structure, that is, differences may be reduced under highly structured interview conditions. These findings suggest the importance of task variables (structure and complexity) in testing matching model predictions.

The self-report measures, tapping cognitive and affective satisfaction and perceived counselor helpfulness, gave clearer and stronger empirical support of matching model theory. Despite interviewer differences in client satisfaction, the disordinal CL X Treatment interaction occurred for both counselors. This suggests that the matching model may be appropriate for many interviewers, regardless of sex, age, or experience differences.

The CL matching model did not predict how clients would perceive their counselors in terms of understanding the thoughts and feelings of the counselees. This definition is similar to the empathy construct used by others (e.g., Carkhuff, 1969). These results represent a failure to replicate findings by Heck and Davis (1973) in which CL interacted with judges' rated empathy. This underlies the importance of using measures from different viewpoints (e.g., clients and judges).

Limitations and Implications

The limitations of this study were as follows: (a) the use of extreme quartiles raises a question about what score should be used as a cutoff point to classify an individual as low CL or high CL; (b) it is not known what effects other levels of structure would have on individuals; (c) subjects were university student volunteers and it is thus not known to what other populations, settings, or "problems" the results might be generalizable; (d) it is not known what effects might result from longer matched and mismatched treatments (e.g., goal attainment, perceived empathy); and (e) it is not known how CL may interact with counselor-offered structure when the counselor needs to convey information to the client.

Results of this study may have implications for counseling practice. We demonstrated that skilled counselors can use both structured and unstructured approaches successfully. Since the different interview treatments were representative of counseling styles, implications for practice are broad. Thus, results suggest that, initially in counseling, an unstructured style such as client-centered or existential methods is more productive for high-CL persons. Structured procedures such as behavioral or rational-emotive counseling are more satisfying and helpful initially for low-CL persons.

In summary, these findings illustrate the importance of measuring Matching Model or Person X Treatment interaction effects on different behavioral outcomes. Results demonstrated that within a counseling interview, the counselee variable of CL interacted with counselor-offered structure to produce predictable effects on perceptions, satisfactions, and verbal behaviors. These findings suggest that it may be important for the counselor to alter his or her interviewing style or intervention program to capitalize on the apparent strengths and preferences of each kind of client.

The results clearly illustrate how counseling, when assessed by treatment "averages," appears to have no effect. Although the specification of counseling effectiveness is problematic, individual differences and multiple measures, both objective and self-report, should be included in future investigations.*

In this section, the findings and implications are discussed. In the limitations section, the issue of external validity is noted ("it is not known to what other populations, settings or 'problems' the results might be generalizable"). The study makes clear that it used a convenient sample of undergraduate stu-

---

*Reference Notes: 1. Hunt, D. E., Greenwood, J., Noy, J. E., & Watson, N. *Assessment of conceptual level: Paragraph Completion Method*. Mimeographed manual, 1973. (Available from D. E. Hunt, Ontario Institute for Studies in Education, Toronto, Canada). 2. Orlinsky, D. E., & Howard, K. I. *Therapy session report, Form P and Form T*. Chicago: Institute for Juvenile Research, 1966. References: Bordin, E. S. *Psychological counseling*. New York: Appleton-Century-Crofts, 1955. Carkhuff, R. R. *Helping and human relations* (2 vols.). Toronto, Canada: Holt, Rinehart & Winston, 1969. Harvey, O. J., Hunt, D. E., & Schroder, H. M. *Conceptual systems and personality organization*. New York: Wiley, 1961. Heck E. J., & Davis, C. S. Differential expression of empathy in a counseling analogue. *Journal of Counseling Psychology*, 1973, *20*, 101-04. Hunt, D. E., & Sullivan, E. V. *Between psychology and education*. Hinsdale, Ill.: Dryden Press, 1974. Jourard, S. M. *Self-disclosure: An experimental analysis of the transparent self*. New York: Wiley, 1971. Kirk, R. E. *Experimental design: Procedures for the behavioral sciences*. Monterey, Calif.: Brooks/Cole, 1968. Posthuma, A. B., & Carr, J. E. Differentiation matching in therapy. *Canadian Psychological Review*, 1975, *16*, 35-43. Stein, M. L. *Counselor ambiguity: Its effect on counselee perceptions, self-exploration, and return behavior*. Unpublished master's thesis, University of Western Ontario, London, Canada, 1973. Strupp, H. H., & Bergin, A. E. Some empirical and conceptual bases for coordinated research in psychotherapy: A critical review of issues, trends and evidence, *International Journal of Psychiatry*, 1969, *7*, 18-90.

dents. It provided a reasonable amount of information, given space limitations, for future replications. It might have been helpful if the researchers had indicated that more extensive information was available elsewhere (for example, a longer report, thesis). In addition, the researchers could have indicated the importance of analogue research in addressing theoretical issues and could have explicitly outlined an extension of the present study.

DESIGN STRATEGIES

Three design strategies are briefly discussed, including factorial designs, intensive designs, and program evaluation. Different methodological concerns are specifically mentioned in relation to particular designs, but it should not be inferred that threats to validity are limited to one type of design strategy. Thus the preceding methodological discussion, although illustrated through a traditional group design, is applicable to all design strategies.

Factorial Designs

The basics of factorial designs are associated with the English tradition of statistics, especially by R. A. Fisher, and agricultural experimentation. Two of these basics are randomization and the simultaneous variation of factors. A classic example is a typical agricultural field trial. The object of a typical trial could be the comparison of a number of alternative fertilizer treatments that were composed of a particular combination of one level from each factor. In the simplest case, each type of fertilizer (nitrogeneous fertilizer, phosphate, and potash) is either present or absent (2 x 2 x 2 factorial design). The experimental area is divided into plots and the different fertilizer treatments are randomly assigned to each plot. The crop yield is then measured for each plot, and from these observations a comparison of treatments can be made.

The logic of factorial designs involves the comparison of performance under different treatment conditions. In counseling research, the primary comparative strategy is to observe differences between persons (groups) who have or have not been exposed to the independent variables. This logic is clearly evident in the widespread use of the treatment/no-treatment strategy in counseling research. In this strategy, persons are randomly assigned to treatment or no-treatment conditions. Treatment effectiveness is determined by the differences between the two groups. The same strategy is used in comparative studies in which there are a number of treatment conditions and control conditions. These strategies can be useful, but there are serious problems, including weak control procedures and/or alternative treatments (for example, differential credibility, lower expectancy, insufficient information about outcome performance) and low informational yield in terms of conceptual development and individual differences. Such limitations suggest the use of factorial designs. The type of factorial design that appears to be potentially informationally rich includes those designs, such as the one illustrated earlier, in which treatment variables are crossed with theoretically relevant personality dimensions. Such designs appear especially relevant for theory testing purposes. From a cognitive-behavioral perspective, such "aptitude X treatment designs" (see Cronbach and Snow, 1976) are given a high priority. This priority appears especially relevant to a field that has accumulated tons of empirical data about comparisons of the Group A versus Group B variety, but very little conceptual wisdom about the process.

Intensive Designs

Many sources can be identified in the emergence of single-case research: the use of the psychoanalytic case study method, practitioner objections to group research, the emergence of the idiographic approach, and the development of a scientific approach to individual phenomena. The case study approach, of course, is often uncontrolled, as in the case of the description of the treatment of Anna O. (Breuer & Freud, 1957), but often the scientific potential of such studies is there. A strong influence on the development of intensive designs must be the criticisms of the clinician against traditional group research. These critics point to numerous inadequacies, including the masking of individual client outcome in group studies (Chassan, 1967; Sidman, 1960), the ethical problems of withholding treatment from a no-treatment group, the practical problems of conducting controlled research in an applied setting (for example, lack of homogeneous client populations), and the general lack of generalizability of laboratory findings to applied settings. These objections led applied researchers to a renewed interest in the uniqueness of the individual. This interest was most eloquently expressed by Gordon Allport (1962) in his discussion of the superiority of the idiographic (individual) approach compared with the nomothetic (group) approach. This same discussion and use of the idiographic approach had been repeated earlier in physiology (Pavlov, Bernard), pharmacological research (Chassan), and operant research with animals (Skinner). Yet it was not until the 1950s and 1960s that the idiographic approach matured into an applied science with a sophisticated and vigorous methodology. It was in the 1950s and 1960s that Shapiro (Shapiro & Ravenette, 1959) demonstrated that an independent variable (therapeutic treatment) could be systematically manipulated within a single case, that Campbell and Stanley (1963) described quasi-experimental designs, that Chassan (1967) clearly outlined the distinctions and the advantages and disadvantages between intensive (single-case) designs and extensive (group) designs, that Sidman (1960) outlined the assumptions and conditions of the experimental analysis of behavior, and that a journal, *Journal of Applied Behavior Analysis*, devoted to intensive research emerged (1968). The 1970s have witnessed a continuation of concern about single-case methodology, especially statistical analysis of time-series data (see Box & Jenkins, 1976; Glass, Wilson, & Gottman, 1975; Gottman & Glass, 1979; McCain & McCleary, 1979). In counseling, counselor researchers have been encouraged to use single-case methods (Anton, 1978; Schmidt, 1974; Thoresen & Anton, 1973, 1974).

The essential feature of intensive research is the gathering of repeated observations over time of specified units (for example, institution, person, family) and examination of the variability. In examining the variability, the criterion for evaluating treatment is the performance of the single unit before intervention (baseline). That is, in single-case research the comparison of interest involves the performance of the same single unit under baseline and treatment conditions, usually replicated a number of times, whereas the comparison of interest in traditional group research concerns the performance of different groups under different conditions. As a simple example, assume that a researcher wanted to assess a particular treatment using a single-case method. Because of practical constraints in the applied setting, the researcher plans to gather repeated observations of a client before introducing the treatment, called a baseline phase (A phase), during treatment (B phase), and after treatment during an extended follow-up period. The data could resemble the simulated data in Figure 5.5. It appears that client performance changed in response to the introduction of treatment and that the change was maintained over an extended period of time. Such an example, called an AB design, may be compatible with applied work and provides graphic illustration of the discontinuity between baseline and treatment conditions, but it does not easily permit cause and effect inferences.

The greatest weakness of this design is its failure to control for the effects of history, that is, other events occurring at the same time as treatment that could account for the change. For example, a weather change or a move to a new location occurring simultaneously with the onset of treatment for shyness may present problems of interpretation. That is, is the gregarious behavior of the client a function of the warmer weather and/or new surroundings that facilitate social contacts or a function of treatment? Such questions cannot easily be resolved by the typical AB design.

Two or more important designs in intensive research include the ABAB or reversal design and the multiple-baseline design. Both of these designs overcome the deficiencies of the previous example. The reversal design is often used in intensive research (Sidman, 1960). The primary purpose of this design is to establish a functional relationship between the target behavior and the treatment through the systematic alteration of the baseline condition (A phase), when no treatment is in effect, and the treatment condition (B phase). Systematic discontinuities in performance associated with variation of the experimental phases, especially when replicated at different points in the design, lend strong support to the establishment of a causal relationship.

While the reversal design is powerful, it also has limitations. Briefly, many of these limits concern practical and ethical issues about the removal

126 / *A Cognitive-Behavioral Approach to Counseling*

FIGURE 5.5 Simulated data.

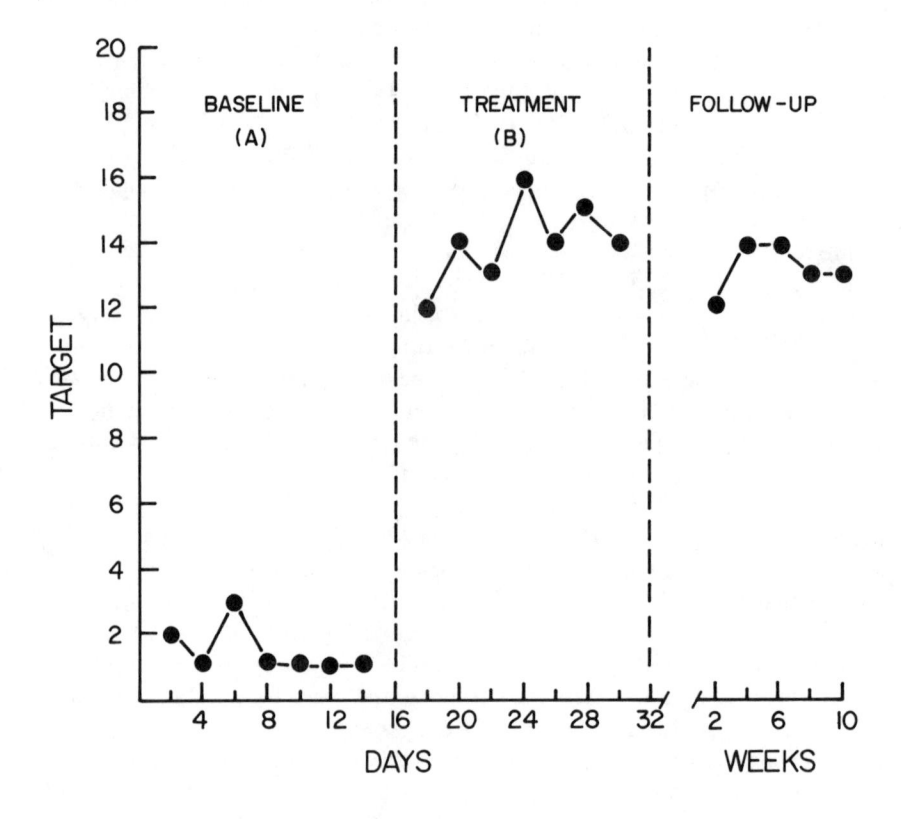

Source: Constructed by the author.

of treatment. That is, it may be impossible to remove the effects of treatment, such as new-skills acquisition, or the removal of treatment may be unethical (self-injurious behavior). Moreover, applied researchers may be more interested in the maintenance of behavior change that the establishment of causal relationships. Other problems occur when two or more different treatments are introduced in a version of the ABAB design. In these cases, evaluation of different interventions is difficult due to the likely confounding of treatment and order effects. Thus researchers should avoid ABAB type designs when the purpose of the inquiry is to compare different treatments.

The multiple-baseline design, used less frequently than the reversal design, establishes functional relationships without withdrawing treatment. The common versions of this design are the multiple baseline across behaviors, across situations, and across subjects. In the across-behaviors version, baseline data are collected across two or more responses. The treatment intervention is then applied to only one response. Baseline conditions remain in effect for the other response(s). This procedure is continued so that treatment is systematically introduced to one response at a time. A causal relationship is demonstrated if each response changes when and only when the intervention is introduced. When performance discontinuities between baseline and treatment phases are replicated across several behaviors, strong evidence for treatment efficacy is provided.

Problems are also apparent in the multiple-baseline version. Since baseline and subsequent treatment interventions serve as separate AB designs for each targeted behavior, with the baseline condition extended to each of the succeeding behaviors until treatment is introduced, it is important that the targeted behaviors be independent of one another. If covariation occurs, the controlling effects of treatment are subject to the limitations of AB designs. Another problem is the number of independent targeted behaviors that are necessary for demonstrating a causal relationship (see Wolf & Risley, 1971).

Several other methodological problems are relevant to intensive research. Two major problems concern data interpretation and external validity. Eyeball tests of performance discontinuities can give distorted assessments of the impact of treatment. Such distortions can often occur under the following conditions: trends in data are present, excessive variability is evident, and/or extreme scores preceding a phase introduction are observed. Under these conditions it appears wise to use statistical evaluation. Conventional statistical methods are inappropriate for analyzing time-series data due to the autocorrelational nature of the data. That is, conventional statistics requires that error terms associated with observations be independent, but in time-series experiments behavior is repeatedly observed over time and events closer to each other in time tend to be more closely associated to each other than to events further removed in time. Thus error terms of consecutive observations are usually correlated. In response to autocorrelated error terms, time-series analysts have used the Autoregressive Integrated Moving Average (ARIMA) models and associated techniques developed by Box and Jenkins (1976). These time-series models transform the data in order to adjust for serial dependency so that the altered scores meet the properties required for statistical analysis. Many authors have discussed these models (for example, Glass et al., 1975; Gottman & Glass, 1979; Kazdin, 1976; McCain & McCleary, 1979), and other quantitative methods for clinical practice (Neufeld, 1977) are available for the applied researcher.

Another problem concerns external validity. The most obvious limitation in single-case research is the unknown relevance of the results found in a single case to other cases. That is, there would be little basis to infer that the efficacy of a treatment procedure established through the use of a single-case experimental design would generalize to other clients, therapists, and settings. This issue has been assumed to be a major obstacle in restricting the use of intensive research. Single-case researchers argue that generalization is not simply a function of extensive or intensive designs. They suggest that traditional group researchers have problems with external validity too because group researchers use a weaker criterion, based on statistical significance of group averages, that does not easily provide insights into the generality of a particular effect for a given client nor ensure a powerful treatment that leads to broad generalization. These single-case researchers point to their conscious strategy of focusing on a single client and selecting interventions that will lead to dramatic changes. Whatever the merit of their arguments, there does not appear to be a satisfactory substitute for adequate specification of variables and replication, regardless of which type of design is used.

Program Evaluation

Within social science and government circles, program evaluation has become a terribly major item. The importance of evaluation has also been noted in the counseling field (for instance, Burck & Peterson, 1975; Oetting, 1976a, 1976b). Many of these writers, explicitly or implicitly, have failed to make a useful conceptual distinction between the different facets of evaluation, including the dimensions of experimental science and policy decision making. This conceptual ambiguity has often led to uncontrolled research and the failure to appreciate the political context of most evaluative research. That is, the separation of evaluation from research has led some investigators away from experimental methodologies. These investigators point to the enormous difficulties encountered in applied settings as their rationale for rejecting these methodologies. Unfortunately, these actions often lead to an emphasis on an immediate solution and are often accompanied by precipitous action. The more difficult task of creating explanatory theories and testing causal hypotheses is an important and often neglected activity in suggesting likely solutions. It may be accurate that many of the design strategies used in experimental science need to be modified by the circumstances of evaluative research, but the realities of applied research do not necessarily have to preclude the use of experimental methods nor render the questions of validity, discussed previously, unimportant.

On the other hand, some evaluation specialists believe that the introduction of scientifically valid findings automatically leads to the implementation of the appropriate decisions. Such decisions are based on the confusion of methodology and policy facets of evaluation research. Policy development uses information about program efficiency, efficacy, and accountability derived from research in formulating policy alternatives, preferences, and decisions. But such information is only one input in policy formulations. Other inputs concern political and pragmatic objectives. In simple terms, evaluation as a research facet provides information, whereas evaluation as policy analysis integrates information from many sources in order to implement political objectives. This conceptual distinction does not imply that the evaluators must become detached from program development and implementation, but it does suggest that evaluation is a multidimensional task and evaluators need to carefully specify their roles and functions. That is, the evaluator may accept the role of evaluative researcher and the task of formal, impartial, and summative appraisal or the evaluator may self-consciously become a change agent and assume the formative task of collecting data relevant to the targeted change. Usually, the tasks of evaluative research involve a combination of research and policy responsibilities. In this book, evaluation is considered, primarily in terms of its research dimension, as one type of strategy within the boundaries of scientific research that uses experimental methods as the appropriate model for evaluating programs (see Campbell, 1971; Stanley, 1972; Wortman, 1975).

Historically, the emergence of program evaluation is related to the expanded role of government in the improvement of the human condition and also, of course, to the development and refinement of research methodologies. A few early precedents of the application of research methodologies to the assessment of programs include the scientific management movement in education, industry, and government. In education, mental tests and other quantitative techniques stimulated by E. L. Thorndike's work were used as evaluative methods in achieving efficiency in the schools. The famous Westinghouse Electric study ("Hawthorne Effect") and the work of Lewin were well-known in industry. Roosevelt's New Deal social programs stimulated the growth of experimental evaluation in government.

In the 1940s and 1950s, program evaluation continued to grow, but it lacked a sophisticated methodology. Lewin's contributions continued in the 1940s. Many applied research programs were carried out during World War II (for example, "American Soldier" studies) and immediately afterward (for instance, family planning).

During the 1960s and 1970s, program evaluation became a growth industry. In the 1960s, a dramatic expansion of social services and demands for accountability occurred. Government was introduced to program budgeting, systems analysis, and cost-benefit analysis. Evidence of impact was required for social program legislation (for example, Title I of the Elementary and Secondary Education Act). At the same time, the literature on the practice of evaluation research grew (for instance, Campbell, 1969; Campbell & Stanley, 1963; Suchman, 1967). By the 1970s, the sophistication of the program-evaluation literature (such as, Struening & Guttentag, 1975) and practice (Cook, Appleton, Conner, Schaffer, Tamkin, & Weber, 1975) had developed. By then, the number of program-evaluatuion studies were in the hundreds, and writers (Burck & Peterson, 1975) in such fields as counseling psychology were calling for more.

Program evaluation has become sophisticated and technical. A full discussion of evaluative research is beyond the scope and purpose of this book. A brief example in occupational mental health is used to highlight some of the important aspects of evaluative research. Assume that a consultant has been contacted by a company officer and a union official about the problem of alcoholism in their plant. The first step is to carefully document the problem so as to suggest a reasonable program. This step is sometimes referred to as needs assessment. This documentation can be derived from interviews and existing records. For instance, records of absenteeism and industrial accidents can be checked. Costs can be estimated for retraining fired alcoholic employees. In addition, pilot experimental research on the effects of alcohol on specific job performances could be conducted. This information could lead to numerous proposals (for example, change in company policy, job redesign) if alcoholism were seen as a major problem by the union and the company. Assuming there is agreement about the seriousness of the problem, the consultant can continue to involve both management and union by sharing the responsibilities of designing the program and evaluation procedures. Through such involvement, the consultant could find out that union and management are interested in reducing absenteeism, industrial accidents, and the firing of employees. Such statements can serve as goals, but further definition will be necessary, that is, determining how much of a reduction in these areas is necessary for a successful outcome. After more discussion, it is suggested that counseling services become available in the plant. Such a suggestion is met with approval and is established with a condition that it be monitored and evaluated.

This example suggests five important steps in program evaluation: needs assessment, setting goals, designing the program, monitoring the program, and evaluating the program. The evaluator needs to be sensitive to the political context and scientific spirit that interact at each step. The commissioning of an evaluation is usually not as straightforward as reported here. It is likely that management and the union are concerned about alcoholism for different reasons and may desire different programs. It is necessary for the consultant-evaluator to appreciate both union and management perspectives and to conduct the program development and evaluation on the basis of mutual sharing. In terms of evaluating the program, it may not be possible to conduct the typical treatment/no-treatment design with random assignment. The consultant could partition volunteer clients receiving the counseling service into light and heavy drinkers and compare their performances with the nonvolunteer groups. Of course, the volunteer and nonvolunteer groups would be nonequivalent and subject to internal validity problems (for example, selection maturation, regression), but pretest information on absenteeism, accidents, and so on would be available for possible cohort designs as well as to serve as potential covariates. It would be best if more than one plant were involved and the consultant could use a multiple-baseline design across plants. Finally, the consultant would need to write the evaluative research reports in a format and from a point of view that reflect both the needs of scientific scholarship and policy decision making.

PRIORITIES

Recent writings of action researchers (Goldman, 1978) appear to renew the scientist-practitioner dichotomy of the 1950s and 1960s. That is, some action researchers, in their apparent zeal to legitimize the less formal research strategies, have concentrated on the limitations of the group-comparison approach and the advantages of alternatives. These arguments tend to mask the strengths and weakness of each design and prevent investigators from asking the more relevant question: What type of design is more appropriate given different relevant questions? Generally speaking, single-case designs are useful in determining clinical accountability, isolating specific components of a treatment package, and pilot testing. Traditional group designs may be more appropriate for outcome studies that compare multicomponent treatments in which individual variability is not a major issue. Program evaluation appears relevant to questions about general programming and the issues of efficiency, consumer satisfaction, and policy development. On the other hand, each of these approaches shares a common scientific orientation, and each strategy must deal with the various questions of validity. Moreover, the differences between the alternative design strategies are not as distinct as presented. There are single-case designs that can be used for comparisons of different treatments (see Leitenberg, 1973). Moreover, program evaluation is not different because it uses so different a design strategy per se, but because evaluative research seeks to answer a different set of questions by incorporating additional facets of evaluation. These additional facets enable program evaluators to deal with political issues and to make interpretable statements when random assignment has not been adequately carried out in the applied setting.

As mentioned earlier, a preference for theory-relevant research has been indicated. In a cognitive-behavioral context, high priority research questions have to do with the systematic examination of interactions among various subject characteristics and treatments. Focusing on one subject does not allow such an examination. Factorial designs enable researchers to analyze the treatment effects separately, according to subject characteristics. Thus such factorial designs receive a relatively higher priority in conceptual development. The other design strategies are necessary, but serve different purposes. In terms of applied-research strategies, a cognitive-behaviorist would suggest that they have been too input-output oriented and need to incorporate more process measures (for example, cognitive variables). These process measures may help assess the impact of treatments or programs on variables other than behavioral performance, such as thinking. Moreover, such findings may broaden our conceptions of treatments and programs and initiate renewed theoretical investigations into the mediators of therapeutic action.

6
PROFESSIONAL DEVELOPMENT

The professional development of applied psychologists, especially counselors and clinicians, has been an issue of lively debate. National conferences on clinical psychology have been held in the United States: the Boulder Conference (Raimy, 1950), the Chicago Conference (Hoch, Ross, & Winder, 1966), and the Vail Conference (Fretz, 1974); and in Canada: Canadian Opinicon Conference (Bernhardt, 1961). The training needs of counseling psychology have also been addressed in national forums (for example, Greystone Conference; Thompson & Super, 1964). Most of these conferences, except perhaps the Vail Conference, have adopted the scientist-professional model. Most programs in clinical and counseling psychology approved by the American Psychological Association have adopted such a model. These scientist-practitioner programs provide doctoral level preparation in which a careful balance between science education and supervised applied experience is attempted. Typically, a student spends from two to three years mastering the academic curriculum, specific bodies of psychological knowledge, and research methodology. During these years, the student is usually introduced to applied experience and issues (ethics) through skill practica, brief practicum placements, and extended clerkships in applied settings. At the conclusion of these years, the student is required to take a year-long internship in an approved setting. After the internship, the student returns to complete his or her doctoral thesis and remaining doctoral requirements.

There have been many complaints about this model (see Peterson, 1968), including constant debates over the right balance between science and practice. In these debates, advocates of each side of the scientist-professional model, proscience or proprofessional, have attempted to separate the two components, to elevate one, and to denigrate the other. Graduate applied programs in many academic departments tend to favor the side of science, while applied experience is often ridiculed and thought to have little value. Parenthetically, professional schools of psychology tend to show the opposite preferences. Each tendency leads to unfortunate consequences.

One such consequence has been the wholesale indictment of the science side of the model. Many critics of academic training programs have pointed to the irrelevance of academic research and rational inquiry to the helping field. Such criticisms are prevalent in counseling psychology (see Rogers, 1973). While they undoubtedly raise cogent points, in the extreme they form a caricature and so distort the role of critical thinking in human experience and therapy that reason itself is identified with dehumanization and antitherapeutic practice. From such an antiintellectual perspective, uncritical innovations and gut reactions come to replace discipline, effort, critical thinking, and scientific study (see Strupp, 1976).

On the other hand, academics are often critical of the work and research of applied psychologists. Traditional academics often believe that applied psychologists belong in professional schools (for example, medicine). From their perspective, the research of applied psychologists does not contribute to basic knowledge. Thus applied psychologists are more technologists than scientists. In addition, an applied psychologist's experience in applied settings does not appear to be academic preparation (for instance, laboratory research), but smacks of professionalism and takes valuable time away from research. Recent efforts by traditional academic departments to broaden their applied programs in response to financial constraints, job-market shifts, and changing student interests may suggest a fundamental change in the traditional negative view of applied psychology. Of course, such efforts may only be the result of having to cope with new realities, with little change in viewpoint. That is, recent program expansion in applied psychology may simply be a necessary evil in order to support the experimentalists and provide training for students in order to make them competitive in searching for jobs. Thus program expansion may suggest little in the way of altering the traditional academic perspective in which the scientific credentials and the psychological identification of applied psychologists are suspect. The impact of the antiprofessional perspective is to disassociate the spirit of scientific investigation from practice and to stimulate unnecessary and frantic searches by practitioners for new identities and new roles (see Fretz, 1977).

Another development resulting from the scientist-professional debates has to do with the unrealistic integration of the two components. Some programs appear to embrace a renaissance strategy in attempting to balance the scientific and professional aspects of applied psychology. The strategy often results in zealous and obsessional attempts to create a curriculum that leads to a complete scientist-professional. That is, it appears that students in such programs are often required to master all knowledge and skills, relevant as well as faddish, before entering the field. In extreme cases, it is assumed that students will be experts in the areas of interest of each faculty member of the program. In terms of the curriculum, more and more courses become required, resulting in extended programs and the indiscriminate integration of the fundamental and trivial aspects of professional education. Students graduating from such programs tend to know a little about a lot of things, having mastered few. In addition, these renaissance programs are often inefficient and create negative consequences for students and faculty. Students appear to have their dependencies unduly extended in such endless programs that prolong their childhood in becoming professionals, resulting in ill feelings toward faculty and in a lack of confidence in their own capabilities. Faculty members may become so preoccupied with the students' adolescent rebellion and their own obsessions and insecurities about ensuring a respectable program that they lose perspective, directing energy from scholarly pursuits to endless conflicts over program development, and eventually become discouraged and prematurely retire from active academic careers.

These endless debates and unfortunate consequences mask an even more important issue in professional development: the failure of most programs to be closely related to psychological theory. It is at this point that a cognitive-behavioral perspective can make a distinct contribution. In the following sections, an attempt is made to explicate the implications of a cognitive-behavioral perspective for professional training in psychology.

SCIENCE EDUCATION

It is apparent that one of the major components of professional development is science education. Typically, students in applied psychology programs obtain their scientific education by taking required courses in methodology and statistics and completing research-theses requirements. From this experience, many clinical and counseling students can often produce technically competent research, but, as discussed earlier, much of this research remains unrelated to the broad mosaic of psychological knowledge. A cognitive model, with its emphasis on theoretical relevance, suggests that students would benefit more if exposed to broad scientific perspectives and specific psychological theories. Such exposure would enable students to relate data to theories and to relate theories and data to broad patterns of knowledge. Such a suggestion clearly implies that technical competence is not the same as perspective, but both are important in science education. This is very similar to the earlier discussion of internal and construct validities, namely, both are of equal importance from a cognitive orientation, but internal validity and construct validity to a large degree reflect different issues of method and theory, respectively. Thus one implication of a cognitive orientation for science education is to provide both technical competence and perspective. Such an implication leads to some specific recommendations about science education in applied psychology.

The aspects of science education selected for discussion are not exhaustive nor have the recommendations been evaluated. The aspects and their corresponding recommendations merely reflect a subjective decision based on the author's experience in graduate education in a psychology department and on their perceived relationship and importance to a cognitive orientation.

Apprenticeship

One of the major aspects of training programs is often overlooked and seldom described in university catalogs and program descriptions. While training programs obviously entail the acquisition of specialized knowledge and skills, programs also entail the acquisition of a critical perspective toward this knowledge and skills. Critical thinking depends on the students' experiences in formal courses and practica but a great deal of learning to be critical occurs through their relationships with research advisors and practicum supervisors through the mechanisms of identification and modeling.

One way of contributing to the development of perspectives in science education is through the use of an apprenticeship model of science practice. In such a model, a tutelage relationship is fostered in which the student is exposed to the perspectives and methods of science through collaboration in doing competent research. In addition, such scientific apprenticeship often leads to the socialization of the student into the profession through formal presentations at conventions and the other benefits that accrue from sponsorship by a professional scientist. The student feels wanted and respected by the faculty sponsor, while the sponsor assumes a personal responsibility for supporting the student's development.

It may be helpful to examine how an apprenticeship model works in practice. Scientific apprenticeship demands a selection system and educational experiences in order to ensure appropriate selection of students and the development of scientific competency, respectively. In the selection system, all applicants are prescreened on the basis of traditional criteria (for example, psychology background, grades, Graduate Record Examination, letters of recommendation, personal description of experience and goals). Such prescreening can be done by a program committee or by a statistical procedure that prescribes certain weights for particular variables (see Goldberg, 1977). After ensuring that students have met the acceptable criteria of traditional requirements, each faculty member is given a chance to select his or her own student on his or her own criteria. The selection by the faculty member often entails a personal obligation to fund the selected student. Such a selection system has many benefits. The prescreening ensures that all accepted students have met the minimal acceptable criteria of the academic unit, while apprentice selection by a faculty member may increase the sense of an apprentice environment in which the student feels appreciated and the faculty mentor feels a sense of responsibility for the student's progress. Moreover, demanding that the selection and support of a student be closely linked would undoubtedly inspire faculty to increase its research endeavors and awarding of grants. Of course, some problems are associated with this system. If the assignment of a student to a faculty mentor through the selection system is closely tied to funding, the resulting assignment may make it difficult for the student to change advisors or interest areas. It may be more problematic if the system allows a few talented faculty members to accumulate most of the students because of their ability to obtain grants or if such a system fosters limited exposure through the pairing of students and faculty of similar orientation. In using an apprentice-selection system, such benefits and costs would have to be carefully evaluated because it is clear that, while the adoption of the scientific apprenticeship model may generate collaboration in scientific research, it also involves risks.

In terms of educating the student in the ways of science, the faculty member can provide learning, practice, and teaching experiences for the student. The student can learn about science from observing the faculty member performing and talking about his or her research. The student should read the faculty member's research and discuss its merits and deficiencies with the faculty member. The student may initially serve as a research assistant in order to obtain the technical skills (for example, computer programming) and the practical experience of conducting experimentation. The basic learning experience takes place in the context of collaboration on research and the resulting tasks. For example, in collaborating on a proposed research topic, the student may be asked, with faculty guidance and feedback, to review the relevant literature with an emphasis on developing a broad, integrative, and conceptual review. Such a review would attempt to relate the specific topic to other relevant bodies of psychological knowledge before becoming enmeshed in the trivial listing of studies according to outcome or the more technical requirements of research criticism. The next step would be to select the major studies in this area and to subject them to criticism based on the canons of scientific research. The faculty member may critique his or her own studies in helping to develop the student's critical abilities.

After a sufficient incubation period, the student is ready to conduct initial independent investigations. In the process, the student can submit a simulated grant to an ad hoc faculty and student committee for review and present the research proposal to his or her peers for critical comment. Such a procedure would provide practice in seeking a grant and in conceptualizing and communicating a program of research, while enabling other students to gain reviewing experience. This independent research could then be conducted for purposes of a thesis, securing an external grant, and/or publication.

Teaching experiences can be generated through research presentations at conventions and in serving as a senior student advisor to new students. Moreover, the dissertation requirements could include a formal public lecture presentation to the university community based on the dissertation research.

Throughout the apprenticeship, the faculty model plays a key role. The relationship can help to develop the aspects of a humane scientific perspective or, because of personal insecurities, lack of motivation, and political considerations, can lead too frustration. As in the selection system, the apprenticeship relationship is not without risks. That is, the relationship can be used to generate research for the faculty member without concern for the student's development or the relationship can become so solely concerned with professional matters that the more personal dimensions of being a professional (for example, work versus family, nonvocational interests) are excluded, leading to a limited conception of the professional role.

Academic Curriculum

The academic curriculum helps students develop the theoretical and methodological foundations of practice. Of obvious importance in providing the student with a scientific perspective is a solid grounding in philosophy of science and in the substantive content areas of psychology and the specialty area.

Exposure to philosophy of science may be through a separate course in the philosophy department or through courses primarily devoted to theories and systems in psychology. The special value of such a topic is that it gives a broad perspective to science in which an understanding of the pretheoretical commitments (passions) of scientific practitioners is provided. Such an understanding may help students avoid the misconceptions of science (see Mahoney, 1976) and the confusion of paradigmatic commitments with science.

The curriculum should have a core program that requires courses in the substantive and specialty areas as suggested by the Steering Committee on Education and Credentialing in Psychology (Wellner, 1977). In terms of the substantive core, course(s) would be required in psychobiology, cognitive science, social psychology, and differential psychology. There are several reasons for the substantive core requirement. First, the substantive core clearly establishes that the practice of psychology is based on the science of psychology. Secondly, the core provides the experience of being confronted with numerous paradigms, which can help the student become more flexible and resist the temptation of paradigmatic idolatry. And third, such exposure stimulates the cross fertilization of theory and practice.

While the substantive core exposes the student to several paradigms and content areas, the specialty core, including foundation, specialty elective, and practicum courses (to be discussed later), enables the student to master the paradigms and content within his or her selected area. For instance, in counseling psychology, a foundations course would introduce beginning students to the fundamental areas of the profession: vocational psychology, psychological adjustment, consultation, prevention, and professional issues (minority groups, ethics). Specialty courses to be taken in subsequent years could include career development, psychological assessment, group counseling, counseling research, counseling theories, normal development, supervision, and consultation. Electives could include counseling courses concerned with different populations (families, children, adolescents, adults, women, minority groups, and so on) and settings (healthcare facilities).

Methodological foundations are provided by courses in statistics, research design and methodology, and psychometrics.

This academic curriculum can contribute to the development of a scientific perspective and to methodological and content competence, but it can also hinder the practice of research. One potential drawback has to do with the amount of time devoted to course work as opposed to conducting research investigations. Inevitably, the more courses required, the less time for doing research. Other related issues often raised in curriculum planning have to do with course priorities and the appropriateness of the course material presented in the substantive core to applied psychology students. The issue on course priorities can be observed in program committee discussions about how many courses are to be required, with such discussions often related to the interests of the faculty rather than to a coherent plan of graduate training. In addition, faculty in applied programs often hear from students about how unrelated the substantive course material is to the students' interests. These observations suggest that beginning students need to be educated concerning the scientific purpose of the substantive core courses so that they will not limit the impact of such courses to the narrow and specialized interests of immediate application.

PRACTICAL EDUCATION

Practicum is pivotal in any applied training program. Generally speaking, practicum has been guided by two approaches: behavioral and psychotherapeutic. In the behavioral-skills curriculum, represented by microcounseling training (see Ivey & Authier, 1978), the approach is to specify the components of helping (skills) and then to systematically train counselors to master these components, using a mastery-learning method. Emphasis of microcounseling is on a skill-mastery approach to practicum. On the other hand, a psychotherapeutic approach, such as advocated by Mueller and Kell (1972), stresses self understanding and emotional insight of the counselor. Such goals are accomplished through therapeutically oriented supervision, based on a dynamic and developmental relationship between supervisor and supervisee. The focus of such supervision is on self understanding of the counselor, including motive, conflicts, and the anxiety that is activated in the parallel and reciprocal processes of counseling and supervision.

On a simplistic level, these two approaches appear to be in conflict. That is, should the focus of practicum lie on personal development or upon the mastery of a body of knowledge and skills? This issue is a variant of the classic argument between psychoanalysis and behaviorism. Does behavior change primarily as a result of insight or as a result experience (behavioral rehearsal)? That is, is the emphasis in learning to be therapeutic on self development or on skill development? This issue is hotly debated under many different guises and at different levels. For instance, a derivative issue has to do with the extent to which supervision should deal with the personality of the supervisee and be viewed as psychotherapy. Of course, there appears to be no logical reason why there must be a necessary division between insight and skill acquisition nor does it seem impossible that the two approaches could be integrated in the training of counselors. It is here that a cognitive perspective, emphasizing a reciprocal relationship between knowing and doing, can guide the development of applied training. In order to elaborate such implications, a stage-model approach to applied training is used.

Practicum experiences in most graduate training programs are often structured developmentally, with students learning basic skills in the prepracticum, practicing skills and receiving feedback on performance during practicum, and teaching basic skills to beginning students in advanced practicum. In addition, the internship provides a twelve-month experience for purposes of integrating the previous phases and the emergence of a professional identity. This developmental structure can easily be described in terms of stages, with distinct emphasis in terms of learning processes and content. Such a conceptualization does not imply mutually exclusive categories, but does provide a practical scheme for organizing applied training. Undoubtedly, the practicum stages overlap, but each stage highlights certain processes and content areas, while at another stage these same processes and knowledge areas may be present but less salient. With such cautions in mind, let us examine each stage and its associated processes and content areas. In so doing, the relevance of the aspects of a cognitive perspective becomes clearer.

Prepracticum

As implied earlier, certain processes are associated with different stages of applied training. That is, learning is often associated with prepracticum, practice with practicum, and teaching others with advanced practicum. In terms of prepracticum, the content of most behaviorally oriented programs usually consists of basic helping skills and an introduction to professional practice (for example, issues, ethics). Such content is usually communicated to the student through observational learning methods: lectures, reading material, and modeling. The goal of the prepracticum stage is skill and knowledge acquisition. While recognizing that learning, practice, and, to some degree (and especially in group prepracticum sessions), teaching others occurs in this stage, the basic assumption in this stage is that the acquisition of specific skills is of primary importance. That is, if the skills are not available to the counselor for use, the counselor's flexibility and creativity in being therapeutic are limited.

This description of prepracticum is usually associated with a behavioral approach (for example, microcounseling). A psychotherapeutic prepracticum would emphasize the importance of being aware of one's affective experience through encounter groups or the use of the Interpersonal Process Recall Method

(IPR) (Kagan et al., 1967). For example, in IPR, the supervisee may be video-recorded while counseling another and then shown the recording immediately after the interaction. The tape is usually viewed by the supervisees with the help of a supervisor (inquirer) who actively encourages the supervisee to recall the underlying feelings and thoughts of the counseling session (for instance, "Can you tell me what you felt at that point?").

From these descriptions, it is apparent from a cognitive perspective that traditional prepracticums, behavioral and psychotherapeutic, have overlooked the importance of the cognitive activity of prepracticum students in their professional development. An overemphasis on skill acquisition leads to an input-output model of professional development that is often experienced as mechanical and unrelated to personal development, while an overreliance on affective experience tends to provide a grossly molar criterion for therapeutic relevance (gut reaction) that precludes a more explicit understanding of how one participates in producing behavior change.

One example of the relevance of cognitive activity to prepracticum concerns the early beliefs of beginning students. These cognitions may often be maladaptive and contribute to inappropriate affect. Two common problematic beliefs have to do with competence, the first with personal competence: "These helping skills are simply not my natural way of helping people." While usually not explicitly stated, this belief is often associated with the anxiety and questioning a person experiences as he or she assumes the role of helping professional. It can indicate difficulties in balancing one's perception of one's personal and professional livess and may indicate a personal ambivalence about one's personal qualities as a helper or about the importance of helping skills. The result of such a belief can be a crisis in confidence or resistance to skill learning since it may be perceived as unsettling or irrelevant. Another problem has to do with performance and mastery expectations: "I must be able to demonstrate these skills without error." Such expectations lead to a great deal of evaluation anxiety and selective attention on negative feedback. Moreover, mastery expectations of students can also affect the faculty in that its mastery expectations become stimulated, leading to attempts by faculty to emulate a mastery model in order to satisfy these demands. Such reciprocal effects can produce a tense training environment in which the main objective of both faculty and students is to avoid making errors, resulting in defensiveness and a loss of creativity that occurs when fear of being wrong overcomes the opportunity to learn from one's errors.

These beliefs can be dealt with in cognitive-restructuring formats. As discussed earlier, the first task of the restructuring process is to make the self-statements associated with learning be therapeutically explicit and then to experiment with more sensible and therapeutically relevant beliefs. This process could be facilitated by using group formats in prepracticum in which the faculty member, adopting a coping-model strategy, shares his or her own personal experience in training. These discussions may help other students share their beliefs. After beliefs have been shared, the group may begin to help each other work out a cognitive-restructuring intervention. Another format that appears helpful in facilitating cognitive development is to use a co-counseling procedure. Co-counseling may be initiated in prepracticum by assigning a student to act as a counselor for a peer. Assignment can be made by random methods, personal choice, sex pairing, or some other procedure. Whatever the assignment method, the arrangement enables each student to serve as a client and as a counselor with different students. These arrangements do not necessarily have to become personal therapy. That is, a co-counseling approach that focuses on a cognitive perspective does not necessarily have to relate the student's (client's) thoughts and feelings to deep psychological problems or personal history, but could relate such beliefs and feelings primarily to the present tasks of learning to be therapeutic and assuming a professional identity.

Practicum

As the student moves from prepracticum to practicum, the emphasis shifts from the learning of discrete skills in laboratory settings to the rehearsal of broad interventions in applied settings. This stage provides practice in integrating the discrete skills into broader strategies and in discriminating the appropriate conditions for their use within the flow of therapeutic interactions. A major process in this stage is supervision. The student is assigned to an experienced supervisor who supervises the student's therapeutic activities. For example, a female student may be placed in a university counseling center for her practicum assignment. Typically, she will be engaged in numerous service activities, one of which would be seeing clients for individual counseling. These counseling sessions could be recorded (audio or video) or observed for purposes of supervision. Individual and group supervisory sessions, in which she would meet with her supervisor and with her practicum colleagues, respectively, to discuss problems and issues, to review her work, and to receive feedback, would generally be held weekly. In traditional supervision, as discussed earlier, the focus of these sessions could be on her use of skills, or her therapeutic work could be more directly related to her personality dynamics. In addition, these sessions could provide opportunities for learning new skills and teaching others, but the important process appears to be supervised practice of broad interventions in applied settings.

Two areas of supervision appear to be neglected by the traditional approaches. The first area is reflective of the inadequate conceptual base of our research and profession, namely, case conceptualization. Behavioral supervisors tend to concentrate on skill production and neglect therapeutic theory, while psychotherapeutic supervisors discourage the formulation of hypotheses about a client's behavior because such rational work is seen as avoiding the primary work of developing supervisee affective understanding.

On the other hand, a cognitive-behavioral supervisor would encourage the process of case conceptualization as a primary dimension in supervision. This encouragement would be based on important assumptions. The first assumption would concern the clinician as an applied scientist. That is, case conceptualization involving the formulation of theoretical hypotheses about a client's behavior would reinforce the continuity between the character of the helping situation and the activities of the scientist. The other assumption would concern the possible therapeutic benefits of relating client problems to psychological theory. For instance, theoretical conceptualization could offer an anxious client an explanation and the counselor a guide for treatment plans and decisions. In addition, the discussion of more theoretical issues in supervision may provide perspective (integration of theory and practice) and enable an excessively anxious and personally involved supervisee to gain some needed space and distance.

The other neglected area of supervision has to do with emotional understanding. The neglect is perhaps more obvious in behavioral supervision (or writings about behavioral supervision). Here the supervisors are portrayed as less concerned about emotional insight of their trainees because such a process is considered to be unnecessary or a product of skillful therapeutic practice. The neglect is less obvious in psychotherapeutic supervision. Here emotional understanding is given a top priority, but, unfortunately, the process tends to be obscured by therapeutic dynamics. The automatic transformation of supervision into therapy can have uptoward consequences for the supervisee: excessive threat, imposed therapy, increased defensiveness, and so on. Moreover, supervision as therapy can become easily distorted into fulfilling the needs of the supervisor and supervisee, while the needs of the client go unmet. Thus emotional reactions of the supervisee can easily be divorced from the counseling/client situation and reanalyzed in terms of personality dynamics. It is this transformation that threatens to obscure the emotional understanding of the supervisee in therapeutic supervision.

On the other hand, cognitive-behavioral supervisors agree with their psychotherapeutic colleagues about the importance of the emotional reactions of the supervisee, but they do not necessarily agree that such reactions must be dealt with in terms of developmental or dynamic therapies. The cognitive-behavioral supervisor would stress the discussion and possible alteration of these reactions in the context of the present counseling situation, in which emotional reactions are triggered by the reciprocal impact of counselor cognitions and client behavior. These discussions and interventions would focus on the relationship of emotional reactions and cognitions of the supervisee during the helping interaction rather than on skills or therapeutic dynamics. Examples of emotional reactions and associated cognitions of beginning counselors may be helpful in elaborating the importance of a cognitive perspective to supervisory practice.

Four common emotional reactions have recently been described by Schmidt (1979): anxiety, anger, guilt, and boredom. Each of these reactions tends to be associated with the specific cognitions of practicum students and can be dealt with in cognitive-restructuring formats.

Anxiety tends to emerge when the counselor senses a loss of control during counseling, often accompanied by such self-statements as "I should know what to do but I don't." Such statements are based on unrealistic expectations concerning counselor control, lead to disruptive attempts to gain control over the client's behavior, and may further anxiety.

Anger can often occur in counseling when the counselor is co-opted by the client to assume the role of the client's advocate. In this situation, anger is usually aimed at the client's environment because the counselor shares the distorted view of the client. For example, a counselor working with an adolescent who is having problems with his or her parents may find him or herself beginning to view the client's parents in a negative way. Such negativity by the counselor may be fostered by such self-statements as "Nobody understands my client (like I do)." In this situation, the counselor's negative reaction can obscure the contribution of the client to the way his or her parents react. Moreover, the counselor may be reexperiencing her own thoughts and feelings about her parents through this encounter.

Feelings of guilt tend to arise from doubts about being a helping person. These doubts often occur during the practicum experience in which errors are perceived or spectacular results are not immediately apparent. These doubts are often in the form of multiple self-statements: "I should be able to help more clients," "I shouldn't make mistakes," and "I shouldn't feel powerful, angry, anxious, or bored." These statements reflect a sense of failure, a sense that somehow one is a poor counselor.

Boredom is often puzzling to the counselor. That is, a counselor may ask "How can I, a helping person, find this client so uninteresting?" It appears that a helping person must always enjoy helping. In addition, it is implied that the client is obligated to interest the counselor. Such faulty assumptions can often mask the significance of such counselor reactions to the therapeutic process.

In dealing with these emotional reactions, it is potentially useful to explore the contribution of cognitive processes. It may be that faulty beliefs are in part responsible for evaluating these emotional reactions as maladaptive. If cognitive interventions could alter these beliefs, perhaps practicum counselors would be more willing to use their emotional reactions as cues for therapeutic interventions, and these counselors would view their mistakes as necessary and useful learning experiences to be approached with boldness.

Advanced Practicum

After sufficient practicum experience, the trainee is often used as a prepracticum supervisor. This sets the stage for advanced practicum in which the basic process is teaching others. Many of the cognitions and feelings experienced as a prepracticum student, a practicum counselor, and a supervisee reoccur as a prepracticum supervisor. One belief that is often a major concern of the supervisor is "I must show the supervisee how competent I am." While such a statement is not often explicitly stated, it is apparent in the behavior of the new supervisor when asked questions or when asked to be observed doing therapy. As indicated earlier, cognitive interventions may be useful in altering these beliefs.

Although "you don't know what you are doing until you teach it to someone else" is a common assumption of the advanced practicum, it has received little attention in the literature. A recent study on supervisory planning (Stone, 1980) revealed that experienced and inexperienced supervisors make few statements concerned with counseling theory when they are planning a skill-oriented supervisory session. While the findings are limited to an analogue situation, they reinforce a recurring theme of this book: the paucity of theoretical development. In terms of this stage, it suggests that new supervisors may want to consider expanding supervisee opportunities for conceptual work. For instance, in teaching the basic helping skills, the supervisor may want to provide alternative theoretical contexts in which these skills can be related and interpreted. That is, the skills of emphatic communication could be conceptualized, in terms of learning theory, as reinforcement strategies or, in information-processing terms, as attending and information-generating strategies. Such conceptual work could facilitate more meaningful linkages between theory and practice, resulting in more meaningful learning.

Another finding in the same study may be worth considering. Stone (1979) found that experienced supervisors focused on the supervisee during planning more than graduate student supervisors and inexperienced supervisors did. This finding suggests that new supervisors spend a great deal of time thinking about mastering unfamiliar content and deciding on the appropriate strategy rather than on the developmental needs of the supervisees. While this planning research is not linked up to thinking during supervision or to outcome, such a finding suggests the potential value of sensitizing new supervisors to their cognitive activities before supervision. This sensitization may enable new supervisors to realize their tendency to focus inwardly on questions of competency and adequacy and to neglect the needs of supervisees.

In dealing with each of these stages of professional training, two major contributions from a cognitive perspective have been highlighted. The first consists of providing a theoretical context in which skill development, case conceptualization, and self development can be understood and evaluated. The other suggests the potential usefulness of examining the cognitive sets of supervisees and supervisors in the learning and teaching of what it means to be therapeutic.

Internship

Thus far the discussion of practice education has been primarily in terms of practicum training and associated learning processes. Such training occurs before the internship experience, but many of these processes continue to be elaborated during the internship. Although not formally conceptualized in the stage model discussed previously, the internship serves as an integrating experience through which professional identity emerges. From a cognitive perspective, there are at least two aspects of the internship experience that need to be emphasized: learning by doing and cognitive sets.

The internship usually provides the student with extended experience in real-life settings. Although previous experiences in practicum may have approximated field situations, they were usually simulated or brief. During the internship, the student is a fulltime member of the staff and the emphasis is on learning by doing. Here is one of the first opportunities for students to develop their sense of responsibility and to observe their competence in demanding environments. From a cognitive perspective, there is little question that learning by doing and self observation are most effective.

Throughout the book, there has been a recognition of the importance of cognitive sets. The internship provides an opportunity for the student to develop a cognitive set that is reflective of a professional identity. While many of the maladaptive beliefs discussed earlier, including beliefs about competency, reemerge in problematic form and have to be reconsidered, it appears that the internship environment is relatively more structured around professional identity development.

One of the most important aspects of this environment is the part played by professional role models. Similar to the faculty sponsor in the academic environment, the professional in the intership setting can model not only in general, but also in terms of ethical practice and personal attitudes toward professional dilemmas.

Another factor in the internship environment has to do with group participation within one's profession and across professions. Such participation can facilitate professional identification through common learning and the experience of working on projects with individuals of different professional background and status.

Each of these factors contributes to the development of a cognitive set in response to the internal questioning of a novice professional, "What is a professional?" Part of becoming a professional concerns the development of a generalized set of attitudes and cognitions. Unfortunately, traditional training programs, including internship programs, have not paid sufficient attention to the affective and cognitive facets of professional development. Hopefully, a cognitive orientation can restore these facets to a position of importance in graduate training without neglecting skill development nor obscuring these facets through therapeutic baptism.

INTEGRATION

Having described the values of science and practice education separately, it may be implied that a cognitive perspective segregates knowing from doing. On the contrary, a cognitive-behavioral model espouses as almost axiomatic the reciprocal relationship between these activities and therefore would strongly encourage the integration of academic and field-center training.

Integration of graduate training experience does not imply sameness, but should indicate the mutual communication of differing perspectives and the mutual responsibilities for professional development of the students within the university and the applied setting. This point of view as been ably articulated by David Shakow (1976): "The fundamental principle . . . is that theory and practicum must be constantly associated and tied together whether in the university or in the field station, and that both types of activity—theory and practicum—start with the very beginning of the program." (p. 556)

There are a number of alternative strategies available to programs that wish to achieve an integrated training experience. Most programs attempt to have both theory and practicum in each year. In the first year, major emphasis is on academic courses at the university, and, at the same time, the university usually provides laboratory practice in interviewing and assessment. The practicum setting provides opportunities for observation and introductory experiences in the areas of ethics, professional issues, and health delivery. In the second year, the university provides additional work in advanced theory and methods, and the field provides practice experiences with associated theory. The third year is the internship year in which the applied setting provides theory related to the internship experience as well as the internship experience itself. The fourth year becomes the year during which dissertation work is done.

This description, while attempting to integrate both theory and practice, seems insufficient. The implication of this traditional program plan is that science, academics, and research primarily occur in the university, while practical experience is only a major concern of the practicum agency. It is true that these agencies have major responsibilities in these areas in most programs, but it does not follow that field settings and universities do not also carry some degree of responsibility for teaching and research and practice, respectively. That is, field settings should be viewed as teaching and research centers that form an integral part of the science education of the student. With such a perspective, courses (such as assessment) would be offered in the applied setting, dissertation work would be done in the field, and research activities (such as intensive studies, program development and evaluation, writing) would become formal requirements of practicum and the internship.

In terms of the university, a commitment to practice would have implications for staffing and curriculum. The academic department could use a rotating faculty position in which qualified practicum-agency psychologists would be given one-year positions in the department. Other staffing arrangements could be made, such as personnel exchanges for a semester between the university and the field setting and adjunct faculty appointments for practicum supervisors. Such arrangements would provide professional role models for students and mutual stimulation for academic and applied faculty. In addition, these staffing arrangements would enable the applied faculty to have access to research resources (for example, thesis committees, consultation, library, computer time) and would give the academic faculty an opportunity to understand the complexity of applied problems. A commitment to practice by the university may also influence course planning and increase interdisciplinary activities. For example, a focal-problem format may be adopted in which the many areas of psychology, including applied psychology, are brought to bear on a single issue, such as anxiety. Thus the course would involve academics from various areas of psychology (for example, psychobiology, cognition, personality) and clinicians and counselors giving input on a single problem. This kind of experience could help develop a scientific perspective and provide an opportunity for academic and professional psychologists to interact.

In sum, a cognitive perspective would suggest that the greater the degree of integration between knowing and doing, between theory and practice, and between university and applied setting, the better the program.

RESEARCH

Unfortunately, these recommendations and suggestions have not been evaluated, since most of the counseling research in graduate training has been concerned with the acquisition of helping skills. From this ever-expanding research, it appears that the teaching method for interaction skill development is less problematic than the questions of whether the skills are retained over long periods, how to assess the impact of learning to be therapeutic, and what to teach. It is these questions that a cognitively based program of research on professional development could address. Let us briefly examine two potential areas of research.

The first has to do with the promise of cognitive-adjunct procedures in facilitating skill retention. Recent research on assertion (Derry & Stone, 1979) has suggested that an added multimodal focus on self-statements tended to enhance, maintain, and generalize gains in comparison with a purely behavioral approach. In terms of counseling-skill training, a recent study (Richardson, 1979) indicated that cognitive modifications of microcounseling procedures facilitated generalization and transfer. Thus it may be important for skill-training programs to consider incorporating cognitive methods that provide broad rules and organization for the generalization of skill use.

Another area has to do with the influence of cognitive processes on affective, self, and professional development of the trainee. Reliable information in this area is almost nonexistent. In attempting to obtain such information, investigators need to conduct preliminary task analyses of the developmental tasks of becoming a helping professional. For example, competent and less competent groups can be identified at different practicum stages or at various levels of experience. These groups would then be exposed to multiple assessments (for example, think-aloud strategies, Interpersonal Recall Method) in order to discern the role of cognitive factors in the development of competence. These assessments would attempt to tap the interpersonal communication systems of trainees as they encounter different developmental tasks. Findings from these task analyses may indicate areas that would be relevant for supervision, teaching, and program planning. For example, low competent groups that differ in real-life assessments from competent groups may not differ from their more competent counterparts in regard to knowledge of the appropriate performance or the ability to demonstrate the performance under laboratory conditions. The crucial difference may be in terms of their cognitions. That is, the high competent group may have little doubt in their minds about their personal competence if their internal statements were mostly positive rather than negative, while the low competent group would be more conflicted if the internal statements of this group were about equally divided between positive and negative. Such hypothetical findings would be similar to those found in the assertion literature (Schwartz & Gottman, 1976) and in sports psychology (Mahoney & Avener, 1977). These findings may also suggest the nature of the difficulties in learning to be therapeutic as well as targets for intervention.

In summary, the cognitively oriented educator has perspectives and a host of procedures available in order to broaden our understanding of professional development. The purpose of a cognitive approach to training is to broaden and clarify the goals and processes. Moreover, a cognitive approach may help identify maladaptive cognitions and reactions as well as provide interventions for their change.

POSTSCRIPT

In the beginning of this project my hope was to explore a cognitive-behavioral perspective within a generic framework of helping. The next logical step in this endeavor is to establish a program of research in order to determine if cognitive science provides adequate explanatory theories of therapy and an adequate base for developing practical applications. In the following paragraphs, I will outline some of the projects that were examined or suggested. Such a procedure will also help us in reviewing the chapters.

Chapter 1 introduced us to the cognitive renaissance and its relation to the helping field. In the introduction, at least two projects suggest themselves. One has to do with history. That is, a detailed historical account of the role of cognition in counseling and psychotherapy would be helpful. Too often, researchers and practitioners in clinical areas are divorced from the historical backgrounds of their respective disciplines, resulting in the unknowing duplication of experimental efforts and the relatively unproductive replication of past semantic conflicts. The other project is conceptual in nature. For instance, the word cognition itself appears to have experienced a common and contemporary malady: inflation. The boundary conditions for cognition and "not cognition" are nonexistent. Such ambiguity may preclude premature rigidity, but confusion and chaos can easily emerge in an area that lacks conceptual clarity.

Chapters 2 through 6 explored the generic functions of therapy from a cognitive-behavioral perspective. Chapter 2 examined the sources of influence in the counseling process. Within this chapter, an interesting project is suggested by an information processing approach to social influence. For example, what is the relationship between therapeutic attitudes and persuasive communications conveyed by the counselor and the client's ability to differentiate and organize facets of personal information? Chapter 3 provided a discussion of the problem identification process. One of the issues to emerge in this chapter concerned the reliability and validity of the reconstruction procedures used in the self-report of cognitive strategies. More work needs to be done on identifying conditions in which cognitive processes play a relatively substantive role and those conditions in which consideration of such processes is unnecessary. Chapter 4 described the major cognitive-behavioral interventions. Major concerns of this chapter focused on clinical significance. Little is known about generalization and maintenance effects. There is need for the systematic study of these interventions with diverse clinical populations. In terms of decision making, future research needs to assess the generalization and maintenance of problem-solving skills learned under laboratory conditions to real-life situations. In addition, the use of these interventions in the areas of vocational psychology and prevention needs evaluation. Chapter 5 discussed research methodology and design. The relationship between research and practice emerged as a contentious issue. Besides a reexamination of philosophy science, critics and advocates of experimental applied research need to conduct research on research in order to obtain some clear evidence about the reciprocal impact of research and practice. Professional development was the topic of Chapter 6. It was revealed that little is known about the impact of learning to be therapeutic on the self-development of the trainee. It seems important to expand our therapeutic training research from an examination of a purely behavioral skills curriculum to an examination of such curricula and therapeutic cognition.

In closing, the writing of this book has convinced me that meaningful research and practice in the areas of counseling and psychotherapy await the integration of cognitive and behavioral psychologies. Perhaps this book can make a contribution to such an integration and provide a stimulus for the critical analysis and reexamination of cognition within therapeutic disciplines.

BIBLIOGRAPHY

Allen, G. J., Chinsky, J. M., Larcen, S. W., Lochman, J. E., & Selinger H. V. *Community psychology and the schools: A behaviorally oriented multi-level preventive approach.* Hillsdale, N.J.: Erlbaum, 1976.

Allport, G. W. The general and the unique in psychological science. *Journal of Personality*, 1962, *30*, 405-22.

American Psychological Association, Task Force on Health Research. Contributions of psychology to health research. *American Psychologist*, 1976, *31*, 263-74.

Anton, J. L. Studying individual change. In L. Goldman (Ed.), *Research methods for counselors: Practical approaches in field settings.* New York: Wiley, 1978.

Astin, A. *The college environment.* Washington, D.C.: American Council on Education, 1968.

Atkinson, J. W. *An introduction to motivation.* Princeton: Van Nostrand, 1964.

Ausubel, D. P., Novak, J.D., & Hanesian, H. *Educational psychology: A cognitive view* (2nd ed.). New York: Holt, Rinehart & Winston, 1978.

Bain, A. J. *Thought control in everyday life.* New York: Funk & Wagnalls, 1928.

Bandler, R., & Grinder, J. *The structure of magic I.* Palo Alto: Science and Behavior Books, 1975.

Bandler, R., & Grinder, J. *The structure of magic II.* Palo Alto: Science and Behavior books, 1976.

Bandura, A. *Principles of behavior modification.* New York: Holt, Rinehart & Winston, 1969.

Bandura, A. Self-efficacy: Towards a unifying theory of behavior change. *Psychological Review*, 1977, *84*, 191-215.

Bandura, A., Adams, N., & Beyer, J. Cognitive processes in mediating behavioral change. *Journal of Personality and Social Psychology*, 1977, *35*, 125-39.

Bannister, D., & Mair, J. M. M. *The evaluation of personal constructs.* New York: Academic Press, 1968.

Barker, R. Ecology and motivation. In M. Jones (Ed.), *Nebraska symposium on motivation.* Lincoln: University of Nebraska Press, 1960.

Barker, R. *Ecological psychology.* Stanford: Stanford University Press, 1968.

Barker, R., & Gump, P. *Big school, small school.* Stanford: Stanford University Press, 1964.

Barker, R. G., & Wright, H. F. *One boy's day.* New York: Harper & Row, 1951.

Barnes, B., & Clawson, E. U. Do advance organizers facilitate learning? Recommendations for further research based on the analysis of thirty-two studies. *Review of Educational Research*, 1975, *45*, 637-59.

Beck, A. T. *Depression: Clinical, experimental, and theoretical aspects.* New York: Hoeber, 1967.

Beck, A. T. *Cognitive therapy and the emotional disorders.* New York: International Universities Press, 1976.

Beck, A. T., Rush, A. J., & Kovacs, M. *Individual treatment manual for cognitive/behavioral psychotherapy of depression.* Philadelphia: University of Pennsylvania, 1976.

Beck, A. T., Ward, C. H., Mendelson, M., Mock, J., & Erbaugh, J. Inventory for measuring depress. *Archives of General Psychiatry.* 1961, *4*, 561-71.

Beck, F. M., Kaul, T. J., & Russell, R. K. Treatment of dental anxiety by cue-controlled relaxation. *Journal of Counseling Psychology*, 1978, *25*, 591-94.

Beck, S. J., & Molish, H. B. *Rorschach's test: II. A variety of personality pictures* (2nd ed.). New York: Grune & Stratton, 1967.

Bem, D. J. Self-perception: An alternative interpretation of cognitive dissonance phenomena. *Psychological Review*, 1967, *74*, 183-200.

Bem, D. J. Self-perception theory. In L. Berkowitz (Ed.), *Advances in experimental social psychology* (vol. 6). New York: Academic Press, 1972.

Bem, S. L. Verbal self-control: The establishment of effective self-instruction. *Journal of Experimental Psychology*, 1967, *74*, 485-91.

Bender, N. Self-verbalization versus tutor verbalization in modifying impulsivity. *Journal of Educational Psychology*, 1976, *68*, 347-54.

Bergin, A. E. The effect of dissonant persuasive communications upon changes in a self-referring attitude. *Journal of Personality*, 1962, *30*, 423-38.

Bergin, A. E., & Strupp, H. H. *Changing frontiers in the science of psychotherapy.* Chicago: Aldine, 1972.

Bernhardt, K. *Training for research in psychology: The Canadian Opinicon Conference, 1960.* Toronto: University of Toronto Press, 1961.

Bertalanffy, L. von. *General systems theory.* New York: George Braziller, 1968.

Block, J. *The Q-sort method in personality assessment and psychiatric research.* Springfield: Charles Thomas, 1961.

Birch, D., Atkinson, J. W., & Bongort, K. Cognitive control of action. In B. Weinger (Ed.), *Cognitive views of human motivation.* New York: Academic Press, 1974.

Blaney, P. H. Contemporary theories of depression: Critique and comparison. *Journal of Abnormal Psychology*, 1977, *86*, 203-23.

Blocher, D. H. *Developmental counseling.* New York: Ronald Press, 1966/1974.

Bolles, R. C. Cognition and motivation: Some historical trends. In B. Weiner (Ed.), *Cognitive views of human motivation.* New York: Academic Press, 1974.

Bordin, E. S. Diagnosis in counseling and psychotherapy. *Educational and Psychological Measurement*, 1946, *6*, 169-84.

Borkovec, T. P., & Nau, S. D. Credibility of analogue therapy rationales. *Journal of Behavior Therapy and Experimental Psychiatry*, 1972, *3*, 257-60.

Box, G. E. P., & Jenkins, G. M. *Time series analysis: Forecasting and control.* San Francisco: Holden-Day, 1976.

Boy, A., & Pine, G. J. *Client-centered counseling in the secondary school.* Boston: Houghton-Miflin, 1963.

Brenner, M. H. *Mental illness and the economy.* Cambridge: Harvard University Press, 1973.

Breuer, J., & Freud, S. *Studies on hysteria.* New York: Basic Books, 1957.

Broadbent, D. E. *Perception and communication.* New York: Pergamon Press, 1958.

Bronfenbrenner, U. Toward an experimental ecology of human development. *American Psychologist*, 1977, *32*, 513-31.

Bruhn, J. Human ecology: A unifying science? *Human Ecology*, 1974, *2*, 105-25.

Burck, H. D., & Peterson, G. P. Needed: More evaluation, not research. *Personnel and Guidance Journal*, 1975, *53*, 563-69.

Callis, R. Diagnostic classification as a research tool. *Journal of Counseling Psychology*, 1965, *12*, 238-47.

Cameron, R. Conceptual tempo and children's problem solving behavior: A developmental task analysis. Ph.D. dissertation, University of Waterloo, 1976.

Campbell, D. T. Reforms as experiments. *American Psychologist*, 1969, *24*, 409-29.

Campbell, D. T., & Fiske, D. W. Convergent and discriminant validation by the multitrait-multimethod matrix. *Psychological Bulletin*, 1959, *56*, 81-105.

Campbell, D. T., & Stanley, J. C. Experimental and quasi-experimental designs for research on teaching. In N. L. Gage (Ed.), *Handbook of research on teaching*. Chicago: Rand McNally, 1963.

Carkhuff, R. R. *Helping and human relations* (2 vols.). New York: Holt, Rinehart & Winston, 1969.

Carnegie, D. *How to stop worrying and start living*. New York: Simon & Schuster, 1948.

Carroll, J. B. Psychometric tests as cognitive tasks: A new "structure of intellect." In L. Resnick (Ed.), *The nature of intelligence*. New York: Erlbaum, 1976.

Cautela, J. R. Covert sensitization. *Psychological Reports*, 1967, *20*, 459-68.

Chassan, J. B. *Research design in clinical psychology and psychiatry*. New York: Appleton-Century-Crofts, 1967.

Chaves, J., & Barber, T. Cognitive strategies, experimenter modeling, and expectation in the attention of pain. *Journal of Abnormal Psychology*, 1974, *83*, 356-63.

Chinsky, J. M., & Rappaport, J. Brief critique of meaning and reliability of "accurate empathy" ratings. *Psychological Bulletin*, 1970, *73*, 379-82.

Chomsky, N. *Syntactic structures*. The Hague: Mouton, 1957.

Chomsky, N. A review of Skinner's Verbal Behavior. *Language*, 1959, *35*, 26-58.

Chomsky, N. Current issues in linguistics theory. In J. A. Fodor, & J. J. Katz (Eds.), *The structure of language: Readings in the philosophy of language.* Englewood Cliffs: Prentice-Hall, 1964.

Chomsky, N. *Aspects of the theory of syntax.* Cambridge: Massachusetts Institute of Technology Press, 1965.

Christensen, C. *Development and field testing of an interpersonal coping skills program.* Toronto: Ontario Institute for Studies in Education, 1974.

Cohen, J. *Statistical power analysis for the behavioral sciences.* New York: Academic Press, 1969.

Cohen, S., Glass, D. C., & Singer, J. E. Apartment noise, auditory discrimination, and reading ability in children. *Journal of Experimental Social Psychology*, 1973, *9*, 407-22.

Comroe, J. H., & Dripps, R. D. Scientific basis for the support of biomedical science. *Science*, 1976, *192*, 105-11.

Cook, T. D., Appleton, H., Conner, R., Schaffer, A., Tamkin, G., & Weber, S. J. *"Sesame Street" revisited: A case study in evaluation research.* New York: Russell Sage Foundation, 1975.

Cook, T. D., & Campbell, D. T. *Quasi-experimentation: Design & analysis issues for field settings.* Chicago: Rand McNally, 1979.

Cornfield, J., & Tukey, J. W. Average values of mean squares in factorials. *Annals of Mathematical Statistics*, 1956, *27*, 907-49.

Coué, E. *The practice of autosuggestion.* New York: Doubleday, 1922.

Cowen, E. L. Baby-steps toward primary prevention. *American Journal of Community Psychology*, 1977, *5*, 1-22.

Craik, F. I. M., & Lockhart, R. S. Levels of processing: A framework for memory research. *Journal of Verbal Learning and Verbal Behavior*, 1972, *11*, 671-84.

Cronbach, L. J., & Furby, L. How we should measure "change"—or should we? *Psychological Bulletin*, 1970, *74*, 68-80.

Cronbach, L. J., & Meehl, P. E. Construct validity in psychological tests. *Psychological Bulletin*, 1955, *52*, 281-302.

Cronbach, L. J., & Snow, R. E. *Aptitudes and instructional methods.* New York: Irvington, 1976.

Davis, G. A. Current status of research and theory in human problem solving. *Psychological Bulletin*, 1966, *66*, 35-54.

Davis, G. A. *Psychology of human problem solving: Theory and practice.* New York: Basic Books, 1973.

Davison, G. C., Tsujimoto, R. N., & Glaros, A. G. Attribution and the maintenance of behavior change in falling asleep. *Journal of Abnormal Psychology*, 1973, *82*, 124-33.

Davison, G. C., & Valins, S. Maintenance of self-attributed and drug-attributed behavior change. *Journal of Personality and Social Psychology*, 1969, *11*, 25-33.

Dell, D. M. Counselor power base, influence attempt, and behavior change in counseling. *Journal of Counseling Psychology*, 1973, *20*, 399-405.

Dell, D. M., & Schmidt, L. D. Behavioral cues to counselor expertness. *Journal of Counseling Psychology*, 1976, *23*, 197-201.

Dember, W. N. Motivation and the cognitive revolution. *American Psychologist*, 1974, *29*, 161-68.

Denney, D. The effects of exemplary and cognitive models and self-rehearsal on children's interrogative strategies. *Journal of Experimental Child Psychology*, 1975, *19*, 476-88.

Derry, P., & Stone, G. L. Effects of cognitive adjunct treatments on assertiveness. *Cognitive Therapy and Research*, 1979, *3*, 213-21.

Dewey, J. *Democracy and education.* New York: Macmillan, 1916.

Dewey, J. *How we think.* Boston: Heath, 1933.

DiGiuseppe, R., Miller, N., & Trexler, L. Outcome studies of rational-emotive therapy. *Counseling Psychologist*, 1977, *7*, 64-72.

DiLoreto, A. O. *Comparative psychotherapy. An experimental analysis.* Chicago: Aldin-Atherton, 1971.

Dolliver, R. H. The relationship of rational emotive therapy to other psychotherapies and personality change. *The Counseling Psychologist*, 1977, *7*, 57-63.

D'Zurilla, T. J., & Goldfried, M. R. Problem solving and behavior modification. *Journal of Abnormal Psychology*, 1971, *78*, 107-26.

Eisenberg, S., & Delancy, D. *The counseling process* (2nd ed.). Chicago: Rand McNally, 1977.

Ekman, P. A. A comparison of verbal and nonverbal behavior as reinforcing stimuli of opinion responses. Ph.D. dissertation, Adelphi University, 1958.

Ellis, A. *Reason and emotion in psychotherapy.* New York: Lyle Stuart Press, 1962.

Ellis, A. *The essence of rational psychotherapy: A comprehensive approach to treatment.* New York: Institute for Rational Living, 1970.

Ellis, A. *Growth through reason: Verbatim cases in rational-emotive psychotherapy.* Palo Alto: Science and Behavior Books, 1971.

Ellis, A. Rational-emotive therapy: Research data that supports the clinical and personality hypotheses of RET and other modes of cognitive-behavior therapy. *The Counseling Psychologist,* 1977, 7, 2-42.

Ellis, A., & Harper, R. A. *A new guide to rational living* (rev. ed.). Englewood Cliffs: Prentice-Hall, 1975.

Endler, N., & Hunt, J. S-R inventories of hostility and comparisons of the proportion of variance from persons, responses, and situations for hostility and anxiousness. *Journal of Personality and Social Psychology,* 1968, 9, 309-15.

Erickson, E. H. *Childhood and society.* New York: Norton, 1950.

Estes, W. K. Reinforcement in human behavior. *American Scientist,* 1972, 60, 723-29.

Estes, W. K. The cognitive side of probability learning. *Psychological Review,* 1976, 83, 37-64.

Evans, J. R., & Cody, J. J. Transfer of decision-making skills learned in a counseling-like setting to similar and dissimilar situations. *Journal of Counseling Psychology,* 1969, 16, 427-32.

Ferreira, A., & Winder, J. D. Family interaction and decision making. *Archives of General Psychiatry,* 1965, 13, 214-23.

Ferster, C. B., Nurnberger, J. I., & Lewitt, E. B. The control of eating. *Journal of Mathematics,* 1962, 1, 87-109.

Feshbach, S. The environment of personality. *American Psychologist,* 1978, 33, 447-55.

Fitts, W. H. *The experience of psychotherapy: What it's like for client and therapist.* Princeton: Van Nostrand, 1965.

Fox, L. Effecting the use of efficient study habits. *Journal of Mathematics,* 1962, 1, 75-86.

Frank, J. D. *Persuasion and healing.* Baltimore: Johns Hopkins Press, 1961/ 1973.

Fretz, B. F. (Ed.). Counseling psychology and the Vail Conference: Analysis of issues in the training of professional psychologists. *The Counseling Psychologist*, 1974, *9*, 64-80.

Fretz, B. F. (Ed.). Professional identity. *The Counseling Psychologist*, 1977, *7*, 4-94.

Gagné, R. M. Problem solving. In A. W. Melton (Ed.), *Categories of human learning.* New York: Academic Press, 1964.

Gagné, R. M. Learning hierarchies. *Educational Psychologist*, 1968, *6*, 1-9.

Gagné, R. M., & Briggs, L. J. *Principles of instructional design.* New York: Holt, Rinehart & Winston, 1974.

Gelatt, H. B. Decision-making: A conceptual frame of reference for counseling. *Journal of Counseling Psychology*, 1962, *9*, 240-45.

Giebink, J. W., Stover, D. S., & Fahl, M. A. Teaching adaptive responses to frustration to emotionally disturbed boys. *Journal of Consulting and Clinical Psychology*, 1968, *32*, 366-68.

Gladstein, G. A. Empathy and counseling outcome: An empirical and conceptual review. *The Counseling Psychologist*, 1977, *6*, 70-79.

Glaser, R. Psychology and instructional technology. In R. Glaser (Ed.), *Training research and education.* Pittsburgh: University of Pittsburgh Press, 1962.

Glass, D. C., Singer, J. E., & Friedman, L. H. Psychic cost of adaption to an environmental stressor. *Journal of Personality and Social Psychology*, 1969, *12*, 200-10.

Glass, G. V. Primary, secondary, and meta-analysis of research. *The Educational Researcher*, 1976, *10*, 3-8.

Glass, G. V., Peckham, P. D., & Sanders, J. R. Consequences of failure to meet assumptions underlying the analysis of variance and covariance. *Review of Educational Research*, 1972, *42*, 237-88.

Glass, G. V., Wilson, V. L., & Gottman, J. M. *Design and analysis of time-series experiments.* Boulder: Colorado Associated University Press, 1975.

Goldberg, L. R. Admission to the Ph.D. program in the Department of Psychology at the University of Oregon. *American Psychologist*, 1977, *32*, 663-68.

Goldfried, M. R. Systematic desensitizatin as training in self-control. *Journal of Consulting and Clinical Psychology*, 1971, *37*, 228-34.

Goldfried, M. R. Reduction of generalized anxiety through a variant of systematic desensitization. In M. F. Goldfried & M. Merbaum (Ed.), *Behavior change through self-control.* New York: Holt, Rinehart & Winston, 1973.

Goldfried, M. R., & Davidson, G. C. *Clinical behavior therapy.* New York: Holt, Rinehart & Winston, 1976.

Goldfried, M. R., Decenteceo, E. T., & Weinberg, L. Systematic rational restructuring as a self-control technique. *Behavior Therapy*, 1974, *5*, 247-54.

Goldfried, M. R., & Merbaum, M. (Eds.), *Behavior change through self-control.* New York: Holt, Rinehart & Winston, 1973.

Goldfried, M. R., & Trier, C. S. Effectiveness of relaxation as an active coping skill. *Journal of Abnormal Psychology*, 1974, *83*, 348-55.

Goldiamond, I. Self-control procedures in personal behavior problems. *Psychological Reports*, 1965, *17*, 851-68.

Goldman, L. A revolution in counseling research. *Journal of Counseling Psychology*, 1976, *23*, 543-52.

Goldman, L. Introduction and point of view. In L. Goldman (Ed.), *Research methods for counselors: Practical approaches in field settings.* New York: Wiley, 1978.

Goldstein, A. P. *Therapist-patient expectancies in psychotherapy.* New York: Pergamon Press, 1962.

Goldstein, A. P., Heller, K., & Sechrest, L. *Psychotherapy and the psychology of behavior change.* New York: John Wiley & Sons, 1966.

Goodman, D. S., & Maultsby, M. C., Jr. *Emotional well-being through rational behavior training.* Springfield, Ill.: Charles C. Thomas, 1974.

Goor, A., & Sommerfeld, R. A. A comparison of problem-solving processes of creative students and non-creative students. *Journal of Educational Psychology*, 1975, *67*, 495-505.

Gottman, J. R., & Glass, G. V. Time-series analysis of interrupted time-series experiments. In T. Kratochwill (Ed.), *Strategies to evaluate change in single subject research.* New York: Academic Press, 1979.

Guilford, J. P. *The nature of human intelligence.* New York: McGraw-Hill, 1967.

Haase, R. F. Power analysis of research in counselor education. *Counselor Education and Supervision*, 1974, *14*, 124-32.

Haley, J. Family experiments: A new type of experimentation. *Family Process*, 1962, *1*, 265-93.

Haley, J. Research on family patterns: An instrument. *Family Process*, 1964, *3*, 41-55.

Hartig, M., & Kanfer, F. The role of verbal self-instructions in children's resistance to temptation. *Journal of Personality and Social Psychology*, 1973, *25*, 259-67.

Hartmann, H. *Ego psychology and the problem of adaption.* New York: International Universities Press, 1958.

Harvey, J. H., Ickes, W. J., & Kidd, R. F. (Eds.). *New directions in attribution research* (vol. 1). Hillsdale, N.J.: Erlbaum, 1976.

Hays, W. L. *Statistics for psychologists.* New York: Holt, Rinehart & Winston, 1963.

Hebb, D. O. *The organization of behavior.* New York: Wiley, 1949.

Heider, F. Social perception and phenomenal causality. *Psychological Review*, 1944, *51*, 358-74.

Heider, F. *The psychology of interpersonal relations.* New York: Wiley, 1958.

Helms, J. E. Counselor reactions to female clients: Generalizing from analoque research to a counseling setting. *Journal of Counseling Psychology*, 1978, *25*, 193-99.

Hill, C., Tanney, M. F., Leonard, M. M., & Reiss, J. A. Counselor reactions to female clients: Types of problems, age of client, and sex of counselor. *Journal of Counseling Psychology*, 1977, *24*, 60-65.

Hoch, E., Ross, A. O., & Winder, C. L. (Eds.). *Professional preparation of clinical psychologists.* Washington, D.C.: American Psychological Association, 1966.

Holland, J. L. Some explorations of a theory of vocational choice: I. One- and two-year longitudinal studies. *Psychological Monographs*, 1962, *76*, (26, whole no. 545).

Holland, J. L. Explorations of a theory of vocational choice and achievement: II. A four-year prediction study. *Psychological Reports*, 1963, *12*, 537-94.

Holland, J. L., & Holland, J. E. Vocational indecision: More evidence and speculation. *Journal of Counseling Psychology*, 1977, *24*, 404-14.

Hollingshead, A., & Redlich, F. *Social class and mental illness.* New York: Wiley, 1958.

Homme, L. E. Perspectives in psychology: XXIV. Control of covenants, the operants of the mind. *Psychological Record*, 1965, *15*, 501-11.

Horan, J. J. *Counseling for effective decision making.* North Scituate, Mass.: Duxbury Press, 1979.

Horan, J. J., Hackett, G., Buchanan, J. D., Stone, C. I., & Demchik-Stone, D. Coping with pain: A component analysis of stress-innoculation. *Cognitive Therapy and Research*, 1977, *1*, 211-21.

Hosford, R. E. Behavioral counseling: A contemporary overview. *The Counseling Psychologist*, 1969, *1*, 1-33.

Hovland, C. I., Janis, I. L., & Kelley, H. H. *Communication and persuasion. Psychological studies of opinion change.* New Haven: Yale University Press, 1953.

Hovland, C. I., Lumsdaine, A. A., & Sheffield, F. D. *Experiments on mass communication.* Princeton: Princeton University Press, 1949.

Huck, S. W., & McLean, R. A. Using repeated measures ANOVA to analyze the data from a pretest-posttest design: A potentially confusing task. *Psychological Bulletin*, 1975, *82*, 511-18.

Hunt, E., Frost, H., & Lunneborg, C. Individual differences in cognition. In G. Bower (Ed.), *The psychology of learning and motivation: Advances in research and theory* (vol. 7). New York: Academic Press, 1973.

Hurdon, C. J., Pepinsky, H. B., & Mearo, N.M. Cônceptual level and structural complexity in language. *Journal of Counseling Psychology*, 1979, *26*, pp. 190-97.

Ivey, A. E., & Authier, J. *Microcounseling: Innovations in interviewing, counseling, psychotherapy, and psychoeducation* (2nd ed.). Springfield: Charles C. Thomas, 1978.

Jackson, D. N. A sequential system for personality scale development. In C. D. Spielberger (Ed.), *Current topics in clinical and community psychology* (vol. 2). New York: Academic Press, 1970.

Jacobson, E. *Progressive relaxation.* Chicago: University of Chicago Press, 1938.

James, W. *The principles of psychology.* New York: Holt, 1890.

Janis, I. L., & Feshbach, S. Effects of fear arousing communications. *Journal of Abnormal and Social Psychology*, 1953, *48*, 78-92.

Jones, E. E., & Davis, K. E. From acts to dispositions: The attribution process in person perception. In L. Berkowitz (Ed.), *Advances in experimental social psychology* (vol. 2). New York: Academic Press, 1965.

Jones, E. E., Kanouse, D. E., Kelley, H. H., Nisbett, R. E., Valins, S., & Weiner, B. (Eds.). *Attribution: Perceiving the causes of behavior.* Morristown: General Learning Press, 1971.

Jones, R. G. A factored measure of Ellis' irrational belief system, with personality and maladjustment correlates. Ph.D. dissertation, Texas Technological College, 1969.

Joyce, B., & Weil, M. *Models of teaching.* Englewood Cliffs: Prentice-Hall, 1972.

Kagan, N., Krathwohl, D., Goldberg, A., Campbell, R. J., Schauble, P. G., Greenberg, B. S., Danish, S. J., Resnickoff, A., Dowes, J., & Bandy, S. B. *Studies in human interaction: Interpersonal recall stimulated by videotape.* Educational Publication Services, College of Education, Michigan State University, East Lansing, Michigan, 1967.

Kahneman, D., & Tversky, A. On the psychology of prediction. *Psychological Review*, 1973, *80*, 237-58.

Kanfer, F. H. Self-management methods. In F. H. Kanfer, & A. P. Goldstein, *Helping people change.* New York: Pergamon Press, 1975.

Kanfer, F. H., & Saslow, G. Behavioral diagnosis. In C. M. Franks (Ed.), *Behavior therapy: Appraisal and status.* New York: McGraw-Hill, 1969.

Kaye, D., Kirschner, P., & Mandler, G. The effect of test anxiety on memory span in a group test situation. *Journal of Consulting Psychology*, 1953, *17*, 265-66.

Kazdin, A. E. Statistical analyses for single-case experimental designs. In M. Hersen, & D. H. Barlow (Eds.), *Single case experimental designs.* New York: Pergamon, 1976.

Kazdin, A. E. Methodological and interpretive problems of single-case experimental designs. *Journal of Consulting and Clinical Psychology*, 1978, *46*, 629-42.

Kazdin, A. E., & Wilcoxon, L. Systematic desensitization and non-specific treatment effects. A methodological evaluation. *Psychological Bulletin*, 1976, *83*, 729-58.

Kelley, H. H. Attribution theory in social psychology. In D. Levine (Ed.), *Nebraska symposium on motivation* (vol. 15). Lincoln: University of Nebraska Press, 1967.

Kelly, G. A. *The psychology of personal constructs.* New York: Norton, 1955.

Kent, R. N., Wilson, G. T., & Nelson, R. Effects of false heartrate feedback on avoidance behavior. An investigation of "cognitive desensitization." *Behavior Therapy*, 1972, *3*, 1-6.

Kerlinger, F. N. The influence of research on education practice. *Educational Researcher*, 1977, *6*, 5-12.

Kiresuk, T. J., & Sherman, R. E. Goal attainment scaling: A general method for evaluating community mental health programs. *Community Mental Health Journal*, 1968, *4*, 443-53.

Kohlberg, L., Yaeger, J., & Hjertholm, E. Private speech: Four studies and a review of theories. *Child Development*, 1968, *39*, 691-736.

Köhler, W. *The mentality of apes.* New York: Harcourt, Brace, & Jovanovich, 1925.

Kopel, S., & Arkowitz, H. The role of attribution and self-perception in behavior change. Implications for behavior therapy. *Genetic Psychology Monographs*, 1975, *92*, 175-212.

Korchin, S. J. *Modern clinical psychology: Principles of intervention in the clinic and community.* New York: Basic Books, 1976.

Kris, E. On preconscious mental processes. In D. Rapaport (Ed.), *Organization and pathology of thought.* New York: Columbia University Press, 1951.

Krumboltz, J. D. Parable of a good counselor. *Personnel and Guidance Journal*, 1964, *43*, 110-26.

Krumboltz, J. D. Behavioral counseling: Rationale and research. *Personnel and Guidance Journal*, 1965, *44*, 383-87.

Krumboltz, J. D. Behavioral goals for counseling. *Journal of Counseling Psychology*, 1966, *13*, 153-59. (a)

Krumboltz, J. D. (Ed.). *Revolution in counseling: Implications of behavioral science.* Boston: Houghton-Mifflin, 1966. (b)

Krumboltz, J. D. Future directions in counseling research. In J. M. Whiteley (Ed.), *Research in counseling.* Columbus, Ohio: Charles E. Merrill, 1967.

Krumboltz, J. D., & Thoresen, C. E. (Eds.). *Behavioral counseling: Cases and techniques.* New York: Holt, Rinehart & Winston, 1969.

Krumboltz, J. D., & Thoresen, C. E. (Eds.). *Counseling methods*. New York: Holt, Rinehart & Winston, 1976.

Kuhn, T. S. *The structure of scientific revolutions*. Chicago: University of Chicago Press, 1962/1970.

Langer, T., & Michael, S. *Life stress and mental health*. New York: Free Press, 1963.

Larcen, S. W., Spivack, G., & Shure, M. *Problem-solving thinking and adjustment among dependent-neglected preadolescents*. Paper presented at the meeting of the Eastern Psychological Association, Boston, 1972.

Lazarus, R. S. *Psychological stress and the coping process*. New York: McGraw-Hill, 1966.

Lazarus, R. S. Cognitive and coping processes in emotion. In B. Weiner (Ed.), *Cognitive views of human motivation*. New York: Academic Press, 1974.

Ledwidge, B. Cognitive behavior modification: A step in the wrong direction. *Psychological Bulletin*, 1978, *85*, 353-75.

Leitenberg, H. The use of single case methodology in psychotherapy research. *Journal of Abnormal Psychology*, 1973, *82*, 87-101.

Levy, L. Fact and choice in counseling and counselor education: A cognitive view point. In C. A. Parker (Ed.), *Counseling theories and counselor education*. New York: Houghton-Mifflin, 1968.

Lewin, K., Lippitt, R., & White, R. Patterns of aggressive behavior in experimentally created "social climates." *Journal of Social Psychology*, 1939, *10*, 271-99.

Loeb, A., Beck, A. T., & Diggory, J. Differential effects of success and failure on depressed and nondepressed patients. *Journal of Nervous and Mental Disease*, 1971, *152*, 106-14.

Loevinger, J. Objective tests as instruments of psychological theory. *Psychological Reports*, 1957, *3*, (monograph no. 9), 635-94.

Luria, A. *The role of speech in the regulation of normal and abnormal behaviors*. New York: Liveright, 1961.

Mahoney, M. J. *Cognition and behavior modification*. Cambridge, Mass.: Ballinger, 1974.

Mahoney, M. J. *Scientist as subject: The psychological imperative*. Cambridge, Mass.: Ballinger, 1976.

Mahoney, M. J. Reflections on the cognitive learning trend in psychotherapy. *American Psychologist*, 1977, *32*, 5-13.

Mahoney, M. J., & Avener, M. Psychology of the elite athlete: An exploratory study. *Cognitive Therapy and Research*, 1977, *1*, 135-41.

Maltz, M. *Psycho-cybernetics*. Englewood Cliffs: Prentice-Hall, 1960.

Marks, P. A., & Seeman, W. *The actuarial description of personality: An atlas for use with the MMPI*. Baltimore: Williams & Williams, 1963.

Maultsby, M. C., Jr., & Ellis, A. *Technique for using rational-emotive imagery*. New York: Institute for Rational Living, 1974.

McCain, L. J., & McCleary, R. The statistical analysis of the simple interrupted time-series quasi-experiment. In T. D. Cook & D. T. Campbell (Eds.), *Quasi-experimentation: Design & analysis issues for field settings*. Chicago: Rand McNally, 1979.

McClelland, D. C. *Power: The inner experience*. New York: Irvington, 1975.

McClelland, D. C., Atkinson, J. W., Clark, R. A., & Lowell, E. L. *The achievement motive*. New York: Appleton-Century-Crofts, 1953.

McFall, R. M., & Lillesand, D. B. Behavior rehearsal with modeling and coaching in assertion training. *Journal of Abnormal Psychology* 1971, *77*, 313-23.

McFall, R. M., & Twentyman, C. T. Four experiments on the relative contributions of rehearsal, modeling, and coaching to assertion training. *Journal of Abnormal Psychology*, 1973, *81*, 199-218.

McGuire, M. T., & Sifneos, P. E. Problem solving in psychotherapy. *Psychiatric Quarterly*, 1970, *44*, 667-73.

McGuire, W. J. The nature of attitudes and attitude change. In G. Lindzey & E. Aronoson (Eds.), *The handbook of social psychology* (vol. 3., 2nd ed.). Reading, Mass.: Addison-Wesley, 1969.

Meichenbaum, D. The effects of instructions and reinforcement on thinking and language behaviors of schizophrenics. *Behaviour Research and Therapy*, 1969, *7* 101-14.

Meichembaum, D. Therapist manual for cognitive behavior modification. Unpublished manuscript, University of Waterloo, 1973.

Meichembaum, D. Theoretical and treatment implications of developmental research on verbal control of behavior. *Canadian Psychological Review* 1975, *16*, 22-7.

Meichembaum, D. *Cognitive behavior modification.* New York: Plenum, 1977.

Meichembaum, D., & Cameron, R. Stress innoculation: A skills training approach to anxiety, Unpublished manuscript, University of Waterloo, 1973.

Meichembaum, D., Gilmore, B., & Fedoravicius, A. Group insight vs. group desensitization in treating speech anxiety. *Journal of Consulting and Clinical Psychology,* 1971, *36,* 410-21.

Meichembaum, D., & Goodman, J. Training impulsive children to talk to themselves: A means of developing self-control. *Journal of Abnormal Psychology,* 1971, *77,* 115-26.

Meichembaum, D., & Turk, D. The cognitive-behavioral management of anxiety, anger, and pain. In P. Davidson (Ed.), *The behavioral management of anxiety, depression and pain.* New York: Bruner Mazel, 1976.

Melzack, R., & Wall, P. Pain mechanisms: A new theory. *Science,* 1965, *150,* 971.

Mendonca, J. D., & Siess, T. F. Counseling for indecisiveness: Problem-solving and anxiety-management training. *Journal of Counseling Psychology,* 1976, *23,* 339-47.

Milgram, S. Behavioral study of obedience. *Journal of Abnormal and Social Psychology,* 1963, *67,* 371-78.

Miller, G. A., & Chomsky, N. Finitary models of language users. In R. D. Luce, R. R. Bush, & E. Galanter (Eds.), *Handbook of mathematical psychology.* New York: Wiley, 1963.

Miller, G. A., Galanter, E., & Pribram, K. *Plans and the structure of behavior.* New York: Holt, Rinehart & Winston, 1960.

Miller, W. R. Psychological deficits in depression. *Psychological Bulletin,* 1975, *82,* 238-60.

Minge, M. R., & Bowman, T. T. Personality differences among nonclients and vocational-educational and personal counseling clients. *Journal of Counseling Psychology,* 1967, *14,* 137-39.

Mischel, W. *Personality and assessment.* New York: Wiley, 1968.

Mischel, W. Toward a cognitive social learning reconceptualization of personality. *Psychological Review,* 1973, *80,* 252-83.

Moos, R. H. *Evaluating correctional and community environments.* New York: Wiley, 1975. (a)

Moos, R. H. *Evaluating treatment environments.* New York: Wiley, 1975. (b)

Moos, R. H. *The human context: Environmental determinants of behavior.* New York: Wiley-Interscience, 1976.

Mueller, W., & Kell, B. *Coping with conflict: Supervising counselors and psychotherapists.* New York: Meredith, 1972.

Murray, H. A. *Explorations in personality.* New York: Oxford University Press, 1938.

Murray, H. A. Preparations for the scaffold of a comprehensive system. In S. Koch (Ed.), *Psychology: A study of science* (vol. 3). *Formulations of the person and the social context.* New York: McGraw-Hill, 1959.

Neisser, U. *Cognitive psychology.* New York: Appleton-Century-Crofts, 1967.

Nelson, C. A., & Hendrick, C. Bibliography of journal articles in social psychology: 1973. *Catalog of Selected Documents in Psychology,* 1974, *4,* 126.

Neufeld, R. W. *Clinical quantitative methods.* New York: Grune & Stratton, 1977.

Newell, A. (Ed.). *Information processing language V manual.* Englewood Cliffs: Prentice-Hall, 1961.

Nisbett, R., & Schachter, S. Cognitive manipulation of pain. *Journal of Experimental Social Psychology,* 1966, *2,* 227-36.

Nisbett, R. E., & Wilson, T. D. Telling more than we know: Verbal reports on mental processes. *Psychological Review,* 1977, *84,* 231-59.

Novaco, R. W. Treatment of chronic anger through cognitive and relaxation controls. *Journal of Consulting and Clinical Psychology,* 1976, *44,* 681.

Oetting, E. R. Evaluative research and orthodox science: Part I. *Personnel and Guidance Journal,* 1976, *55,* 11-15. (a)

Oetting, E. R. Planning and reporting evaluative research: Part II. *Personnel and Guidance Journal,* 1976, *55,* 60-64. (b)

Ojemann, R. H. Incorporating psychological concepts in the school curriculum. In H. P. Clarizo (Ed.), *Mental health and the educative process.* Chicago: Rand McNally, 1969.

Osborn, A. F. *Applied imagination: Principles and procedures of creative problem-solving* (3rd ed.). New York: Scribner's, 1963.

Osgood, C. E., Suci, G. J., & Tannenbaum, P. H. *The measurement of meaning.* Urbana: The University of Illinois Press, 1957.

Paivio, A. Neomentalism. *Canadian Journal of Psychology*, 1975, *29*, 263-91.

Palkes, H., Stewart, M., & Kahana, B. Porteus' maze performance after training in self-directed verbal commands. *Child Development*, 1968, *39*, 817-26.

Park, R. *Human communities.* Chicago: University of Chicago Press, 1925.

Parnes, S. J., & Meadow, A. Effects of "brainstorming" instructions on creative problem solving by trained and untrained subjects. *Journal of Educational Psychology*, 1959, *50*, 171-76.

Parsons, F. *Choosing a vocation.* Boston: Houghton Mifflin, 1909.

Patterson, C. H. Comment. *Personnel and Guidance Journal*, 1964, *43*, 124-26.

Paul, G. L. *Insight versus densensitization in psychotherapy: An experiment in anxiety reduction.* Stanford: Stanford University Press, 1966.

Paul, G. L. Behavior modification research: Design and tactics. In C. M. Franks (Ed.), *Behavior therapy: Appraisal and status.* New York: McGraw-Hill, 1969.

Peale, N. V. *The power of positive thinking.* Englewood Cliffs: Prentice-Hall, 1960.

Pepinsky, H. B. The selection and use of diagnostic categories in clinical counseling. *Applied Psychological Monographs* (no. 15), 1948.

Peterson, D. The doctor of psychology program at the University of Illinois. *American Psychologist*, 1968, *23*, 511-16.

Peterson, W. W., & Birdsall, T. G. The theory of signal detectability. University of Michigan, Electronic Defense Group, *Technical Report No. 13*, 1953.

Piaget, J. Piaget's theory. In P. H. Mussen (Ed.), *Carmichael's manual of child psychology* (vol. 1). New York: Wiley, 1970.

Pierce, A. The economic cycle and the social suicide rate. *American Sociological Review*, 1967, *32*, 457-62.

Platt, J., & Spivack, G. Problem-solving thinking of psychiatric patients. *Journal of Consulting and Clinical Psychology*, 1972, *39*, 148-51.

Platt, J., & Spivack, G. Means of solving real-life problems: I. Psychiatric patients versus controls, and cross-cultural comparisons of normal females. *Journal of Community Psychology*, 1974, *2*, 45-48.

Price, R. Analysis of task requirements in schizophrenic concept identification performance. *Journal of Abnormal Psychology*, 1968, *73*, 285-94.

Proshansky, H., Ittelson, W., & Rivlin, L. (Eds.). *Environmental psychology*. New York: Holt, Rinehart & Winston, 1970.

Raimy, V. C. (Ed.). *Training in clinical psychology*. Englewood Cliffs: Prentice-Hall, 1950.

Rapaport, D. The theory of ego autonomy: A generalization. *Bulletin of the Menninger Clinic*, 1958, *22*, 13-35.

Rapaport, D., Gill, M. M., & Schafer, R. *Diagnostic psychological testing* (2 vols.). New York: International Universities Press, 1945.

Rice, L. N., & Wagstaff, A. K. Client voice quality and expressive style as indexes of productive psychotherapy. *Journal of Consulting Psychology*, 1967, *31*, 557-63.

Rich, A. R., & Schroeder, H. E. Research issues in assertiveness training. *Psychological Bulletin*, 1976, *83*, 1081-96.

Richardson, B. The role of cognition in microcounseling. Ph.D. dissertation, University of Western Ontario, London, Canada, 1979.

Riopelle, A. J. (Ed.). *Animal problem solving*. Baltimore: Penguin, 1967.

Rogers, C. R. *Counseling and psychotherapy: Newer concepts in practice*. Boston: Houghton-Mifflin, 1942.

Rogers, C. R. *Client-centered therapy*. Boston: Houghton-Mifflin, 1951.

Rogers, C. R. The necessary and sufficient conditions of therapeutic personality change. *Journal of Consulting Psychology*, 1957, *21*, 95-103.

Rogers, C. R. A theory of therapy, personality, and interpersonal relationships, as developed in the client-centered framework. In S. Koch (Ed.), *Psychology: A study of science. Study I. Conceptual and systematic* (vol. 3). New York: McGraw-Hill, 1959.

Rogers, C. R. *On becoming a person*. Boston: Houghton-Mifflin, 1961.

Rogers, C. R. Some new challenges. *American Psychologist*, 1973, *28*, 379-87.

Rogers, C. R. Empathic: An appreciated way of being. *The Counseling Psychologist*, 1975, *5*, 2-10.

Rogers, T. B., Kuiper, N. A., & Kirker, W. S. Self-reference and the encoding of personal information. *Journal of Personality and Social Psychology*, 1977, *35*, 677-88.

Rosenthal, R., & Rosnow, R. L. (Eds.). *Artifact in behavioral research.* New York: Academic Press, 1969.

Ross, L., Rodin, J., & Zimbardo, P. G. Toward an attribution therapy: The reduction of fear through induced cognitive-emotional misattribution. *Journal of Personality and Social Psychology*, 1969, *12*, 279-88.

Rotter, J. B. *Social learning and clinical psychology.* Englewood Cliffs: Prentice-Hall, 1954.

Rotter, J. B. Generalized expectancies for internal versus external control of reinforcement. *Psychological Monographs*, 1966, *80* (1, whole no. 609).

Rotter, J. B., Chance, J. E., & Phares, E. J. (Eds.). *Applications of a social learning theory of personality.* New York: Holt, Rinehart & Winston, 1972.

Russell, M. L., & Thoresen, C. E. Teaching decision-making skills to children. In J. D. Krumboltz, & C. E. Thoresen (Eds.), *Counseling methods.* New York: Holt, Rinehart & Winston, 1976.

Russell, R. K., & Sipich, J. F. Cue-controlled relaxation in the treatment of test anxiety. *Journal of Behavior Therapy and Experimental Psychiatry*, 1973, *4*, 47-49.

Russell, R. K., & Wise, F. Treatment of speech anxiety by cue-controlled relaxation and desensitization with professional and paraprofessional counselors. *Journal of Counseling Psychology*, 1976, *23*, 583-86.

Schachter, S. The interaction of cognitive and physiological determinants of emotional state. In C. Spielberger (Ed.), *Anxiety and behavior.* New York: Academic Press, 1966.

Schachter, S., & Singer, J. E. Cognitive, social, and physiological determinants of emotional state. *Psychological Review*, 1962, *69*, 379-99.

Scheid, A. B. Client's perception of the counselor: The influence of counselor introduction and behavior. *Journal of Counseling Psychology*, 1976, *23*, 503-08.

Schmidt, J. A. Research techniques for counselors: The multiple baseline. *Personnel and Guidance Journal*, 1974, *53*, 200-06.

Schmidt, J. P. Psychotherapy supervision: A cognitive-behavioral model. *Professional Psychology*, 1979, *10*, 278-84.

Schultz, J. H., & Luthe, W. *Autogenic training: A psychophysiologic approach in psychotherapy.* New York: Grune & Stratton, 1959.

Schutz, A. *On phenomenology and social relations.* Chicago: University of Chicago Press, 1970.

Schwartz, R., & Gottman, J. Toward a task analysis of assertive behavior. *Journal of Consulting and Clinical Psychology*, 1976, *44*, 910-20.

Secord, P. F., & Backman, C. W. *Social psychology* (2nd ed.). New York: McGraw-Hill, 1974.

Seligman, M. E. P. Depression and learned helplessness. In R. J. Friedman & M. M. Katz (Eds.), *The psychology of depression: Contemporary theory and research.* Washington, D.C.: V. H. Winston, 1974.

Seligman, M. E. P. *Helplessness: On depression, development, and death.* San Francisco: W. H. Freeman, 1975.

Shabow, D. What is clinical psychology? *American Psychologist*, 1976, *31*, 553-60.

Shannon, C. E. A mathematical theory of communication. *Bell System Technical Journal*, 1948, *27*, 379- 423, 623-56.

Shantz, C. U. *The development of social cognition.* Chicago: University of Chicago Press, 1975.

Shapiro, A. K. The placebo effect in the history of medical treatment: Implications for psychiatry. *The American Journal of Psychiatry*, 1959, *116*, 298-304.

Shapiro, A. K., & Morris, L. A. Placebo effects in medical and psychological therapies. In S. L. Garfield & A. E. Bergin (Eds.), *Handbook of psychotherapy and behavior change* (2nd ed.). New York: Wiley, 1978.

Shapiro, D., & Schwartz, G. E. Biofeedback and visceral learning: Clinical applications. *Seminars in Psychiatry*, 1972, *4*, 171-84.

Shapiro, M. B., & Ravenette, A. T. A preliminary experiment of paranoid delusions. *Journal of Mental Science*, 1959, *105*, 295-312.

Shaw, B. F. Comparison of cognitive therapy and behavior therapy in the treatment of depression. *Journal of Consulting and Clinical Psychology*, 1977, *45*, 543-51.

Shelton, J. L., & Ackerman, J. M. *Homework in counseling and psychotherapy.* Springfield, Ill.: Charles C. Thomas, 1974.

Shure, M. B., & Spivack, G. Means-ends thinking, adjustment, and social class among elementary school aged children. *Journal of Consulting and Clinical Psychology*, 1972, *38*, 348-53.

Shure, M. B., & Spivack, G. *A preventive mental health program for young "inner city" children: The second (kindergarten) year.* Paper presented at the meeting of the American Psychological Association, Chicago, 1975.

Shure, M. B., Spivack, G., & Jaeger, M. Problem-solving thinking and adjustment among disadvantaged preschool children. *Child Development,* 1971, *42,* 1791-1803.

Sidman, M. *Tactics of scientific research: Evaluating experimental data in psychology.* New York: Basic Books, 1960.

Simon, S. B., Howe, L., & Kirschenbaum, H. *Values clarification: A practical handbook of strategies for teachers and students.* New York: Hart, 1972.

Singer, J. *Imagery and daydream methods in psychotherapy.* New York: Academic Press, 1974.

Skinner, B. F. *Science and human behavior.* New York: Macmillan, 1953.

Skinner, B. F. *Verbal behavior.* New York: Appleton-Century-Crofts, 1957.

Skinner, B. F. An operant analysis of problem solving. In B. Kleinmuntz (Ed.), *Problem solving: Research, method, and theory.* New York: Wiley, 1966.

Smith, M. L., & Glass, G. V. Meta-analysis of psychotherapy outcome studies. *American Psychologist,* 1977, *32,* 752-60.

Smith, R. D., & Evans, J. R. Comparison of experimental group guidance and individual counseling as facilitators of vocational development. *Journal of Counseling Psychology,* 1973, *20,* 202-08.

Spivack, G., & Shure, M. B. *Social adjustment of young children: A cognitive approach to solving real-life problems.* San Francisco: Jossey-Bass, 1974.

Stanley, J. C. (Ed.). *Preschool programs for the disadvantaged: Four experimental approaches to early childhood education.* Baltimore: Johns Hopkins University Press, 1972.

Stein, M. L., & Stone, G. L. Effects of conceptual level and structure on initial interview behavior. *Journal of Counseling Psychology,* 1978, *25,* 96-102.

Stephenson, W. *The study of behavior: Q-technique and its methodology.* Chicago: University of Chicago Press, 1953.

Stewart, N. R., & Winborn, B. B. A model for decision making in systematic counseling. *Educational Technology,* 1973, *69,* 13-15.

Stewart, N. R., Winborn, B. B., Johnson, R. G., Burks, H. M., Jr., & Engelkes, J. R. *Systematic counseling.* Englewood Cliffs: Prentice-Hall, 1978.

Stone, G. L. Effect of simulation on counselor training. *Counselor Education and Supervision*, 1975, *14*, 199-203.

Stone, G. L. Effects of experience on supervisor planning. *Journal of Counseling Psychology*, 1980, *27*, 84-88.

Stone, G. L., Hinds, W. C., & Schmidt, G. Teaching mental health behaviors to elementary school children. *Professional Psychology*, 1975, *6*, 34-40.

Stone, G. L., & Noce, A. Cognitive training for young children: Expanding the counselor's role. *Personnel and Guidance Journal*, 1980, *58*, 416-20.

Storms, M. D., & McCaul, K. D. Stuttering, attribution, and exacerbation. Unpublished manuscript, University of Kansas, 1975.

Storms, M. D., & McCaul, K. D. Attribution processes and emotional exacerbation of dysfunctional behavior. In J. H. Harvey, W. J. Ickes, & R. F. Kidd (Eds.), *New directions in attribution research* (vol. 1). Hillsdale, N.J.: Erlbaum, 1976.

Storms, M. D., & Nisbett, R. E. Insomnia and the attribution process. *Journal of Personality and Social Psychology*, 1970, *16*, 319-25.

Strickland, B. R. Internal-external expectancies and health-related behaviors. *Journal of Consulting and Clinical Psychology*, 1978, *46*, 1192-211.

Strong, S. R. Counseling: An interpersonal influence process. *Journal of Counseling Psychology*, 1968, *15*, 215-24.

Strong, S. R. Social psychological approach to psychotherapy research. In S. L. Garfield & A. E. Bergin (Eds.), *Handbook of psychotherapy and behavior change* (2nd ed.). New York: Wiley, 1978.

Strong, S. R., & Dixon, D. N. Expertness, attractiveness, and influence in counseling. *Journal of Counseling Psychology*, 1971, *18*, 562-70.

Strong, S. R., & Schmidt, L. D. Expertness and influence in counseling. *Journal of Counseling Psychology*, 1970, *17*, 81-87.

Struening, E. L., & Guttentag, M. *Handbook of evaluation of research* (2 vols.). Beverly Hills: Sage, 1975.

Strupp, H. Clinical psychology, irrationalism, and the erosion of excellence. *American Psychologist*, 1976, *31*, 561-71.

Suchman, E. A. *Evaluative research: Principles and practices in public service and social action programs.* New York: Russell Sage, 1967.

Suinn, R. M. Removing emotional obstacles to learning and performance by visuomotor behavioral rehearsal. *Behavior Therapy*, 1972, *3*, 308-10.

Suinn, R. M., & Richardson, F. Anxiety management training: A nonspecific behavior therapy program for anxiety control. *Behavior Therapy*, 1971, *2*, 498-510.

Super, D. E. *The psychology of careers.* New York: Harper & Row, 1957.

Thompson, A. P. Client misconceptions in vocational counseling. *Personnel and Guidance Journal*, 1976, *55*, 30-33.

Thompson, A. S., & Super, D. E. (Eds.). *The professional preparation of counseling psychologists: Report of the 1964 Greystone Conference.* New York: Teachers College Press, 1964.

Thoresen, C. E. Behavioral counseling: An introduction. *The School Counselor*, 1966, *14*, 13-21.

Thoresen, C. E., & Anton, J. L. Intensive counseling. *Focus on Guidance*, 1973, *6*, 1-11.

Thoresen, C. E., & Anton, J. L. Intensive designs in counseling research. *Journal of Counseling Psychology*, 1974, *21*, 553-59.

Thoresen, C. E., & Mahoney, M. J. *Behavioral self-control.* New York: Holt, Rinehart & Winston, 1974.

Thorndike, E. L. *Animal intelligence*, New York: Macmillan, 1911.

Thorndike, E. L. *The elements of psychology* (2nd ed.). New York: A. G. Seiler, 1922.

Tinsley, H. E. A., & Weiss, D. J. Interrater reliability and agreement of subjective judgments, *Journal of Counseling Psychology*, 1975, *22*, 358-76.

Tolman, E. C. *Purposive behavior in animals and man.* New York: Appleton, 1932.

Truax, C. B. A scale for the measurement of accurate empathy. *Psychiatric Institute Bulletin*, Wisconsin Psychiatric Institute, University of Wisconsin, 1961, *1*, 12.

Truax, C. B., & Carkhuff, R. R. *Toward effective counseling and psychotherapy: Training and practice.* Chicago: Aldine, 1967.

Tukey, J. W. *Exploratory data analysis.* Reading, Mass.: Addison-Wesley, 1977.

Tyler, L. *The work of the counselor* (3rd ed.). New York: Appleton-Century-Crofts, 1969.

Valins, S., & Ray, A. A. Effects of cognitive desensitization on avoidance behavior. *Journal of Personality and Social Psychology*, 1967, *7*, 345-50.

Vroom, V. A. *Work and motivation.* New York: Wiley, 1964.

Vygotsky, L. *Thought and language.* New York: Wiley, 1962.

Wachtel, P. L. *Psychoanalysis and behavior therapy: Toward an integration.* New York: Basic Books, 1977.

Weimer, W. B. *Psychology and the conceptual foundations of science.* Hillsdale, N.J.: Erlbaum, 1976.

Weimer, W. B. *Notes on methodology.* Hillsdale, N.J.: Erlbaum, 1977.

Weiner, B. *Theories of motivation.* Chicago: Markham, 1972.

Weiner, B. *Achievement motivation and attribution theory.* Morristown, N.J.: General Learning Corporation, 1974. (a)

Weiner, B. An attributional interpretation of expectancy-value theory. In B. Weiner (Ed.), *Cognitive views of human motivation.* New York: Academic Press, 1974. (b)

Weisenberg, M. Pain and pain control. *Psychological Bulletin,* 1977, *84,* 1008-44.

Weiss, R. L., Hops, H., & Patterson, G. R. A framework for conceptualizing marital conflict: A technology for altering it, some data for evaluating it. In L. A. Hamerlynck, L. C. Handy, & E. J. Marsh (Eds.), *Behavior change: Methodology, concepts, and practice.* Champaign, Ill.: Research Press, 1973.

Wellner, A. M. (Ed.). Education and credentialing in psychology, II. *Clinical Psychologist,* 1977, 31, *1,* 4-10.

Wertheimer, M. *Productive thinking.* New York: Harper, 1959.

Wexler, D. A. A cognitive theory of experiencing, self-actualization, and therapeutic process. In D. Wexler & L. Rice (Eds.), *Innovations in client-centered therapy.* New York: Wiley, 1974.

Wexler, D. A., & Butler, J. M. Therapist modification of client expressiveness in client-centered therapy. *Journal of Consulting and Clinical Psychology,* 1976, *44,* 261-67,

Wilkins, W. Expectancy of therapeutic gain: An empirical and conceptual critique. *Journal of Consulting and Clinical Psychology,* 1973, *40,* 69-77.

Williamson, E. G. *How to counsel students: A manual of techniques for clinical counselors.* New York: McGraw-Hill, 1939.

Williamson, E. G. *Counseling adolescents.* New York: McGraw-Hill, 1950.

Williamson, E. G. *Vocational counseling.* New York: McGraw-Hill, 1965.

Williamson, E. G., & Biggs, D. A. Trait-factor theory and individual differences. In H. M. Burks, Jr., & B. Stefflre (Eds.), *Theories of counseling.* New York: McGraw-Hill, 1979.

Williamson, E. G., & Darley, J. G. *Student personnel work.* New York: McGraw-Hill, 1937.

Wolf, M. M., & Risley, T. R. Reinforcement: Applied research. In R. Glaser (Ed.), *The nature of reinforcement,* New York: Academic Press, 1971.

Wolpe, J. *Psychotherapy by reciprocal inhibition.* Stanford: Stanford University Press, 1958.

Wolpe, J. *The practice of behavior therapy* (2nd ed.). New York: Pergamon Press, 1973.

Wolpe, J., & Lang, P. J. *Fear Survey Schedule.* San Diego: Educational and Industrial Testing Service, 1964.

Wortman, P. M. Evaluation research: A psychological perspective. *American Psychologist,* 1975, *30,* 562-75.

Yabroff, W. Learning decision making. In J. D. Krumboltz & C. E. Thoresen (Eds.), *Behavioral counseling: Cases and techniques.* New York: Holt, Rinehart & Winston, 1969.

AUTHOR INDEX

Ackerman, J. M., 44
Adams, N., 35, 78
Adler, A., 50
Allen, G. J., 85
Allport, G. W., 124
Anton, J. L., 125
Appleton, H., 130
Arkowitz, H., 2
Astin, A., 46
Atkinson, J. W., 2, 34, 40
Ausubel, D. P., 28, 30
Authier, J., 139
Avener, M., 149

Back, K. W., 25
Backman, C. W., 25, 30
Bain, A. J., 58
Bandler, R., 23, 78, 79, 82, 83, 84
Bandura, A., 2, 3, 4, 12, 29, 30, 35, 71, 75, 77-78, 85
Bandy, S. B., 44
Bannister, D., 36
Barber, T., 97
Barker, R., 46
Barnes, B., 29
Bartlett, F. C., 2
Bateson, G., 47
Beck, A. T., 2, 3, 4, 39, 40, 50, 55-56, 84
Beck, F. M., 64
Beck, S. J., 34
Bekhterev, V. M., 9
Bem, D. J., 75, 77
Bem, S. L., 58
Bender, N., 60
Bergin, A. E., 26, 29, 54, 109
Bernard, C., 124
Bernhardt, K., 133
Bertalanffy, L. von, 13
Beyer, J., 35, 78

Bieri, J., 110
Biggs, D. A., 6
Binet, A., 2
Birch, D., 2
Birdsall, T. G., 3
Blaney, P. H., 20
Bloch, J., 37
Blocher, D. H., 18
Bolles, R. C., 2
Bongort, K., 2
Bordin, E. S., 32, 109
Borkovec, T. P., 98
Bower, M., 47
Bowman, T. T., 19
Box, G. E. P., 125, 128
Boy, A., 18
Brenner, M., 47
Breuer, J., 124
Briggs, L. J., 13
Broadbent, D. E., 3
Bronfenbrenner, U., 37
Bruhn, J., 46
Buchanan, J. D., 60
Burck, H. D., 128, 130
Burks, H. M., Jr., 13
Butler, J. M., 82

Callis, R., 32
Cameron, R., 41, 65
Campbell, D. T., 37, 90, 91, 124, 129, 130
Campbell, R. J., 44
Carkhuff, R. R., 21, 22, 110, 121
Carnegie, D., 58
Carr, J. E., 109
Carroll, J. B., 39
Cartwright, D., 25
Cautela, J. R., 2
Chance, J. E., 75
Chassan, J. B., 124

Chaves, J., 97
Chinsky, J. M., 22, 85
Chomsky, N., 3, 78
Christensen, C., 72
Clark, R. A., 34
Clawson, E. U., 29
Cody, J. J., 72, 73
Cohen, J., 104
Cohen, S., 47
Comroe, J. H., 88
Comte, A., 10
Conner, R., 130
Cook, T. D., 90, 91, 107, 130
Cornfield, J., 107
Coué, E., 58
Cowen, E. L., 72
Craik, F. I. M., 22, 23, 69
Cronbach, L. J., 37, 102, 124
Danish, S. J., 44
Darley, J. G., 6, 32
Davis, C. S., 121
Davis, G. A., 66, 72
Davis, K. E., 75
Davison, G. C., 21, 51, 75, 77
Decenteceo, E. T., 2, 52
Delaney, D., 68
Dell, D. M., 27
Dember, W. N., 2
Demchik-Stone, D., 60
Denney, D., 61
Derry, P., 148
Descartes, R., 9
Deutsch, M., 25
Dewey, J., 6, 7, 19, 21, 66,
Diggory, J., 39
DiGiuseppe, R., 53
DiLoreto, A. O., 53-54
Dixon, D. N., 27
Dolliver, R. H., 50
Dowes, J., 44
Dripps, R. D., 88
D'Zurilla, T. J., 2, 15, 66, 67, 69, 70, 86

Eisenberg, S., 68
Ekman, P. A., 29
Ellis, A., 2, 3, 4, 44, 50-53, 56, 57, 59
Endler, N., 46

Engelkes, J. R., 13
Epstein, S., 64
Erbaugh, J., 39
Erickson, E. H., 2
Estes, W. K., 29, 70
Evans, J. R., 72, 73

Fahl, M. A., 72
Fedoravicius, A., 57
Ferreira, A., 47
Ferster, C. B., 61
Feshbach, S., 28, 48
Festinger, L., 25
Fisher, R. A., 123
Fiske, D. W., 37
Fitts, W. H., 19
Fox, L., 61
Frank, J. D., 2, 3, 15, 20, 26, 28, 29, 58
Fretz, B., 133, 134
Freud, S., 50, 124
Friedman, L. H., 77
Frost, H., 39
Furby, L., 102

Gagné, R. M., 13, 41
Galanter, E., 3, 71
Gelatt, H. B., 73
Giebink, J. W., 72
Gill, M. M., 34
Gilmore, B., 57
Gladstein, G. A., 22
Glaros, A. G., 75
Glaser, R., 13, 14
Glass, D., 47, 77
Glass, G. V., 53, 88, 102, 125, 128
Goldberg, A., 44
Goldberg, L. R., 136
Goldfried, M. R., 2, 15, 19, 21, 51, 52, 63, 64, 66, 67, 69, 70, 86
Goldman, L., 87, 88, 131
Goldiamond, I., 61
Goldstein, A. P., 26, 29
Goodman, D. S., 52
Goodman, J., 59, 60
Goor, A., 42, 43, 45
Gottman, J. M., 41, 45, 125, 128, 149

Gottman, J. M., 41, 45, 125, 128, 149
Greenberg, B. S., 44
Greenwood, J., 110
Grinder, J., 23, 78, 79, 82, 83, 84
Guilford, J. P., 42
Gump, P., 46
Guthrie, E. R., 9
Guttentag, M., 130

Haase, R. F., 104
Hackett, G., 60
Haley, J., 47
Hanesian, H., 28, 30
Harper, R., 51
Hartig, M., 60
Hartmann, H., 2
Harvey, J. H., 75
Harvey, O. J., 110
Hays, W. L., 103
Hebb, D. O., 3
Heck, E. J., 121
Heider, F., 1, 75
Heller, K., 26
Helms, J. E., 107
Hendrick, C., 74
Hill, C., 107
Hinds, W. C., 85
Hjertholm, E., 58
Hoch, E., 133
Holland, J. E., 73
Holland, J. L., 46, 73
Hollingshead, A., 47
Homme, L. E., 62
Hops, H., 72
Horan, J. J., 60, 65, 67, 73
Horney, K., 50
Hosford, R. E., 10
Hovland, C. I., 25, 27, 28
Howard, K. I., 111
Howe, L., 70
Huck, S. W., 102
Hull, C. L., 9
Hume, D., 9
Hunt, D. E., 109, 110, 112
Hunt, E., 39
Hunt, J. McV., 46
Hurndon, C. J., 113

Ickes, W. J., 75
Ittelson, W., 46
Ivey, A. E., 139

Jackson, D. D., 47
Jackson, D. N., 37
Jacobson, E., 63
Jaeger, M., 72
James, W., 66
Janis, I. L., 25, 27, 28, 64
Jenkins, G. M., 125, 128
Jensen, A., 89
Johnson, R. G., 13
Jones, E. E., 75
Jones, R. G., 45, 51
Jourard, S., 111
Joyce, B., 13
Jung, C., 2

Kagan, J., 60
Kagan, N., 44, 141
Kahana, B., 58
Kahneman, D., 29
Kanfer, F., 10, 19, 60
Kanouse, D. E., 75
Katona, G., 47
Kaul, T. J., 64
Kaye, D., 20
Kazdin, A. E., 29, 64, 97, 104, 128
Kell, B., 139
Kelley, H. H., 1, 25, 27, 75
Kelly, G. A., 2, 3, 36, 59, 110
Kent, R. N., 75
Kerlinger, F. N., 87, 89, 90
Kidd, R. F., 75
Kilpatrick, W., 21
Kiresuk, T. J., 72
Kirker, W. S., 69, 81
Kirschenbaum, H., 71
Kirschner, P., 20
Koffka, K., 2
Kohlberg, L., 58
Köhler, W., 2, 66
Kopel, S., 2
Korchin, S. J., 34
Kovacs, M., 55
Krathwohl, D., 44
Kris, E., 2

Krumboltz, J. D., 10, 11, 12, 18, 73, 87
Kuhn, T. S., 1
Kuiper, N. A., 69, 81

Lang, P. J., 35
Langer, T., 47
Larcen, S. W., 85
Lazarus, R. S., 2, 29, 64, 85
Ledwidge, B., 57
Leitenberg, H., 131
Leonard, M. M., 107
Levy, L., 4
Lewin, K., 2, 25, 46, 129
Lewitt, E. B., 61
Lillesand, D. B., 42
Lippitt, R., 25
Lochman, J. E., 85
Locke, J., 9
Lockhart, R. S., 22, 23, 69
Loeb, A., 39
Loevinger, J., 37
Lowell, E. L., 34
Lumsdaine, A. A., 28
Lunneborg, C., 39
Luria, A., 2, 58, 59
Luthe, W., 62

Mahoney, M. J., 1, 4, 12, 13, 19, 35, 53, 57, 89, 138, 149
Mair, J. M. M., 36
Maltz, M., 58
Mandler, G., 20
Marks, P. A., 33
Maultsby, M. C., Jr., 52
McCain, L. J., 125, 128
McCaul, K. D., 77
McCleary, R., 125, 128
McClelland, D. C., 27, 34
McFall, R. M., 41, 42
McGuire, M. T., 72
McGuire, W. J., 26, 27, 28
McLean, R. A., 102
Meadow, A., 69
Meara, N., 113
Meehl, P., 37
Meichenbaum, D., 1, 2, 3, 4, 28, 45, 55, 56-57, 58, 59, 60, 64, 65

Melzack, R., 64
Mendelson, M., 39
Mendonca, J. D., 73, 85
Merbaum, M., 2, 19
Michael, S., 47
Milgram, S., 27
Miller, G. A., 3, 71
Miller, N. J., 53, 54
Miller, W. R., 40
Minge, M. R., 19
Minuchin, S., 47
Mischel, W., 2, 12, 35, 37, 46
Mock, J., 39
Molish, H. B., 34
Moos, R. H., 37, 46-47
Morris, L. A., 97
Mueller, W., 139
Murray, H. A., 34, 35, 46

Nau, S. D., 98
Neisser, U., 3, 4
Nelson, C. A., 74
Nelson, R., 76
Neufeld, R. W. J., Jr., 128
Newell, A., 3
Nisbett, R. E., 43, 70, 75
Noce, A., 86
Novaco, R. W., 65
Novak, J. D., 28, 30
Noy, J. E., 110
Nurnberger, J. I., 61

Oetting, E. R., 128
Ojemann, R. H., 72
Orlinsky, D. E., 111
Orne, M. T., 64
Osborn, A. F., 66, 69
Osgood, C. E., 36

Paivio, A. V., 38-39
Palkes, H., 58
Park, R., 47
Parnes, S. J., 69
Patterson, C. H., 18
Patterson, D. G., 6
Patterson, G. R., 72
Paul, G. H., 58, 62
Pavlov, I., 9, 124

182 / A Cognitive-Behavioral Approach to Counseling

Peale, N. V., 58
Peckham, P. D., 102
Pepinsky, H. B., 32, 113
Peterson, D., 133
Peterson, G. P., 128, 130
Peterson, W. W., 3
Phares, E. J., 75
Piaget, J., 1, 2
Pierce, A., 47
Pine, G. J., 18
Plato, 79
Platt, J., 72
Posthuma, A., 109
Pribram, K., 3, 71
Price, R., 41
Proshansky, H., 46

Raimy, V. C., 133
Rapaport, D., 2, 34
Rappaport, J., 22
Ravenette, A. T., 124
Ray, A. A., 75
Redlich, F., 47
Reiss, J. A., 107
Resnickoff, A., 44
Rice, L. N., 25, 83
Rich, A. R., 41
Richardson, B., 148
Richardson, F., 62, 63, 64
Riopelle, A. J., 72
Risley, T. R., 127
Rivlin, L., 46
Rodin, J., 75
Rogers, C. R., 7, 8, 9, 21, 22, 37, 133
Rogers, T. B., 69, 81
Roosevelt, F. D., 129
Rosenthal, R., 97
Rosnow, R. L., 97
Ross, A. O., 133
Ross, L., 75
Rotter, J. B., 2, 3, 75, 76
Rush, A. J., 55
Russell, M. L., 73
Russell, R. K., 62, 63

Sanders, J. R., 102
Saslow, G., 11
Satir, V., 47

Schachter, S., 24, 25, 64, 75
Schafer, R., 34
Schaffer, A., 130
Schauble, P. G., 44
Scheid, A. B., 27
Schmidt, G., 85
Schmidt, J. A., 125
Schmidt, J. P., 143
Schmidt, L. D., 27
Schroder, H. M., 109
Schroeder, H. E., 41
Schultz, J. H., 62
Schutz, A., 1
Schwartz, G. E., 2
Schwartz, R., 41, 45, 149
Sechrest, L., 26
Secord, P. F., 25, 30
Seeman, W., 32
Seligman, M. E. P., 2, 20
Selinger, H. V., 85
Shakow, D., 147
Shannon, C. E., 3
Shantz, C. U., 1
Shapiro, A. K., 29, 97
Shapiro, D., 2
Shapiro, M. B., 124
Shaw, B. F., 56
Sheffield, F. D., 28
Shelton, J. L., 44
Sherman, R. E., 72
Shure, M., 45, 72, 85
Sidman, M., 124, 125
Siess, T. F., 73, 85
Sifneos, P. E., 72
Simon, S. B., 71
Singer, J. E., 2, 24, 47, 74, 75, 77
Sipich, J. F., 62, 63
Skinner, B. F., 9, 41, 62, 66, 68, 124
Smith, M. L., 53
Smith, R. D., 73
Snow, R. E., 124
Sommerfeld, R. A., 42, 43, 45
Spivack, G., 45, 72, 85
Stanley, J. C., 72, 90, 91, 124, 129, 130
Stein, M. L., 108, 112, 114
Stephenson, W., 37
Stewart, M., 58

Stewart, N. R., 13, 14, 73
Stone, C. I., 60
Stone, G. L., 42, 68, 85, 86, 108, 145, 148
Storms, M. D., 75, 77
Stover, D. S., 72
Strickland, B. R., 76
Strong, S. R., 18, 26, 27
Struening, E. L., 130
Strupp, H. H., 9, 54, 109, 133
Suchman, E. A., 130
Suci, G. J., 36
Suinn, R. M., 62, 63, 64
Sullivan, A., 109
Super, D. E., 85, 133

Tamkin, G., 130
Tannenbaum, P. H., 46
Tanney, M. F., 107
Thibaut, J. W., 25
Thompson, A. P., 84
Thompson, A. S., 133
Thoresen, C. E., 10, 11, 12, 19, 35, 73, 125
Thorndike, E. L., 9, 41, 66, 129
Tinsley, H. E. A., 100
Tolman, E. C., 2
Trexler, L., 53, 54
Trier, C. S., 63
Truax, C. B., 21, 22
Tsujimoto, R. N., 75
Tukey, J. W., 90, 107
Turk, D., 65
Tversky, A., 29
Twentyman, C. T., 41
Tyler, L., 32, 38

Valins, S., 75, 77
Vroom, V. A., 12, 85
Vygotsky, L., 58

Wachtel, P. L., 37
Wagstaff, A. K., 25, 83
Wall, P., 64
Ward, C. H., 39
Watson, G., 21
Watson, J., 9
Weber, S. J., 130
Weil, M., 19
Weimer, W. B., 89, 102
Weinberg, L., 2, 52
Weiner, B., 1, 2, 75
Weisenberg, M., 65
Weiss, D. J., 100
Weiss, R. M., 72
Wellner, A. M., 138
Wertheimer, M., 2, 41
Wexler, D. A., 2, 9, 12, 22, 69, 82
White, R., 25
Wilcoxon, L., 29, 64, 97
Wilkins, W., 29
Williamson, E. G., 6, 7, 18, 32, 66
Wilson, G. T., 76
Wilson, T. D., 43, 70
Wilson, V. L., 125, 128
Winborn, B. B., 73
Winder, C. L., 133
Winder, J. D., 47
Wise, F., 64
Wolf, M. M., 127
Wolpe, J., 28, 35, 62
Wortman, P. M., 129
Wright, H. F., 46
Wynne, L., 47

Yabroff, W., 73
Yaeger, J., 58

Zimbardo, P. G., 75

SUBJECT INDEX

advanced practicum, 144-45
anxiety, 19-20
anxiety management training, 62-64
assessment: behavioral, 34-35; dynamic, 33-34; methodological, 32, 37-38; phenomenological, 36-37; psychometric, 33 (*see also* cognitive-behavioral: assessment; environmental assessment)
attribution, description, 74-75; precursors, 74-75 (*see* attribution therapy
attribution therapy: applications, 74-76; evaluation, 78; locus of control, 76-77; self-attribution, 78 (*see* attribution)

Beck's cognitive therapy, 55-56
behavioral theory, mediational themes, 11-12; outline, 9-11; precursors, 9-10

client-centered theory: mediational themes, 9; outline, 7-9; precursors, 7
client characteristics, initial stage of counseling, 19-20
cognition: trends, 1-2; counseling, 5 (*see* cognitive psychology)
cognitive-behavioral: assessment, 38-45; interventions, 49-86; perspective, 3-5
cognitive psychology, history, 2-4 (*see* cognition)
cognitive restructuring, 50-58 (*see* Beck's cognitive therapy, self-statement therapy)
construct validty: description, 95; method bias, 96-97; nonspecific effects, 97-99; stimulus sampling, 96; theory, 95-96; treatment validity, 99-100
coping skills training: antecedents, 62; conceptualization, 62; rationale, 63; skills, 63; discrimination training, 63; rehearsal, 63; evaluation, 64, 65 (*see* anxiety management training, cue-controlled relaxation, problem solving, stress innoculation training)
counseling process: framework, 12-15; stages, 15, 17
credibility (*see* expertness, 27-28)
cue-controlled relaxation, 62-63

design strategies, 123-32 (*see* factorial designs, intensive designs, and program evaluation)

empathy, description, 22; information processing, 22-25
environmental assessment developments, 45-46; perceptually-based approaches, 46-47 (*see* human ecology)
expectations, 29-30
experimental psychology, 39-40
expertness, 27-28 (*see* credibility)
external validity, description, 105-07

factorial designs, 123-24

goals, controversy, 18; establishment goals, 19-20; self-management, 19

human ecology: Barker's approach,

184

46; family, 47; physical environment, 47 (*see* environmental assessment)

information processing: empathy, 22-25; levels of processing, 22-23
intensive designs, 110-28
internal validity: description, 91; differential mortality, 91-93; reactive conditions, 93-95
internship, 145-46

language therapy: description, 78-80; empathy, 23-24; evaluation, 82-83; processes, 79-82
mediation, 4-5
models thinking: applications, 14-15, 17; methodology, 14; perspective, 13; precursors, 13-14
motivation, 20

neomentalism, 38

practicum, 142-44
prepracticum, 140-42
prevention, 85-86
problem solving: antecedents, 66; conceptualization, 66-67; counseling process, 14-15; evaluation, 72-73; stages, 67-72
professional training: academic curriculum, 138-39; debate, 133-35; integration, 146-48; practitioner training, 139-46; research, 148-49; scientist training, 135-38 (*see* advanced practicum, practicum, prepracticum)
program evaluation, 128-31

Q-sort, 37

rationales, 28-29
relationship conditions: functions, 21; information processing, 21-25; precursors, 21
REP test, 36
research: basic vs. applied, 87-91; illustration, 108-22; priorities, 108-22 (*see* construct validity, external validity, internal validity, statistical conclusion validity, design strategies)

self instructions: antecedents, 58-59; evaluation, 60-61; methodology, 59-60
self management: description, 61; development, 61; precursors, 61-62 (*see* coping skills training)
self observation, 35
self-statement therapy: description, 27, 55; evaluation, 57-58; rationale, 56-57; strategies, 57-58
semantic differential, 36
situational tests, 35
social influence: components, 25-26; counseling, 26-27; information processing, 30-31; precursors, 25 (*see* credibility, expectations, expertness, rationales)
statistical conclusion validity: clinical significance, 104-05; description, 100; precision, 100-01; statistics, 101-04
stress-innoculation training: antecedents, 64; evaluation, 65; procedures, 64-65

task analysis: applications, 41-42; background, 40-41; procedures, 41
trait and factor theory: mediational themes, 7; outline, 6; precursors, 6

vocational psychology: information processing, 84-85

ABOUT THE AUTHOR

GERALD L. STONE is associate professor of Education and coordinator of the Counseling Psychology Program at the University of Iowa, Iowa City. Until 1979, he was associate professor of Psychology and coordinator of the Applied Psychology Program at the University of Western Ontario, London, Ontario, Canada.

Dr. Stone has been widely published in the areas of psychology and education. His articles have appeared in the *Journal of Counseling Psychology, Professional Psychology, Canadian Journal of Behavioural Science, Cognitive Therapy and Research, Personnel and Guidance Journal*, and *Counselor Education and Supervision*.

Dr. Stone holds a B.A. from the University of California at Los Angeles, a B.D. from Princeton Theological Seminary, and an M.A. and Ph.D. from Michigan State University.